Haifeng Shen

Collaborative Programming on the Internet: Environments

Haifeng Shen

Collaborative Programming on the Internet: Environments

VDM Verlag Dr. Müller

Imprint

Bibliographic information by the German National Library: The German National Library lists this publication at the German National Bibliography; detailed bibliographic information is available on the Internet at http://dnb.d-nb.de.

Cover image: www.purestockx.com

Publisher:
VDM Verlag Dr. Müller Aktiengesellschaft & Co. KG , Dudweiler Landstr. 125 a, 66123 Saarbrücken, Germany,
Phone +49 681 9100-698, Fax +49 681 9100-988,
Email: info@vdm-verlag.de

Zugl.: Brisbane, Griffith University, 2003

Produced in USA and UK by:
Lightning Source Inc., La Vergne, Tennessee, USA
Lightning Source UK Ltd., Milton Keynes, UK
BookSurge LLC, 5341 Dorchester Road, Suite 16, North Charleston, SC 29418, USA

ISBN: 978-3-639-01242-2

Abstract

Software systems are getting larger and more complex, while the requirements are becoming vaguer and more rapidly changing. These trends make current software development more and more likely a team work. To integrate multiple developers into a coherent structured management process and make team software development a positive-sum game for both higher productivity and better quality, many team software development methodologies have been proposed and practised. An emerging methodology is collaborative programming, which allows a group of programmers to work together on the same source code for design, implementation of individual components, and integration of individual components. Compared with other team software methodologies that only address needs in some phases or situations, collaborative programming is more adaptive to the variety of different phases or situations in a team software development process.

A core technical component in collaborative programming is collaborative editing, which allows a group of programmers to view and edit the same source code. To support different phases or situations in an Internet-based collaborative programming process, collaborative editing must meet the requirements of supporting unconstrained, responsive, real-time collaborative editing; unconstrained, syncretic, non-real-time collaborative editing; and smooth, flexible switching between real-time and non-real-time collaborative editing. This thesis research contributes several novel techniques to address these requirements, and an Internet-based collaborative programming environment to integrate those techniques.

These research contributions have advanced state-of-the-art technologies on collaborative editing for supporting Internet-based collaborative programming. First, we contribute a collaborative highlighting gestural communication technique for unconstrained, responsive, real-time collaborative editing. This technique is particularly effective in improving the quality of real-time interaction on text-based source code documents. The contribution to the operational transformation technology is the extension of the technology to support group awareness. It includes a package of operational transformation functions and transformation control algorithms for consistency maintenance in collaborative highlighting, and a flexible undo solution that has the capability of undoing any highlighting operation at any time.

Second, we contribute a flexible operation-based merging technique for unconstrained, syncretic, non-real-time collaborative editing, which is efficient and has the capability of textually integrating all changes, and automatically detecting and resolving syntactic conflicts according to application-dependent user-specified policies. The contribution to the operational transformation technology is the extension of the technology to support unconstrained, syncretic, non-real-time collaborative editing. Its includes a log compression algorithm, a textual merging algorithm, and a syntactic merging algorithm.

Moreover, we contribute a flexible notification technique to support flexible collaborative editing: unconstrained, responsive, real-time collaborative editing; unconstrained, syncretic, non-real-time collaborative editing; and smooth, flexible switching between them. The contribution to the operational transformation technology is the extension of the technology to support flexible collaborative editing. It includes a new transformation control algorithm that has a linear time complexity, two notification algorithms that support propagation and acceptance of any notifications at any time, and a notification propagation protocol that is efficient for both real-time and non-real-time collaborative editing.

Table of Contents

List of Figures

Publications derived from this research

1. Haifeng Shen and C. Sun. Improving Real-time Collaboration with High-lighting. In *International Journal of Future Generation Computer Systems*, North-Holland, Elsevier Science Publisher, to appear July 2003.

2. Haifeng Shen and C. Sun. Flexible Notification for Collaborative Systems. In *Proceedings of ACM Conference on Computer-Supported Cooperative Work*, pages 77–86, New Orleans, Louisiana, USA, ACM Press, November 2002.

3. Haifeng Shen and C. Sun. Flexible Merging for Asynchronous Collaborative Systems. In *Proceedings of Tenth International Conference on Cooperative Information Systems*, pages 304–321, University of California, Irvine, USA, Springer Verlag, November 2002.

4. Haifeng Shen and C. Sun. RECIPE: A Web-based Environment for Supporting Real-time Collaborative Programming. In *Proceedings of International Conference on Networks, Parallel and Distributed Processing*, pages 283–288, Tsukuba, Japan, ACTA Press, October 2002.

5. Haifeng Shen and C. Sun. Highlighting: A Gesturing Communication Tool for Real-time Collaborative Systems. In *Proceedings of the 5th IEEE International Conference on Algorithms and Architectures for Parallel Processing*, pages 180–187, Beijing, China, IEEE computer society, October 2002.

6. Haifeng Shen and C. Sun. A Log Compression Algorithm for Operation-based

Version Control Systems. In *Proceedings of IEEE 26th Annual International Computer Software and Application Conference*, pages 867–872, Beijing, Oxford, England, IEEE computer society, August 2002.

7. Haifeng Shen and C. Sun. Collaborative Highlighting for Real-time Group Editors. In *Proceedings of International Conference on Innovative Internet Computing Systems*, pages 39–50, Khlungsborn, Germany, Springer Verlag, June 2002.

8. Haifeng Shen and C. Sun. Operation-based revision control systems. In *Proceedings of ACM GROUP 2001 Workshop on Collaborative Editing Systems*, Online proceeding: http://www.research.umbc.edu/~jcampbel/Group01/ WS-Papers.htm, Boulder, Colorado, USA, September 2001.

9. Haifeng Shen and C. Sun. RECIPE: a prototype for Internet-based real-time collaborative programming. In *Procedings of ACM CSCW 2000 Workshop on Collaborative Editing Systems*, Online proceeding: http://csdl.tamu.edu/~lidu/ iwces2/papers/index.html, Philadelphia, USA, December 2000.

Systems derived from this research

1. RECIPE (REal-time Collaborative Interactive Programming Environment): A Web-based Real-time Collaborative Programming Environment. Demonstrated at *ACM CSCW 2000 Workshop on Collaborative Editing Systems*, Philadelphia, USA, December 2000. URL: http://reduce.qpsf.edu.au/~hfshen/recipe/

2. FORCE (Flexible Operation-based Revision Control Environment): A Web-based Source Code Editor with Integrated Flexible Revision Control Support. URL: http;//reduce.qpsf.edu.au/force/

3. NICE (Notification-flexible Collaborative Editing): A Web-based Collaborative Edting System with Flexible Notification Support. Demonstrated at *ACM CSCW 2002 Workshop on Collaborative Editing Systems*, New Orleans, Louisiana, USA, November 2002. URL: http://reduce.qpsf.edu.au/nice/

Acknowledgements

I would like to express my most sincere appreciation to my supervisor, Professor Chengzheng Sun, who has looked after me throughout the four years of my PhD study. He has taught me every aspect of how to be successful in academia and his pursuit for research excellence has set a good example for me. Without his supervision and advice, I could not have done this.

No words can express my gratitude to my beloved wife, who has provided me with emotional and family support, which has carried me through some difficult time. She deserves more than half of my achievements.

I am indebted to my parents. They have patiently supported me throughout my years of studies. Without their support, this would not be possible.

I owe my friends, Jisheng Han, Jiuyong Li, and Junhu Wang, for their companionship and encouragement during these years. I would like to thank my colleagues, David Chen, Aguido Horatio Davis, Jingzhi Guo, Qian Xia, and Maria Aneiros, for the knowledge I have gained from discussions, debates, and various fun activities.

Chapter 1

Introduction

A computer system consists of hardware and software, where hardware is the "body" and software is the "heart and soul" [140]. Software keeps a computer system alive and trains it for more cognitive functions. Like human society, where the evolution of human being's intelligence and knowledge has been significantly quicker than the evolution of human beings' physical body, computer systems have manifested faster growing software than hardware in the past decades. A variety of sophisticated software systems make computer systems more intelligent, more knowledgable, and capable of performing more tasks.

1.1 Trends in software development

Software development is changing over time. Some major trends in software development are described as follows:

1.1.1 Larger and more complex software

A trend in software development is that software systems are getting larger and larger. We still remember that Microsoft *Windows 3.1* operating system [106] was shipped with less than ten 3.5" floppies, not larger than 12 Megabytes. But its successor, *Windows 2000* [89], is now shipped with a CD-ROM, at least 360 Megabytes, 30 times larger than its predecessor *Windows 3.1*. Despite the growing size of software systems, their development cycles should not be prolonged accordingly because speed-to-market is a key to retaining a competitive edge in market [15].

What happens when software development exceeds its time targets and is late to market? As widely reported in the press, Novell's handling of the word processing system *WordPerfect* is an example of how dilatory software development can devastate a software system's market future. In 1994, Novell purchased *WordPerfect* for over $855 million in an effort to create an integrated software product to compete with Microsoft *Office* suite but later sold it to Corel for only $186 million. The calamitous 80% drop in market value is the result of Novell's inability to keep apace with Microsoft in the race to bring new software features to market. The key to speed up software development for the sake of reducing cycle time is to employ more developers to work on the same software project [51].

Another trend in software development is that software systems are getting more and more complex. As we know, when the *Mosaic* web browser [7] was first developed at *NCSA* at the University of Illinois in Urbana-Champaign a decade ago, it could only interpret nothing more than a very limited set of basic HTML tags. But now its successor, Microsoft *Internet Explorer* [31], is far more sophisticated; able to interpret frames, forms, stylesheets, scripts, Java applets, ActiveX Web controls, and so on. A complex software system requires different expertise possessed by different developers to contribute to. For example, the development of a sophisticated web browser requires many developers with different backgrounds, some specialized in XML and stylesheets, some specialized in script languages, some specialized in Java virtual machine, some specialized in ActiveX controls, and so on.

1.1.2 Vaguer and more rapidly changing software

Another major trend in software development is that the requirements of software systems are becoming more and more vague and rapidly changing. In a conventional software development process, the requirements of a software system should be clearly provided by users once and for all. According to the analysis of the requirements, developers design the software system that delivers those features, then implement and test the system to make sure the features are really delivered, and finally ship the system to the users. Such a conventional software development process was the waterfall model, as shown in Figure 1.1.

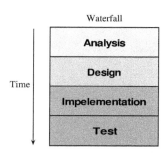

Figure 1.1: The waterfall model of software development process

However, users may not be able to tell what they exactly want because they do not know at that time. They may contradict themselves and change their minds from time to time. Moreover, users' requirements may not all be exactly captured by developers. Because the long development cycles of the waterfall model could not adapt to rapid changes, a software development process should be made of shorter and iterative development cycles in order to incorporate changes as quickly as possible. As shown in Figure 1.2 (Iterative), the waterfall model should be adapted to iterations. If iterations are so frequent that all those activities are actually blended, a little at a time, throughout the entire software development process [4], as shown in Figure 1.2 (XP), a new lightweight software development process, named *Extreme Programming* (XP), comes into being. XP is every effective for a team of software engineers to become a productive unit that embrace changes and incorporate them quickly into an evolving system [90].

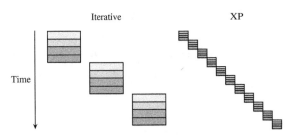

Figure 1.2: Frequent iterations lead to extreme programming

Extreme programming (XP) is a software development methodology that favours informal and immediate communication over the detailed and specific work products required by any number of traditional design methods [149]. It is well suited for small or mid-size teams to develop software with vague or rapidly changing requirements and copes with changes by delivering software early and often and by absorbing feedback from deliveries into the development culture and then ultimately into the code [149]. For the sake of success, *XP* prescribes a combination of special practices in which pair programming is an essential one [5, 90, 149, 150]. Pair programming [26, 150] is a practice in which two programmers work side-by-side at one computer, continuously collaborating on the same design, algorithm, code, or test, which fits well within XP for a number of reasons ranging from quality and productivity to vocabulary development and cross training [149], in particular:

- A pair of developers is more likely to better interpret the requirements and design the system closer to those requirements.
- A partner who has been tracking the intention of a programmer is more suited to judge the expressiveness of the program and find errors in the program.
- A pair of developers can help each other maintain the distinct disciplines of testing the implementation.

1.2 Team software development methodologies

Trends in software development have revealed the fact that current software development is more likely a team work rather than an individual business. Adding more developers to a project may help reduce development cycle time, but may also have the opposite effect of low productivity, since coordination complexities make large teams more difficult to manage [15]. Therefore, effective methodologies for team software development are needed to integrate developers into a coherent, structured management process, and make team software development a positive-sum game for both higher productivity and shorter cycle times [51].

1.2.1 Pair programming

Not many methodologies are available for facilitating team software development. As mentioned in the previous section, pair programming is a major methodology heavily used in extreme programming for team software development, where all production code is written by a pair of programmers. Anecdotal and initial statistical evidence [26, 98, 150] indicates that pair programming can not only improve productivity but also improve the quality of software products. In pair programming, two programmers work together, collaborating in real-time on the same design, algorithm, code, or test, in the way of exchanging ideas to tackle the complexities of software development and continuously performing inspections on each other's work to remove defects as early as possible [149].

As shown in Figure 1.3, pair programming normally requires that two programmers sit side-by-side at one computer; one manipulates the keyboard and mouse while the other performs system design, problem solving, and code reviewing. This kind of pair programming is inadequate in reality. First of all, it is too restrictive for two programmers to share one computer because they may need to switch their roles from time to time and may even need to manipulate input devices at the same time. For instance, if one programmer finds an error in the code written by the other when performing reviewing, it would be much easier for her/him to just fix the error rather than interrupting her/his partner to tell her/him where the error is and how to fix it.

Figure 1.3: Pair programming

Moreover, it is not always practical or achievable for two programmers to sit side-by-side at one computer. A programmer may belong to multiple pairs in fulfilling different pair programming tasks [147], but it is hard for her/him to sit by a programmer in an office for a period of time and then leave for another office (by walk, by car, by train, or even by air) to sit by another programmer for another period of time. Furthermore, because of the globalization of organizations, two programmers working on the same pair programming task could be located over different places; economics and organizational factors could even make them spread over continents [77]. It is out of the question to make them sit side-by-side unless one of them has to take a travel.

Therefore, as shown in Figure 1.4, virtual pair programming [148] where two programmers work at their own computers, connected by network, to collaborate in real-time on the same design, algorithm, code, or test, by means of specially designed software tools, is an essential complement to pair programming.

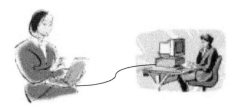

Figure 1.4: Virtual pair programming

Most of the supporting software systems emulate the effect of two programmers manipulating the same computer, in the way that they take turns to generate input events from their own keyboards/mice and they see exactly the same view of the shared application at the same time. These systems, although slightly different in implementation, actually exploit the same technique of *shared window*, which uses a centralized architecture in which inputs from users at multiple sites are merged and delivered to a single instance of the application, and any change to the graphical output of the application is broadcast to all sites. These systems are typified by *VNC* (Virtual Network Computing) [111], which allows a single entire desktop environment to be accessed and manipulated from multiple places simultaneously; Microsoft *Net-meeting* [87], which allows a single entire desktop environment or some applications within the desktop environment in a *Windows* operating system to be accessed and manipulated from multiple places simultaneously; and HP *SharedX* [60], which allows some applications based on the X protocol in a *Unix* operating system to be accessed and manipulated from multiple places simultaneously.

These systems have been used for virtual pair programming experiments [146, 147] but the results were not so encouraging. The performance was acceptable on

some platforms [146] but inefficient on other platforms, even on a 10Megabit LAN
(Local Area Network) [147]. The reasons are twofold. First all of, the shared window
technique is generally not responsive because in response to a local input, the input
event first has to be transferred across the network to the application, then is applied
onto the application, and finally, changes to the graphical output of the application
have to be transferred back across the network. But compared with LAN, the Internet
has higher latency and more nondeterministic traffic congestion, so the response would
be much worse. Moreover, the shared window technique normally demands high
network bandwidth in order to transfer graphical pixels across the network in short
time. But compared with LAN, the Internet has less network bandwidth, so the
performance would be much worse. In addition to the low efficiency, shared window
systems are restrictive because they force all participants to see exactly the same view
of the shared application all the time and prohibit participants from simultaneously
generating input events to the application.

1.2.2   Software configuration management

Another major methodology for team software development is *SCM* (Software Configuration Management), which is the discipline that enables software developers to
control the evolution of complex software development [50]. It was initially proposed
for keeping track of the evolvement of a software project by means of versioning in
order to support rebuilding, composition, and backtracking. Now it is used widely for
software development, and, besides being the mechanism to keep track of an evolving software project, it is also an effective mechanism to facilitate and coordinate
cooperative work [50] in team software development.

A software configuration consists of a combination of files and directories. The
software configuration evolves as the inside files or directories are changed and the
evolvement of the software configuration is tracked by keeping significant phases as

versions in a repository. As shown in Figure 1.5, cooperative work among team members is managed by the mechanism of *Copy-Modify-Merge* [32]: each member first makes a separate copy of a version from the repository as a local workspace at her/his site, then modifies the copied files inside the local workspace, and finally merges the modified files in the local workspace with corresponding files in a version to generate a new version in the repository, or to generate a new workspace at the local site.

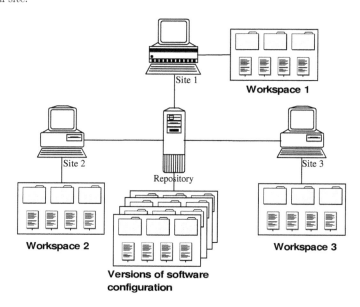

Figure 1.5: Concurrent work supported by Copy-Modify-Merge

Merging is the process of integrating different pieces of work done in a concurrent way by multiple users on the same document, which is a key technique for *SCM* to support concurrent work on the same document. Early SCM systems, such as *RCS* (Revision Control System) [142], do not support merging since when a file is checked out from the repository by a user, it will be locked until it has been checked in by the same user, in order to prevent other users from attempting to concurrently modify the file. Therefore, these systems only support concurrent work on different files and cooperative work on the same file has to be sequentialized. But later SCM systems, including influential open source systems such as *CVS* (Concurrent Version System) [10, 56] and *Subversion* [27], and leading commercial products such as *ClearCase* [1] and *Continuus* [19, 34], all support merging.

Textual merging is available in almost all SCM systems [28], which heuristically compares two plain text files line by line with a reference to their common ancestor. If a line is present in a file but not in the common ancestor, it was added and must be kept in the merged file; if a line is present in the ancestor but not in the file, it was removed and must be removed from the merged file. If changes occurred in different lines, they can all be automatically integrated into the merged file. But if changes occurred in the same line, the textual merging algorithm is unable to decide how to merge them and it is up to the user to manually merge them. Textual merging, though simple, proved to be very useful in SCM systems [18].

Object merging that merges concurrent changes to the attributes of shared objects is desirable to handle files consisting of general objects such as graphic objects, bitmap pixels, tree nodes, and tables, etc. But object merging has not been mature enough to be adopted in any SCM system [50]. Some work has been done on merging concurrent changes to the attributes of graphic objects in real-time collaborative graphic editing [23, 135]. Some work has been done on merging concurrent changes to bitmap graphics in real-time bitmap-based collaborative graphic editing [144]. Some work has been done on merging concurrent changes to tree nodes in real-time collaborative editing of tree-structured *SGML* (Standard General Markup Language) documents [36]. These previous work, though primarily proposed for real-time collaborative editing of object-based documents, has laid foundations for object merging in the context of SCM.

However, these previous work is neither mature enough nor directly applicable to object merging for SCM due to the fundamental difference between real-time collaborative editing and SCM. Unlike textual merging, object merging is more conflict-prone, where a conflict occurs when an attribute of an object is concurrently changed to two different values. In real-time collaborative editing, when a conflict occurs, the users who made the conflicting changes can resolve the conflict by means of interaction. On the contrary, in SCM, if a conflict could not be automatically resolved by the underlining object merging algorithm, it could not count on the users to resolve it because they may not be both "on the spot". Furthermore, conflicts do not accumulate in real-time collaborative editing because they can be resolved when occurring. In contrast, conflicts could be accumulated in SCM to such a large scale that it is infeasible for users to manually resolve them. In conclusion, object merging in SCM should be capable of detecting and resolving conflicts with as little human intervention as possible.

Textual merging and object merging are low level merging mechanisms, which are based on individual lines in plain text documents or individual objects in object-based documents. Syntactic merging and semantic merging are high level merging mechanisms that take advantage of the syntax and the semantics of the documents to be merged. Syntactic merging [18] exploits the context-free syntax of the documents to be merged and aims at achieving a syntactically correct result. Although syntactic merging has been studied for a long time, it has only been realized in a few research prototypes [18, 145], which are, however, too slow to be practically usable, at least for programming languages [50]. Semantic merging [11] takes into account the semantics of the documents to be merged and performs sophisticated analysis in order to detect conflicts between changes; however, it is hard to come up with a definition of semantic conflict that is neither too strong nor too weak while determinable [28]. The semantic merging algorithms developed so far are applicable only to simple programming languages (not C or C++) [11, 13, 69]. It is still a long way for semantic merging to be practically usable.

To extend SCM to the Internet environment in supporting geographically distributed team software development, there are some urgent issues to be addressed. One issue is efficiency. The textual merging algorithm, though heuristic and simple, is actually inefficient. On the one hand, it requires a lot of network bandwidth to transfer documents over the network back and forth [122, 124] and a long time to compute deltas between documents by text differentiation algorithms [71, 88, 93, 94]. On the other hand, a lot of non-conflicting changes cannot be merged together automatically, and still need human intervention by means of real-time interaction.

Another issue is scalability and availability. Most SCM systems only support a single centralized repository, which does not scale to the Internet environment and could become a bottleneck for availability. A further issue is web support. On the one hand, as the web becomes ubiquitous, SCM deserves to become a standard service on the Internet [50]. Therefore, *BSCW* (Basic Service for Collaborative Work) [68], *WedDAV* [43, 44] and *DeltaV* [70] are currently working in that direction. On the other hand, the web produced a new kind of artifacts: the web pages, which are evolving and highly related with each other, certainly requiring configuration management. Special consideration needs to be given to web pages because: the number of pages is significantly larger than the number of program source files, the time between changes is significantly shorter, and the number of contributors who are not necessarily computer specialists is significantly larger [35].

1.3 Collaborative programming

Collaborative programming is an emerging methodology for team software development, which allows a group of programmers to work together on the same source code for design, implementation, and integration. Design includes partitioning the source code into individual components, structuring relations between individual components, and making specifications for individual components. Implementation includes coding, debugging, testing, and documenting individual components according to their specifications in a programming language, where documentation is to add comments on various places in individual components in order to improve the readability of the code. Integration includes debugging and testing the source code with integrated individual components, and documenting comments in individual components to reflect the integration process.

A team software development process should consist of different phases from design, implementation of individual components, to integration of individual components. Therefore, the way of collaboration among team members in a software development should be adaptive to these different phases. In particular:

- In the design phase, the source code is initially empty and there is no obvious rule for team members to develop the source code. Because of the vague and explorative nature of the software system to be developed, all team members should work out a feasible way to partition the system into components, structure relations between components, and make specifications for components, by means of brainstorming and frequent interaction. Therefore, most collaboration in this phase would be in real-time (synchronous).

- In the implementation phase, individual team members have been assigned with individual components to work on. Those working on different components work concurrently and independently, with little interaction. Those working on the same component could sometimes interact frequently for coding, debugging, testing, and documenting the same component, or sometimes work independently on different parts of the same component for isolated functions with little interaction. Therefore, collaboration in this phase could be in either real-time (synchronous) or non-real-time (asynchronous), or a combination of both.

- In the integration phase, individual components are integrated into the same source code, which needs to be thoroughly tested and debugged to ensure all components work well together. Any changes resulting from the integration should be well documented in corresponding components for the sake of readability of the source code. Because integration involves interrelated components implemented by individual team members, they should work interactively to find and fix bugs that hinder the integration, and to document changes in their own components in the process of debugging and testing. Therefore collaboration in this phase should be mainly in real-time (synchronous).

Furthermore, in a team software development process, for those situations where real-time collaboration is difficult to achieve because the network connecting collaborators is unreliable (e.g., in mobile and wireless computing environments) or collaborators are separated geographically in different time zones, non-real-time collaboration can be used to support team software development. When situations change in favour of real-time collaboration, tasks that definitely need real-time collaboration can then be fulfilled.

In conclusion, collaborative programming is distinguished from pair programming and SCM in that collaborative programming respects the variety of different phases or situations in a team software development process and makes itself flexible enough to be contingent upon the variety. In contrast, pair programming or SCM only addresses some phases or situations and could not adapt to the variety of different phases or situations. For example, pair programming only addresses the need for real-time collaboration in which a common goal can be reached by frequent interaction but does not address the need for non-real-time collaboration in which concurrent work can be made to the same source code by means of noninteractive cooperation. SCM is just opposite to pair programming; it only addresses the need for noninteractive cooperation but does not address the need for interactive collaboration.

1.3.1 The case for collaborative programming

The emergence of collaborative programming is the response to many surveys on team software development and collaborative writing. Blackburn *et al.* [15] divided a concurrent software development process into isolated and non-isolated stages and simultaneous activities should be made in different ways at different stages. Magnusson [85] pointed out that the work in development and maintenance of software systems typically alternates between group tasks and individual assignments. As a result, collaborative software development needs to support development in both asynchronous mode for individual assignments and synchronous mode for group tasks. Dewan and Riedl [37] stressed the importance of allowing engineers to collaborate both synchronously and asynchronously and allowing them to switch between close and loose collaboration in concurrent software engineering in order to enable engineers to maximize collaboration despite differences in work styles or time zones.

An empirical study of how people are actually collaborating in writing by Posner and Baecker [102] concludes that both real-time and non-real-time strategies and processes are used in different phases of a collaborative writing project and a system must support both styles and allow a smooth transition between them. Rhyne and Wolf [110] also argued the necessity of an integrated model that includes both real-time and non-real-time capabilities. On the one hand, the lack of non-real-time capability in a real-time application makes it difficult for a person to review the events that occurred before s/he joined. One the other hand, not being able to switch from a non-real-time mode to a real-time mode makes it difficult for a group of people to interactively discuss the same issue.

In conclusion, technology that strictly enforces limited approaches and that is not sufficiently flexible will constrain the group work process and likely lead to frustration and eventually lack of use of the prescriptive technology [102]. Therefore, as advocated by Koch [77] and Posner [102], technical support should be provided in as flexible a way as possible without being enforced and technology needs to be flexible and permissive, allowing groups to change strategies and processes at any time during the project with minimal distraction. Collaborative programming is therefore proposed to realize these philosophies for team software development.

1.3.2 Collaborative editing

There are many technical components in collaborative programming, such as collaborative design, collaborative implementation, collaborative debugging, collaborative testing, and collaborative documentation. Each technical component has a number of issues to be tackled, such as:

- *Group awareness* - group awareness allows each participant to be informed of the work done by others in a team working environment, including the presence of other participants, the creation and availability of new objects, changes to the objects, etc [41, 66].

- *Access control* - control access to shared artifacts by multiple users [47, 40, 64].

- *Concurrency control* - in a collaborative environment, multiple users may attempt to access shared resources concurrently and it is important to control concurrent access so as to ensure the results of concurrent access are predictable [46, 54, 79, 118, 130].

Because collaborative programming is to support collaboration on the basis of shared source code while source code has to be manipulated by means of editing, a core technical component in collaborative programming is collaborative editing, which allows a group of programmers to view and edit the same source code. In particular:

- In the design phase, a group of programmers need to collaboratively edit the same source code in real-time to define new components, structure relations between components, and make specifications for components, by means of brainstorming and frequent interaction. Therefore, real-time (synchronous) collaborative editing is needed in this phase.

- In the implementation phase, programmers working on different components need to independently edit their own components with little interaction. Programmers working on the same component may sometimes collaboratively edit the same component in real-time for coding, debugging, testing, and documentation, or sometimes independently edit different parts of the same component for isolated functions with little interaction. Therefore real-time (or synchronous) or non-real-time (or asynchronous) collaborative editing, or a combination of both is needed in this phase.

- In the integration phase, programmers need to collaboratively edit the same source code with integrated components implemented by individual programmers in real-time, by means of frequent interaction and discussion, in order to write testing programs, find and fix bugs hindering the integration, and document comments on changes in individual components during the process of debugging and testing. Therefore, real-time (synchronous) collaborative editing is needed in this phase.

1.3.3 Requirements for collaborative editing

To support different phases or situations in an Internet-based collaborative programming process, some requirements for collaborative editing are identified as follows:

- Real-time collaborative editing is needed to support phases or situations that require frequent interaction among participants. Real-time collaborative editing should be *responsive* and *unconstrained*.

- Non-real-time collaborative editing is needed to support phases or situations that do not require frequent interaction among participants. Non-real-time collaborative editing should be *unconstrained* and *syncretic*.

- Switching between real-time and non-real-time collaborative editing is needed to support transit between different phases or situations. Switching should be *smooth* and *flexible*.

First, a collaborative editing system is *responsive* in the sense that local response should ideally be as good as that in single-user editors. Non-real-time collaborative editing is certainly responsive because it usually uses single-user editors. However, real-time collaborative editing is generally supported by specially designed group editors, which should be equally responsive. Second, a collaborative editing system is *unconstrained* in the sense that it should support concurrent editing of the same document without imposing any restrictions to users' actions. In other words, users should be allowed to edit any part of a shared document in any manner at any time in either real-time or non-real-time collaborative editing. Third, a collaborative editing system is *syncretic* in the sense that it should be able to integrate different pieces of work done by multiple users on the same document. Real-time collaborative editing is syncretic because the specially designed group editors have mechanisms to ensure users' actions be integrated in the same shared document in real-time. Non-real-time collaborative editing should be syncretic in the sense that changes made to the shared document by multiple users over any length of time should be automatically integrated.

Finally, switching between real-time and non-real-time collaborative editing should be *smooth* in the sense that transit from real-time to non-real-time collaborative editing or vice versa should not cause any distraction to users. Users should still do collaborative editing in their normal ways without paying much attention to the mode change. Moreover, switching between real-time and non-real-time collaborative editing should be *flexible* in the sense that any user should be allowed to transit from real-time to non-real-time collaborative editing or vice versa at any time without any restriction. With the guide of the identified requirements for collaborative editing, we will review some representative techniques and systems for real-time collaborative editing, non-real-time collaborative editing, and switching between real-time and non-real-time collaborative editing, and outline our major contributions to collaborative editing for supporting Internet-based collaborative programming.

1.4 Real-time collaborative editing

Real-time collaborative editing has been studied for over a decade and quite a lot of systems have been developed to demonstrate real-time collaborative editing techniques. The architecture of these systems can be classified into two main categories: centralized architecture and replicated architecture [63].

1.4.1 Centralized architecture

Centralized architecture [79] uses a central server that runs a single instance of the shared editing program with a single copy of the shared document. Inputs from participants at multiple sites are merged and delivered to the single instance of the editing program and any change to the graphical output of the editing program is broadcast to all sites. Real-time collaborative editing systems facilitated by various shared window systems like *VNC* [111], Microsoft *Netmeeting* [87], or HP *SharedX* [60] all fall into this category.

Real-time collaborative editing systems with centralized architecture are generally collaboration-transparent systems, which provide the shared use of existing single-user applications through mechanisms that are transparent to the applications and developers [80], and can be used to collaborate in legacy applications that were developed with no support of collaboration in mind [6]. But there are a few exceptions, which are specially designed collaboration-aware systems to support real-time collaborative editing with centralized architecture. For example, the *Make frame on display* feature in *Emacs* text editor allows a single Emacs to talk to multiple frames distributed on multiple X Windows displays [20]. Each frame is a terminal of the shared Emacs for accepting inputs from keyboard or mouse and transmitting them to Emacs, and displaying outputs propagated from Emacs. Inputs from multiple frames are floor controlled [33], which means only one frame is available for accepting inputs at any instant of time.

Another example is *MMM* (Multi-device Multi-User Multi-Editor) shared editors [12], which support the sharing of a hierarchy of editors on a single screen among a group of users for conference applications. Input events from all users are placed in the same queue, where actions are responded differently. Mandatory actions such as text inputs on the same text editor are floor controlled and handled in the order in which they are received. Optional actions such as dragging or resizing rectangle editors are allowed to be generated simultaneously and handled in the way that the editor selects the user who has been least recently served so that the editor is equally responsive to all users.

Generally speaking, real-time collaborative editing with centralized architecture is simple and easy to implement, and can be used to collaborate in legacy applications that were developed with no support of collaboration in mind. But it is unable to meet the requirements of collaborative editing for supporting Internet-based collaborative programming for the following reasons: first, it is not responsive [6, 60] because in response to a local input, the input event first has to be transferred across the network to the application, then is applied onto the application, and finally changes to the graphical output of the application have to be transferred back across the network. Because the Internet has higher latency and more nondeterministic traffic congestion, compared to LAN, Internet-based real-time collaborative editing with centralized architecture is even less responsive. Moreover, real-time collaborative editing with centralized architecture does not support unconstrained work because inputs from multiple users are floor-controlled and collaboration is supported in a tightly coupled style that forces all users to view the same portion of the shared document all the time.

1.4.2 Replicated architecture

Real-time collaborative editing with replicated architecture is able to overcome the shortcomings in centralized architecture, which is more suitable to be used for supporting Internet-based collaborative programming. In replicated architecture, the shared editing program and the shared document are replicated at all collaborating sites. Local changes are applied to the local replica of the shared document and reflected on the local user interface of the shared editing program immediately, which ensures a good local response. User inputs may not be restricted by floor control and consequently unconstrained work may be supported.

Local changes are propagated to remote sites to keep all replicas consistent. The benefit of propagating changes is twofold. First of all, changes made to the shared document are significantly smaller than the output pixels from the editing program. Therefore propagation of changes makes network resources utilized efficiently. Moreover, propagation of local changes can be controlled to support both tightly coupled and loosely coupled collaboration styles.

Replication is a major technique to hide communication latency and support responsive real-time collaborative editing, but it may cause inconsistency problems, that is, replicas of the shared document could become inconsistent at different sites. Consistency maintenance is a key issue in collaborative editing with replicated architecture [47, 137] and has attracted major research attention for a long time.

1.4.3 Consistency maintenance techniques

Sun *et al.* [137] presented a consistency model, which has been widely accepted as a theoretical framework for consistency maintenance in real-time collaborative editing with replicated architecture. In this framework, consistency is maintained if the following properties have been preserved:

- *Convergence*: when the same set of operations have been executed at all sites, all replicas of the shared document are identical.

- *Causality Preservation*: operations are always performed in their natural cause-effect order at all sites despite nondeterministic communication latencies.

- *Intention Preservation*: for any operation O, the effects of executing O at all sites are the same as the execution effect by applying O on the document state from which O was generated, and the effects of executing O does not change the effects of concurrent operations.

In essence, the *convergence* property ensures the consistency of the final results *at the end* of a collaborative editing session; the *causality-preservation* property ensures the consistency of the execution orders of causally ordered operations *during* a collaborative editing session; and the *intention-preservation* property ensures that the effects of executing an operation at remote sites achieve the same effect as executing this operation at the local site at the time of its generation, and that the execution effects of concurrent operations do not interfere with each other. The consistency model imposes an execution order constraint on causally ordered operations only, but leaves it open for execution order of concurrent operations as long as the convergence and intention-preservation properties are maintained. The consistency model effectively specifies, on the one hand, what assurance a collaborative editing system promises to its users, on the other hand, what properties the underlining consistency maintenance techniques must support.

Causal ordering by means of timestamping [52, 78, 107] is a well-known technique for causality preservation, which relies on a timestamping scheme based on a data structure called *State Vector* [46, 137] to capture the causal relationships among operations. The causal ordering relation between two operations is defined in terms of their generation and execution sequences [78, 137].

Definition 1.1. Causal ordering relation "$\rightarrow$"

Given two operations O_a and O_b generated at sites i and j, then O_a is causally before O_b, denoted as $O_a \rightarrow O_b$, *iff*:

1. $i = j$ and the generation of O_a *happened before* the generation of O_b, or

2. $i \neq j$ and the execution of O_a at site j *happened before* the generation of O_b, or

3. there exists an operation O_x such that $O_a \rightarrow O_x$ and $O_x \rightarrow O_b$.

In this approach, local operations can be executed immediately after their generation, so responsiveness is good. But some remote operations that arrive out of causal order are selectively delayed until all causally preceding operations have been executed in order to ensure that operations are always performed in their natural cause-effect order at all collaborating sites despite of nondeterministic network communication latencies [46, 137]. Another commonly used technique is to use a central *propagator* to relay all operations generated from collaborating sites [134], if communication channels between the central *propagator* and collaborating sites are reliable and order-preserving. The causal ordering approach can achieve causality preservation only, but it does not address the problems of divergence and intention violation.

Convergence can be achieved by various concurrency control techniques, which can be divided into two categories: pessimistic concurrency control that prevents divergence from occurring and optimistic concurrency control that allows divergence to occur but provides mechanisms to resolve it. Turn-taking is a pessimistic concurrency control technique in which participants take turns to manipulate the shared data and only one participant at a time has the floor to operate [79, 63]. Since there is only a single active user at any instant of time, all three consistency properties can be preserved but at the cost of not supporting concurrent editing. Consequently, this approach is limited to just situations where having a single active participant fits the dynamics of the session [46], and ill-suited to application environments where the nature of collaboration is characterized by concurrent streams of activities from multiple users [38]. Turn-taking has been adopted in several real-time collaborative editing systems such as *GroupKit* [114].

Locking is another pessimistic concurrency control technique, where an object (e.g., a word, a line, or a section, etc.) is first locked before it is going to be updated. This way, only one user at a time is able to update a object, which can prevent multiple users from generating conflicting editing operations over the same object [86, 130]. However, unless the granularity of locking is the whole document (thus resorting to the turn-taking protocol), none of the three consistency properties can be ensured by locking since the occurrence of those inconsistency problems is independent of whether or not editing operations refer to the same object [137]. Moreover, locking increases response time due to the overhead of requesting and releasing locks in distributed environments.

Serialization exploits a global time ordering defined for operations, where operations may be generated concurrently but the execution effects will be the same as if all operations were executed in the same *total order* [137] at all sites. This can be achieved either by pessimistically delaying the execution of an operation until all totally preceding operations have been executed [78], or optimistically executing operations upon their arrival or generation without regard to their ordering, but using a repairing technique such as *undo/redo* to repair out-of-order execution effects [74, 63]. Serialization can solve the problem of divergence, but has the following problems: first, the intention violation problem cannot be solved by serializing concurrent operation in any order. We will have an example in the following section. Second, the causality violation problem remains unsolved if operations are executed upon their arrival in the optimistic case, or if the total ordering is inconsistent with the causal ordering in the pessimistic case [137]. Third, responsiveness may not be good if operations are not executed immediately after their generation in the pessimistic case. Finally, there is an unpleasant possibility that an operation will appear on the user's screen and later disappear as the result of the undo in the optimistic case [46, 128]. Optimistic serialization based protocols have been adopted in several real-time collaborative editing systems such as *Prospero* [39] and *Groove* [95].

Operational transformation [46, 136] is an innovative optimistic concurrency control technique for both intention preservation and convergence without imposing any restrictions on users' activities. In this technique, local operations are executed immediately after their generation, therefore local response is good. Remote operations may need to be transformed before their execution so that the execution of the same set of properly transformed operations in different orders could produce identical document states [46]. Operational transformation is often combined with the causal ordering approach to achieve all three consistency properties. Operational transformation approach has been adopted in several real-time collaborative editing systems such as *GROVE* [47], *REDUCE* [137], *JAMM* [6], and *Hydra* [49].

1.4.4 Operational transformation

Because operational transformation technique is the foundation of our research, we would like to briefly introduce some background knowledge about operational transformation [137, 136]. In a real-time collaborative editing system that uses operational transformation technique for optimistic concurrency control, concurrent operations need to be transformed against each other before execution. The concurrent relation between two operations is defined as follows.

Definition 1.2. Concurrent relation "$\|$"

Given two operations O_a and O_b, O_a is concurrent with O_b, denoted as $O_a \parallel O_b$, *iff* neither $O_a \rightarrow O_b$ nor $O_b \rightarrow O_a$.

Concurrent operations are transformed against each other by two types of primitive transformation functions [137]: one is the *Inclusion Transformation* function – $IT(O_a, O_b)$, which transforms operation O_a against operation O_b in such a way that the impact of O_b is effectively included in the parameters of the output operation O_a'; and the other is the *Exclusion Transformation* function – $ET(O_a, O_b)$, which transforms O_a against O_b in such a way that the impact of O_b is effectively excluded from the parameters of the output operation O_a'.

The following definitions are used to describe the precondition and the postcondition of primitive transformation functions.

Definition 1.3. Operation context "CT"

Given an operation O, its *context*, denoted as CT_O, is the document state on which O is defined.

Definition 1.4. Context preceding relation "$\mapsto$"

Given two operations O_a and O_b, O_a is *context preceding* O_b, denoted as $O_a \mapsto O_b$, *iff* $CT_{O_b} = CT_{O_a} \circ [O_a]$.

Definition 1.5. Context equivalent relation "$\sqcup$"

Given two operations O_a and O_b, O_a is *context equivalent* O_b, denoted as $O_a \sqcup O_b$, ***iff*** $CT_{O_a} = CT_{O_b}$.

The precondition for $O_a' = \textbf{IT}(O_a, O_b)$ transformation is $O_a \sqcup O_b$ and its post-condition is $O_b \mapsto O_a'$. Furthermore, transformation has the following two properties to meet:

Definition 1.6. List equivalent relation "≡"

Given any two lists of operations L_a and L_b storing editing operations performed on the document state S_0, then L_a and L_b are equivalent, denoted as $L_a \equiv L_b$, ***iff*** $S_0 \circ L_a = S_0 \circ L_b$.

Based on the definition of list equivalent relation, two transformation properties are described as follows:

Property 1.1. *Transformation Property 1(TP1)*

Given two operations O_a and O_b, if $O_a' = \textbf{IT}(O_a, O_b)$ and $O_b' = \textbf{IT}(O_b, O_a)$, then $[O_a, O_b'] \equiv [O_b, O_a']$.

Property 1.2. *Transformation Property 2(TP2)*

Given three operations O, O_a and O_b, if $O_a' = \textbf{IT}(O_a, O_b)$ and $O_b' = \textbf{IT}(O_b, O_a)$, then $\textbf{IT}(\textbf{IT}(O, O_a), O_b')) = \textbf{IT}(\textbf{IT}(O, O_b), O_a'))$.

Furthermore, the precondition for $O_a' = \textbf{ET}(O_a, O_b)$ transformation is $O_b \mapsto O_a$ and its postcondition is $O_b \sqcup O_a'$. In addition, inclusion transformation and exclusion transformation has the following reversibility property to meet:

Property 1.3. *Reversibility Property (RP)*

Given any two operations O_a and O_b, if $O_b' = \textbf{ET}(O_b, O_a)$, then $O_b = \textbf{IT}(O_b', O_a)$.

The reversibility property should be met in defining exclusion transformation functions. But in reality, it is difficult to define exclusion transformation functions that always meet the reversibility property due to the information loss in defining inclusion transformation functions [137].

Various transformation control algorithms have been devised to control the transformation process in order to meet the above preconditions, postconditions, and transformation properties. Representative algorithms are *dOPT* [46], *adOPTed* [109], *GOT* [137], and *GOTO* [136]. But none of them is able to always meet all those conditions and properties. *adOPTed* [109], *GOT* [137], and *GOTO* [136] algorithms are able to meet transformation preconditions and postconditions but may violate transformation property 2(TP2). The *dOPT* algorithm could even violate transformation preconditions and postconditions.

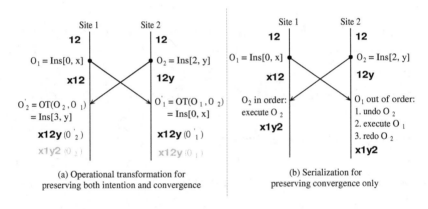

(a) Operational transformation for
preserving both intention and convergence

(b) Serialization for
preserving convergence only

Figure 1.6: Operational transformation versus serialization

An example is given to show how operational transformation technique can be used to preserve intention and convergence. As shown in Figure 1.6(a), the shared document initially contains characters 1 and 2, replicated at two sites *Site 1* and *Site 2*. *Site 1* performs an operation $O_1 = \mathbf{Ins}[0, x]$ to insert character x at position 0 (i.e., before character 1) while *Site 2* concurrently performs another operation $O_2 = \mathbf{Ins}[2, y]$ to insert character y at position 2 (i.e., after character 2). Because $O_2 \parallel O_1$, when O_2 arrives at *Site 1*, it should be transformed against the concurrent operation O_1 by the transformation function $O_2' = \mathbf{IT}(O_2, O_1) = \mathbf{Ins}[3, \text{y}]$ before execution. Because $CT_{O_2} \sqcup CT_{O_1}$ with $CT_{O_2} = CT_{O_1} = 12$, the precondition of $\mathbf{IT}(O_2, O_1)$ has been met. As a result, execution of O_2' on the current document state $x12$ is able to preserve O_2's intention of inserting character y after character 2, and preserve convergence in the document state $x12y$. In contrast, if O_2 were executed as-is, character y would be inserted before character 2, which violates O_2's intention and leads to divergent document states: $x1y2$ at *Site 1* and $x12y$ at *Site 2*.

By comparison, if optimistic serialization is applied to the same example, presuming O_1 is totally before O_2 according to the global ordering, Figure 1.6(b) shows how convergence is maintained while intention is not preserved. When O_2 arrives at *Site 1*, it is in the correct order and therefore is executed as-is, leading to the result that character y has been inserted before character 2, which apparently violates O_2's intention. When O_1 arrives at *Site 2*, it is out of the order. So O_2 is first undone, then O_1 is executed, and finally O_2 is redone. O_2 inserted character y after character 2, but when it is undone and then redone, it inserts character y before character 2, which apparently violates O_2's intention. Nevertheless, the two sites are convergent since their document states are the same: $x1y2$.

1.4.5 Focuses and contributions

In recent years, major research attention has been paid to consistency maintenance by means of operational transformation technique in real-time collaborative editing systems. By comparison, our research on real-time collaborative editing has been focused on another important issue - group awareness, which allows each participant to be informed of the work done by others [41, 62, 66]. Gestural communication tools are a kind of group awareness tools, which they are particularly more important for improving the quality of real-time interaction in real-time collaborative editing of shared source code. In a collaborative programming process, programmers often need to collaboratively edit the same source code file in the form of brainstorming, exchanging ideas, or close discussion. Therefore, gestural communication tools are very useful for them to draw attention to particular parts in a source code, indicate relations between various parts in a source code, show intentions about what they are about to do, suggest emotional reactions, and so on.

One major contribution of our research on unconstrained, responsive, real-time collaborative editing is a useful collaborative *highlighting* gestural communication tool [126] for improving the quality of real-time interaction. Two major issues have been identified in collaborative highlighting. One is consistency maintenance and the other is collaborative undo. So, the major contribution to the operational transformation technique is the extension of the technique, originally proposed for consistency maintenance in real-time collaborative editing, to support group awareness, by means of collaborative highlighting. It includes a package of operational transformation functions and transformation control algorithms for consistency maintenance in collaborative highlighting, and a flexible undo solution that has the capability of undoing any highlighting operation at any time. To test the correctness of the collaborative highlighting technique and to demonstrate the feasibility and usefulness of the collaborative highlighting tool, collaborative highlighting has been implemented in the *REDUCE* (Real-time Distributed Unconstrained Collaborative Editing) system [138].

1.5 Non-real-time collaborative editing

Non-real-time collaborative editing has been practiced since the emergence of single-user editors. People normally do non-real-time collaborative editing without using specially designed collaborative editors.

1.5.1 Related techniques and systems

There are three basic forms of non-real-time collaborative editing. One is *turn-taking* where participants take turns to change the shared document and only one participant at a time is allowed to perform changes. This form of non-real-time collaborative editing was initially coordinated by pure human social protocols but was later facilitated by some software systems. One example is *Prep* [97], which supports non-real-time collaborative editing between co-authors and commenters in the form of authoring and commenting. Another example is *MESSIE* [119] that supports non-real-time collaborative editing via Email to transfer the shared document around a group of collaborators. Other examples are shared workspace systems like *BSCW* [68] and *WebDAV* [44], which lock the shared document before it is going to be modified by a collaborator. An obvious disadvantage of this form is that it does not allow multiple participants to edit the shared document concurrently, which is inadequate for meeting the specified requirements of collaborative editing for supporting collaborative programming.

Another form is *Split-Combine* [85] where the shared document is first split into partitions, then each collaborator makes changes in her/his own partition independently, and finally the updated partitions are combined to become the updated shared document. This form of non-real-time collaborative editing does support concurrent editing of the shared document. But it is neither easy nor always feasible to split a shared document into independent partitions that can be concurrently modified by individual collaborators without any knowledge about what has happened to other partitions. If partitions are interrelated syntactically or semantically but changes in individual partitions have been made without any knowledge of these interrelations, it could be very difficult to combine updated partitions into a desirable updated document. Although this approach is still practised in real world, its application is rather ad hoc and there is no software system supporting the *split* or *combine* process.

Copy-Modify-Merge [32] is a widely used form of non-real-time collaborative editing, where each collaborator is first given a full copy of the shared document, then does changes in her/his own copy, and finally merges changes in all copies together. This form of non-real-time collaborative editing suits collaborative programming because it allows participants to concurrently edit the shared document and allows concurrent changes to be automatically integrated into the final updated document by means of merging. This approach has been adopted in various SCM systems such as *CVS* [10, 56], *Subversion* [27], *ClearCase* [1], and *Continuus* [19, 34] for supporting non-real-time collaborative editing of shared documents and version control of evolving shared documents.

1.5.2 Focuses and contributions

There are a lot of issues in non-real-time collaborative editing, such as group awareness, access control, data management, workspace management, web support, and so on, but our research has been focused on merging, which is the core technical component in the *Copy-Modify-Merge* approach, to support unconstrained, syncretic, non-real-time collaborative editing of the same document. On the one hand, existing merging algorithms are inefficient to be used in the Internet environment because they are inefficient in utilizing network resources and time-consuming. On the other hand, existing merging algorithms are not syncretic enough because some non-conflicting changes are unable to be automatically merged and some conflicting changes are unable to be automatically detected and resolved.

One major contribution of our research on unconstrained, syncretic, non-real-time collaborative editing is a flexible operation-based merging technique, which is efficient and has the capability of textually integrating all changes concurrently made by multiple users and automatically detecting and resolving syntactic conflicts according to application-dependent user-specified policies. Major issues in flexible operation-based merging include compression of logs that store user-performed editing operations to ensure the efficiency of operation-based merging [122], a textual merging algorithm that is able to textually integrate all changes with their intentions correctly preserved [124], and a syntactic merging algorithm that is able to automatically detect and resolve syntactic conflicts according to application-dependent user-specified policies [124].

So, the major contribution to the operational transformation technique is the extension of the technique, originally proposed for supporting unconstrained, responsive, real-time collaborative editing, to support unconstrained, syncretic, non-real-time collaborative editing. It includes a log compression algorithm, a textual merging algorithm, and a syntactic merging algorithm. The flexible operation-based merging technique has been implemented in the *FORCE* (Flexible Operation-based Revision Control Environment) source code editor with integrated flexible version control support for the purpose of testing the correctness, demonstrating the feasibility and usefulness, and investigating system design and implementation issues.

1.6 Switching between real-time and non-real-time collaborative editing

As specified in the requirements of collaborative editing for collaborative programming, a very important requirement is that smooth, flexible switching between real-time and non-real-time collaborative editing should be supported in order to adapt to different phases or situations in a collaborative programming process.

1.6.1 Related techniques and systems

A naive approach for switching between real-time and non-real-time collaborative editing is to simply use separate real-time and non-real-time collaborative editing systems and manually switch between these two systems from time to time. This approach has two major problems. First, it is difficult to achieve smooth switching between these two different systems because they were designed without any knowledge of each other and are likely to be incompatible in the sense that they view their data differently and do not provide any mechanism to share data between them [110]. For example, a group of programmers use a SCM system such as *CVS* [10] to do non-real-time collaborative editing of a shared source code file. When there is a need for them to switch to the real-time collaborative editing mode in order to interactively tackle an urgent issue by using a real-time collaborative editing system such as *REDUCE* [138], the switch process will not be smooth because the *REDUCE* system is unable to automatically obtain a proper document to start with. In fact, all participants have to stop non-real-time collaborative editing and reconcile a proper document for *REDUCE* to start with. Moreover, it is difficult to achieve flexible switching by allowing any participant to switch to any one of the two systems at any time. In the above example, before switching from non-real-time collaborative editing to real-time collaborative editing, all participants have to run a protocol involving a number of merging rounds to obtain a convergent copy of the shared source code file. That protocol could take several minutes or even hours to complete [9], depending on how far those copies are divergent and how effective the merging algorithm is.

Turn-taking is a concurrency control mechanism used by both real-time and non-real-time collaborative editing. Therefore, a commonly used approach for supporting switching between real-time and non-real-time collaborative editing is to use turn-taking as the common concurrency control mechanism to prevent inconsistent copies from happening. A representative system is the *SEPIA* hypertext authoring system [67], which allows work to be done in three different modes: *individual, loosely coupled,* and *tightly coupled.* When working on a document without concurrent users, an author works in *individual* work mode, which is a typical non-real-time collaborative editing mode. Multiple users are not allowed to do concurrent individual work on the same document but are allowed to take turns to do individual work on the same document.

When a co-author works on a document already used by another author, all concurrent users shift into *loosely coupled* mode, where multiple users collaboratively edit the same document in real-time by the technique of turn-taking in which the document may be edited by one user at a time while others may see the changes in real-time. If some co-author in a loosely coupled session feels the need for a real-time conference, the co-author can initiate a tightly coupled session with a group of specified loosely coupled collaborators to join in. In a tightly coupled session, collaborators work in the way of *WYSIWIS* (What You See Is What I See) [129] by shared views [41, 62], telepointers [6, 115], and audio communication but real-time collaborative editing is still based on turn-taking.

This approach does support smooth, flexible switching between real-time and non-real-time collaborative editing [67]. But, as discussed in Section 1.4, turn-taking is a pessimistic concurrency control technique that does not support concurrent work. So, the disadvantage of this approach is that unconstrained concurrent editing is not supported in either real-time or non-real-time collaborative editing, which consequently does not meet the requirements of collaborative editing for collaborative programming.

1.6.2 Focuses and contributions

Notification is an essential feature in both real-time and non-real-time collaborative systems, which determines when, what, and how changes made by one user are propagated, applied, and reflected on other users' interfaces [46, 125]. Therefore, our research has been focused on supporting smooth, flexible switching between real-time and non-real-time collaborative editing from the perspective of notification. One major contribution of our research on smooth, flexible switching between real-time and non-real-time collaborative editing is a flexible notification technique to support flexible collaborative editing that integrates unconstrained, responsive, real-time collaborative editing, unconstrained, syncretic, non-real-time collaborative editing, and smooth, flexible switching between real-time and non-real-time collaborative editing.

A major issue in the flexible notification technique is that an efficient consistency maintenance solution is required for flexible collaborative editing. So the major contribution to the operational transformation technique is the extension of the technique, originally proposed for consistency maintenance in real-time collaborative editing, to support consistency maintenance in flexible collaborative editing. It includes a new transformation control algorithm that has a linear time complexity, two notification algorithms that support propagation and acceptance of any notifications at any time, and a notification propagation protocol that is efficient for both real-time and non-real-time collaborative editing. The flexible notification technique has been implemented in the web-based flexible collaborative editing system *NICE* (Notification-flexible Collaborative Editing) for the purpose of testing the correctness, demonstrating the feasibility, and providing a vehicle to do a usability study and motivate future research on flexible collaborative editing.

1.7   Thesis outline

The rest of the thesis is organized as follows: Chapter 2 presents a novel collaborative highlighting technique, including technical solutions for supporting consistency maintenance and flexible collaborative undo in real-time collaborative editing. Chapter 3 presents a flexible operation-based merging technique, including issues and technical solutions in applying operation-based merging to supporting textual and syntactic merging in non-real-time collaborative editing of text documents. Chapter 4 presents a flexible notification technique, including a framework for unifying real-time and non-real-time collaborative systems and technical solutions for consistency maintenance

37

in flexible collaborative editing. Chapter 5 presents an Internet-based collaborative programming environment *RECIPE* (Replicated Collaborative Interactive Programming Environment) that integrates the proposed techniques on collaborative editing for supporting collaborative programming. Finally Chapter 6 concludes the thesis with a summary of major contributions and future work.

Chapter 2

Real-time collaborative highlighting

In the design phase of a collaborative programming process, programmers need to collaboratively edit the same source code to define new components, their relations, and their specifications by means of brainstorming. In the integration phase of a collaborative programming process, programmers need to collaboratively edit the same source code to find and fix bugs, and document changes that have been made in individual components to reflect the integration process. While various external communication tools such as audio, video, and text chatting [87, 73] have proven useful in facilitating real-time interaction, internal communication tools such as telepointer [6, 113] are even more valuable for drawing attention to particular artifacts and their relations. In this chapter, we present a novel internal gestural communication tool - *highlighting*, which is even more useful than telepointer in facilitating real-time interaction on text-based source code documents.

2.1 Introduction

Highlighting is a common feature in most single-user editors, which provides users with a mechanism of emphasizing important text in order to support non-real-time collaboration between the author and readers. This feature is naturally necessary and even more valuable in multi-user collaborative editors. First, besides supporting non-real-time collaboration, highlighting can be used to help real-time collaboration, such as highlighting key points in brainstorming, discussing interesting topics, and debugging programs. Second, highlighting may be used for other purposes that have never been used in single-user editors. Highlighting can be used for providing awareness hints. For instance, when doing some crucial tasks in an area, a user can highlight the area to warn others to avoid updating the same area.

Finally, highlighting can be used as a complementary tool to telepointer, a gestural communication tool for supporting real-time discussion. Telepointer [6, 113, 115] is a well-known and commonly used tool in real-time collaborative applications for indicating remote users' cursor or mouse locations [6]. It can serve as a mechanism of gestural communication through which participants indicate relations between the artifacts on the display, draw attention to particular artifacts, show intentions about what they are about to do, suggest emotional reactions, and so on [115]. However, telepointing has limitations. First, a telepointer can indicate a focus on only one character and may not make much sense for text documents. Moreover, a telepointer dynamically moves around a document and the user cannot see its history track, hence it is incapable of simultaneously keeping multiple focuses and difficult to indicate relations among multiple artifacts in a document. Highlighting can overcome these drawbacks in telepointing because a highlight is designed to cover a region rather than a single character and multiple highlights can be simultaneously kept in a document.

To illustrate the above points, an example is shown in Figure 2.1. In this scenario, a teacher checks English errors in a document and a student concurrently corrects the errors pointed out by the teacher in the same document. In Figure 2.1(a), the teacher's telepointer moves from one error to another. The teacher has to wait for the student to correct the current error before moving to the next one because once his telepointer moves to the next error, the information on previous errors (shown as grey telepointers) will disappear. Moreover, those telepointers could not precisely tell where the errors are. For instance, the last telepointer pointed at character *o* in the word *not*. But the error was not character *o*. Instead, the error was the answer *not old*, which should be in this case something like *16 years old*. By contrast, in Figure 2.1(b), all errors have been simultaneously highlighted and these highlights can indicate precisely where the errors are. As a result, the teacher and the student can work concurrently at their own paces.

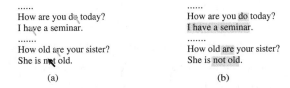

(a)   (b)

Figure 2.1: Telepointing versus highlighting

However, it is non-trivial to extend single-user highlighting to collaborative highlighting. First, the representation of highlights on the user interface in collaborative editors should be designed studied because it is necessary to distinguish different users' highlights in order to provide group awareness support. Group awareness [2, 42, 62, 65] is a fundamental and challenging issue in collaborative applications and the user interface design has a fundamental impact on other issues.

Second, concurrent operations and nondeterministic communication latency may cause inconsistency problems [47, 137]. In particular, concurrent highlighting operations may overshadow each other in different ways at different sites, concurrent insertion or deletion operations may change some document segments on which highlighting operations were performed, and nondeterministic communication latency may cause operations to arrive out of order. Consistency maintenance is another fundamental and challenging issue in collaborative applications with replicated architecture [6, 9, 47, 137].

Finally, collaborative undo of highlighting operations is needed for error recovering, try-and-failure, backtracking, and focus-changing [61, 141, 151, 123] during a real-time collaborative editing session. It is very challenging to achieve collaborative undo in general [8, 24, 25, 103, 108, 131]. Most existing solutions focus on undoing insertion and deletion operations [103, 108, 131] for text documents or graph editing operations for graphic documents [24, 144]. No work has been done on the undo of highlighting operations and no existing solution can be directly applied to the undo of highlighting operations.

Major differences between highlighting and insertion/deletion operations make solutions of consistency maintenance and collaborative undo for insertion and deletions operations not directly applicable to highlighting operations. The differences between highlighting operations and insertion/deletion operations are twofold. First, highlighting operations do not add or remove characters but change certain attribute of characters. Therefore, character positions in a document cannot be changed as the result of highlighting operations. Moreover, the effects of multiple highlighting operations may overlap each other. Although the effects of multiple graphic editing operations may also overlap each other [24], the difference between highlighting operations and graph editing operations is that highlighting operations are performed on sequential characters while graph editing operations are performed on independent objects.

The rest of the chapter is organized as follows: the representation of highlights on the user interface is discussed in the following section. The next section addresses the issue of consistency maintenance and presents technical solutions accordingly. A flexible undo solution is described after that and it has the capability of supporting collaborative undo of any operation at any time. Finally, the chapter is concluded with a summary of contributions and future work.

2.2   Representation of highlights

In single-user editors, a highlight is usually represented by changing the background colour of a sequence of characters to a randomly chosen colour that is different from the document background colour. In multi-user collaborative applications, colours are commonly used to differentiate operations performed by different users in order to provide some sort of group awareness support [2, 65]. Each user in a collaborative session is represented by a unique colour, which is called the user's *ID* colour. For example, in some collaborative editors [47], the foreground colour of the characters inserted by a user is set to the user's *ID* colour. The same approach can also be used to differentiate highlighting operations performed by different users in multi-user collaborative editors. For example, the *MMM* shared editor [12] has already demonstrated the use of colours to differentiate highlighting operations performed by different users.

The representation of highlights on the user interface is a fundamental issue in collaborative editors. There are many design choices. For example, in *MMM* shared editor [12], each highlight is marked by an underline in the *ID* colour of the user who performed the highlighting operation. Multiple overlapping highlights are represented by multiple underlines stacked beneath the text. The major merit of this approach is that it can simplify solutions to the issues of consistency maintenance and collaborative undo. But its drawback is also obvious. It uses a different representation for the same function supported in single-user editors. Therefore this approach may discourage users from learning, using and adopting the collaborative version of the single-user editor.

It is important that a multi-user collaborative application emulates the user interface of the corresponding single-user application in order to encourage users who are used to the single-user application to learn, use and adopt the multi-user collaborative version. Therefore, as shown in Figure 2.2, the representation of a highlight on the user interface in collaborative editors is represented as changing the background colour of a sequence of characters to a colour that is different from the document background colour. To differentiate highlighting operations performed by different users, the *ID* colour of the user who performs a highlighting operation is chosen as that background colour. On the basis of this representation of highlights on the user interface, we will address the issues of consistency maintenance and collaborative undo and present our technical solutions accordingly.

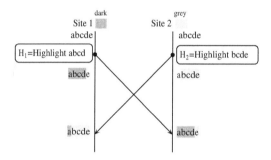

Figure 2.2: Highlights represented as changes of background colours

First, some notations need to be introduced for representing highlighting operations. A highlighting operation can be simply denoted as $\mathbf{Hlt}[P, N]$ to highlight a sequence of N characters starting from position P. However, undoing a highlighting operation must recover highlighting regions that have been overshadowed by the highlighting operation. To support the recovery of highlighting regions, highlighting regions overshadowed by a highlighting operation should be maintained inside that operation. The data structure OHL (Overshadowed Highlighting List) is used to maintain that information, where each element is called an OHR (Overshadowed Highlighting Region) denoted by a tuple $\langle S,\ L,\ C\rangle$, representing an overshadowed highlighting region in colour C (*null* will be used if the region has not been highlighted) covering a sequence of L characters starting from position S.

As a result, a highlighting operation that covers a sequence of N characters starting from position P and overshadows m OHRs will be denoted as $H = \mathbf{Hlt}[P,\ N,\ OHL]$ where $OHL = [\langle S_i,\ L_i,\ C_i\rangle \mid 1 \leq i \leq m]$. If $\langle S_i,\ L_i,\ C_i\rangle$ are sorted according to S_i's value, it must be $S_i = S_{i-1} + L_{i-1}$ $(1 \leq i \leq m)$, $P = S_1$, and $N = \sum_{i=1}^{m} L_i$. A highlighting operation H's inverse operation $\overline{H}$ is denoted as $\mathbf{Uhlt}[P,\ N,\ OHL]$, which means to recover background colours for a sequence of N characters starting from position P by highlighting a sequence of L_i characters starting from position S_i in colour C_i for any i $(1 \leq i \leq m)$. A special highlighting operation is dehighlighting, which clears highlights covered by a specified region. A dehighlighting operation can also be denoted as $\mathbf{Hlt}[P,\ N,\ OHL]$. The only difference is the colour for a dehighlighting operation is not the ID colour of the user who performs the operation but the background colour of the document. Solutions for consistency maintenance and collaborative undo of highlighting operations are directly applicable to dehighlighting operations. Therefore highlighting and dehighlighting operations will not be differentiated in the following discussions.

An insertion/deletion operation is denoted as $\mathbf{Ins/Del}[P,\ N,\ S]$ to represent inserting/deleting a string S of N characters at position P. For an insertion/deletion operation E, $P(E)$ denotes its position parameter, $N(E)$ denotes its length parameter, and $S(E)$ denotes its text parameter. For a highlighting operation $H = \mathbf{Hlt}[P,\ N,\ OHL]$, $P(H)$ denotes its position parameter, $N(H)$ denotes its length parameter, and $OHL(H)$ denotes its OHL parameter. For an operation O, $T(O)$ denotes its type parameter and $C(O)$ denotes the ID colour of the user who performs O.

An example is shown in Figure 2.3 to illustrate highlighting operations and their inverses. *Site 1* performed highlighting operation H_1 to highlight characters a, b, c, and d in its *ID* colour *dark*. After its execution, $H_1 = \mathbf{Hlt}[0, 4, [\langle 0, 4, null \rangle]]$, where $OHR = \langle 0, 4, null \rangle$ representing a region of four characters (i.e., a, b, c, and d) that has not been highlighted by any operation before H_1 was performed. Subsequently, *Site 2* performs highlighting operation H_2 to highlight characters b, c, d, and e in its *ID* colour *grey*. After its execution, $H_2 = \mathbf{Hlt}[1, 4, [\langle 1, 3, dark \rangle, \langle 4, 1, null \rangle]]$, where $OHR = \langle 1, 3, dark \rangle$ representing a region of three characters (i.e., b, c, and d) that was highlighted in dark, and $OHR = \langle 4, 1, null \rangle$ representing a region of one character (i.e., e) that has not been highlighted by any operation before H_2 was performed.

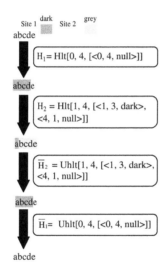

Figure 2.3: Highlighting operations and their inverses

Then *Site 2* performed H_2's inverse operation $\overline{H_2}$ to undo H_2'effect. After the execution of $\overline{H_2} = \mathbf{Uhlt}[1, 4, [\langle 1, 3, \text{dark} \rangle, \langle 4, 1, \text{null} \rangle]]$, characters b, c, and d are recovered to the dark background colour and character e is recovered to the document's background colour. Finally, *Site 1* performed H_1' inverse operation $\overline{H_1} = \mathbf{Uhlt}[0, 4, [\langle 0, 4, \text{null} \rangle]]$ to undo H_1's effect. After that, characters a, b, c, and d are recovered to the document's background colour.

2.3   Consistency maintenance

The consistency model proposed by Sun *et al.* [137] addresses inconsistency problems caused by concurrent insertion/deletion operations and can also be used to address inconsistency problems for collaborative highlighting in real-time collaborative editing systems.

2.3.1   General causality violation problem

Consider a document with characters A, B, and C, replicated at three sites *Site 1*, *Site 2*, and *Site 3*, as shown in Figure 2.4. *Site 1* performs an insertion operation $E = \mathbf{Ins}[1, 2, \text{xy}]$ to insert characters x and y at position 1 (i.e., between characters A and B). Subsequently *Site 2* performs a highlighting operation $H = \mathbf{Hlt}[1, 2, [\langle 1, 2, \text{null} \rangle]]$ to highlight a region of two characters from position 1 (i.e., characters x and y). According to Definition 1.1, $E \rightarrow H$ because the execution of E at *Site 2* happened before the generation of H.

After both operations have been executed at these three sites, results at *Site 1* and *Site 2* are both correct because the causal ordering relation between operations E and H have been correctly preserved. However, the causal relation was not preserved at *Site 3*, where the highlighting operation H was executed before the insertion operation E, leading to the result that characters B and C instead of characters x and y have been highlighted. Since the highlighting operation H was executed out of causal order, it refers to the wrong text BC rather than the correct text xy that has not

yet been inserted. This is a typical causality violation problem and the well-known
causal ordering technique [52, 78, 107] can be directly used to solve this problem.
This technique relies on a timestamping scheme based on a data structure named
State Vector [46, 137] to capture causal relations among operations. Operations that
arrive out of causal order are selectively delayed. In this example, when H arrives at
Site 3, H's state vector indicates that an operation that is causally before H has not
yet arrived. So the execution of H will be delayed until E that is causally before H
arrives and is executed.

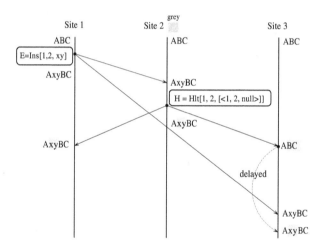

Figure 2.4: An example of causality violation

2.3.2   Divergence caused by concurrent overshadowing high-lighting operations

In Figure 2.2, H_1 and H_2 are concurrent highlighting operations and their highlighting
regions are overlapping in the sense that they both attempt to highlight a region of
three characters b, c, and d. Concurrent overlapping highlighting operations executed

in different orders at different sites may generate different overshadowed highlights at different sites. Therefore, in addition to the divergence problem defined in terms of different document contents at different sites and caused by concurrent insertion and deletion operations [137], a special divergence problem in collaborative highlighting is the divergent effects of overshadowed highlights although document contents may still be identical at all sites.

Although various pessimistic concurrency control techniques such as locking [130] and turn-taking [79] can be used to prevent such a divergence problem from happening, they are unsuitable for supporting real-time collaborative editing due to poor responsiveness and lack of concurrent work support [46]. As introduced in Chapter 1, optimistic serialization technique is responsive and can support concurrent work. It can be used to tackle the divergence problem by ensuring the final result is as if operations are executed in the same order at all sites. But its disadvantage is that a *undo-redo* repairing process may cause an unpleasant flash on the user interface [46, 128]. The proposed solution in this thesis is to emulate serialized effects, although operations are not executed in the same order at all sites. Like the optimistic serialization technique, this solution is responsive and supports concurrent work. Local highlighting operations are executed immediately on generation without any restriction. When a remote highlighting operation arrives out of order, a novel repairing process is used to achieve the serialized effect according to a global order and it does not cause any flash on the user interface.

The proposed solution is based on the operational transformation technique [136]. Briefly speaking, local highlighting operations are executed immediately. When a remote highlighting operation arrives in the right order, it will be executed as-is. Otherwise, it is transformed against concurrent highlighting operations to include their effects before execution. In the meantime, those concurrent highlighting operations are also transformed against this highlighting operation to include its effect. By means of transformation, the execution effect of the remote operation is as if it was executed before those concurrent highlighting operations that should be executed afterwards according to a global order. To implement this approach, each highlighting operation is timestamped with a state vector and each site maintains a data structure called HB (History Buffer) to store all executed local and remote operations. Based on the total ordering relation defined by Sun *et al.* [137], the *HOSE* (Highlighting Operation Serialization Emulation) algorithm for preserving convergence with only highlighting operations is defined as follows:

Algorithm 2.1. $HOSE(H_{new}, HB)$: $EH_{new} = [H_{new}^1, \cdots, H_{new}^n]$

At site k, m highlighting operations have been executed and saved in $HB = [H_1, \cdots, H_m]$. When a new highlighting operation H_{new} is generated locally, it will be executed immediately as-is and appended to HB, which then becomes $[H_1, \cdots, H_m, H_{new}]$. When a new highlighting operation H_{new} arrives from a remote site,

1. Scan HB from left to right to find the first operation that is totally after H_{new}. If no one is found, H_{new} will be executed as-is and then appended to HB, which becomes $[H_1, \cdots, H_m, H_{new}]$. If the highlighting region covered by H_{new} overshadows highlighting regions covered by $H_1, \cdots, H_m$, it should be placed on the top layer. Therefore, **OHL**(H_{new}) should be replaced with new *OHRs* collected in the process of H_{new}'s execution.

2. Otherwise, suppose H_k ($1 \leq k \leq m$) is found. Transform H_{new} against the list of concurrent operations $[H_k, \cdots, H_m]$ to achieve H_{new}'s execution form EH_{new}, and in the meantime, transform the list of operations $[H_k, \cdots, H_m]$ against H_{new}. EH_{new} may contain more than one highlighting operation because H_{new} could be split into a list of highlighting operations covering smaller highlighting regions in the process of transformation. Details about transformation are referred to the function of $EH_{new} = $ **transformDo**($H_{new}, [H_k, \cdots, H_m]$).

3. Finally, execute highlighting operations in $EH_{new} = [H_{new}^1, \cdots, H_{new}^n]$ and insert H_{new} into HB at the position before H_k, which then becomes $[H_1, \cdots, H_{k-1},$ $H_{new}, H_k, \cdots, H_m]$.

The **transformDo**(H, L) function returns H's execution form by including the effects of concurrent operations in list L in such a way that H was executed before the list of operations in L. In the meantime, the list of operations in L also take into account H's effect in such a way that they were executed after H.

Function 2.1. *transformDo(H, L): EH = [H¹, ⋯, Hⁿ]*

```
{  EH = [H];
   for (j = 0; j < sizeof(L); j++)
   { EH' = [ ];
     for (k = 0; k < sizeof(EH); k++)
     { EH' += IT_EH(EH[k], L[j]);
       if T(H) == Hlt
          IT_HH(L[j], EH[k]);
       else if T(H) == Uhlt
          IT_HU(L[j], EH[k]);
     }
     EH = EH';
   }
   return EH;
}
```

The transformation function **IT_EH**(H_1, H_2) is to achieve H_1's execution form by inclusively transforming operation H_1 against operation H_2. The highlighting region covered by H_1 and overshadowed by H_2 is removed from H_1 in order to emulate the effect that H_1 was executed before H_2. After transformation, H_1's execution form could consist of 0, 1, or 2 highlighting operation(s).

Function 2.2. *IT_EH(H_1, H_2): [H_1^i | i = 0, 1, 2]*

{ **if** $T(H_1)$ == *Hlt* //H_1 is a highlighting operation

  { [$\langle P_i, L_i \rangle$ | i = 0, 1, 2] = **Transform-EH**($P(H_1)$, $N(H_1)$, H_2);

    switch (sizeof([$\langle P_i, L_i \rangle$ | i = 0, 1, 2]))

    { **case** 0: **return** [ ];

            break;

      case 1: **return** [H_1^1 = **Hlt**[P_1, L_1, OHL(H_1)]];

            break;

      case 2: **return** [H_1^1 = **Hlt**[P_1, L_1, OHL(H_1)], H_1^2 = **Hlt**[P_2, L_2, OHL(H_1)]];

            break;

    }

  } **else if** $T(H_1)$ == *Uhlt* //H_1 is the inverse of a highlighting operation

  { OHL_{new} = [ ];

    for (j=0; j<**sizeof**(OHL(H_1)); j++)

    { OHR = OHL(H_1)[j];

      [$\langle P_i, L_i \rangle$ | i = 0, 1, 2] = **Transform-EH**(OHR.S, OHR.L, H_2);

      switch (sizeof([$\langle P_i, L_i \rangle$ | i = 0, 1, 2]))

      { **case** 0: **break**;

        case 1: OHL_{new} += [$\langle P_1, L_1, OHR.C \rangle$];

            break;

        case 2: OHL_{new} += [$\langle P_1, L_1, OHR.C \rangle$, $\langle P_2, L_2, OHR.C \rangle$];

            break;

      }

    }

    return [H_1^1 = **Uhlt**[$P(H_1)$, $N(H_1)$, OHL_{new}]];

  }

}

Function 2.3. *Transform-EH(P, L, H): [⟨P_i, L_i⟩ | i = 0, 1, 2]*

{ if P≤P(H) and P+L≤P(H)+N(H)

   return [⟨P, P(H) - P⟩];

  else if P≥P(H) and P+L≤P(H)+N(H)

   return [ ];

  else if P≥P(H) and P+L≥P(H)+N(H)

   return [⟨P(H) + N(H), P + L - P(H) - L(H)⟩];

  else if P≤P(H) and P+L≥P(H)+N(H)

   return [⟨P, P(H) - P⟩, ⟨P(H) + N(H), P + L - P(H) - L(H)⟩];

  else

   return [⟨P, L⟩];

}

Transformation function IT_HH (H_2, H_1) is defined to transform a highlighting H_2 against another highlighting H_1 in such a way that H_1's effect is included in H_2 to order to emulate the effect that H_2 was executed after H_1.

Procedure 2.1. *$IT\_HH(H_2, H_1)$*

{ for (i=0; i<**sizeof**(OHL(H_2)); i++)

  { OHR = OHL(H_2)[i];

   if P(H_1)≤OHR.S and P(H_1)+N(H_1)≤OHR.S+OHR.L

   { OHL(H_2) += [⟨OHR.S, P(H_1)+N(H_1)-OHR.S, C(H_1)⟩];

   OHR.S = P(H_1) + N(H_1);

   OHR.L = OHR.S + OHR.L -(P(H_1) + N(H_1));

   } else if P(H_1)≤OHR.S and P(H_1)+N(H_1)≥OHR.S+OHR.L

   OHR.C = C(H_1);

   else if P(H_1)≥OHR.S and P(H_1)+N(H_1)≥OHR.S+OHR.L

   { OHL(H_2) += [⟨P(H_1), OHR.S+OHR.L-P(H_1), C(H_1)⟩];

   OHR.L = P(H_1) - OHR.S;

} **else if** P(H_1)$\geq$OHR.S **and** P(H_1)+N(H_1)$\leq$OHR.S+OHR.L

{ OHL(H_2) += [$\langle$P(H_1), N(H_1), C(H_1)$\rangle$,

$\langle$P(H_1)+N(H_1), OHR.S+OHR.L-(P(H_1)+N(H_1)), OHR.C$\rangle$];

OHR.L = P(H_1) - OHR.S;

}

}

}

Transformation function IT_HU (H_2, $\overline{H_1}$) is defined to transform a highlighting operation H_2 against the inverse of a highlighting operation H_1 to exclude H_1's effect from H_2. This function is designed to support undo of the highlighting operation H_1.

Procedure 2.2. $IT\_HU(H_2, \overline{H_1})$

{ /*find the OHR in OHL(H_2) that stores H_1's information*/

for (i=0; i<**sizeof**(OHL(H_2))); i++)

{ **if** P(H_1)$\leq$OHL(H_2)[i].S **and** OHL(H_2)[i].S+OHL(H_2)[i].L$\leq$P(H_1)+N(H_1)

and OHL(H_2)[i].C=C(H_1)

{ OHR_2 = OHL(H_2)[i];

break;

}

}

/*remove H_1's information from H_2 and incorporate OHL(H_1) into OHL(H_2)*/

for (j=0; j<**sizeof**(OHL(H_1))); j++)

{ OHR_1 = OHL(H_1)[j];

if OHR_2.S$\leq$$OHR_1$.S **and** OHR_2.S+OHR_2.L$\leq$$OHR_1$.S+$OHR_1$.L

{ OHR_1.L = OHR_2.S + OHR_2.L - OHR_1.S;

OHR_1.C = OHR_2.C;

} **else if** OHR_2.S$\leq$$OHR_1$.S **and** OHR_2.S+OHR_2.L$\geq$$OHR_1$.S+$OHR_1$.L

{ OHR_1.C = OHR_2.C;

} **else if** $OHR_2.S{\geq}OHR_1.S$ **and** $OHR_2.S{+}OHR_2.L{\geq}OHR_1.S{+}OHR_1.L$

{ $OHR_1.S = OHR_2.S$;

$\quad OHR_1.L = OHR_1.S + OHR_1.L - OHR_2.S$;

$\quad OHR_1.C = OHR_2.C$;

} **else if** $OHR_2.S{\geq}OHR_1.S$ **and** $OHR_2.S{+}OHR_2.L{\leq}OHR_1.S{+}OHR_1.L$

{ $OHR_1.S = OHR_2.S$;

$\quad OHR_1.L = OHR_2.L$;

$\quad OHR_1.C = OHR_2.C$;

}

}

}

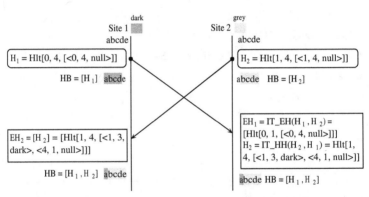

Figure 2.5: HOSE algorithm to solve the divergence problem

The divergence problem in Figure 2.2 can be solved by the *HOSE* algorithm as shown Figure 2.5. At *Site 1*, after the execution of H_1, $H_1 = $ **Hlt**$[0, 4, [\langle 0, 4, \text{null} \rangle]]$, $HB = [H_1]$, and characters a, b, c, and d are highlighted in dark. When remote operation $H_2 = $ **Hlt**$[1, 4, [\langle 1, 4, \text{null} \rangle]]$ arrives, it will be executed as-is because it is totally after H_2. After the execution of H_2, OHL(H_2) is replaced with new *OHR*s.

Therefore, $H_2 = \mathbf{Hlt}[1, 4, [\langle 1, 3, \text{dark}\rangle, \langle 4, 1, \text{null}\rangle]]$, $HB = [H_1, H_2]$, and characters b, c, d, and e are highlighted in grey while character a remains highlighted in dark. At *Site 2*, after the execution of H_2, $H_2 = \mathbf{Hlt}[1, 4, [\langle 1, 4, \text{null}\rangle]]$, $HB = [H_2]$, and characters b, c, d, and e are highlighted in grey. When the remote operation H_1 arrives, because it is totally before H_2, its execution form $EH_1 = \mathbf{IT\_EH}(H_1, H_2)$ $= [\mathbf{Hlt}[0, 1, [\langle 0, 4, \text{null}\rangle]]]$ and H_2 is updated by $\mathbf{IT\_HH}(H_2, H_1) = \mathbf{Hlt}[1, 4, [\langle 1, 3, \text{dark}\rangle, \langle 4, 1, \text{null}\rangle]]$. After the execution of the highlighting operation in EH_1, character a is highlighted in dark while other characters remain highlighted in grey.

To remind the user at *Site 2* that H_1's intention is to highlight characters a, b, c, and d rather than only character a in dark, characters b, c, d will be rotated from being highlighted in dark and grey for a period of time to visualize the effect that characters b, c, d were initially highlighted in dark but then highlighted in grey by another highlighting operation. After the execution of EH_1, highlighting operation H_1 is inserted into HB at the position before H_2, which then becomes $[H_1, H_2]$. *Site 1* and *Site 2* are convergent after H_1 and H_2 have been executed at both sites.

2.3.3 Intention violation of highlighting operations caused by concurrent insertion/deletion operations

When highlighting operations are mixed with insertion/deletion operations, concurrent insertion or deletion operations may change some document segments on which highlighting operations were performed. As a result, the intentions of highlighting operations may be violated and the intention violation problem may further cause divergence problem. Consider a document with characters a, b, c, d, and e, replicated at two sites, as shown in Figure 2.6. *Site 1* performed a deletion operation $E = \mathbf{Del}[1, 1, a]$ to delete the character at position 1 (i.e., character a). Concurrently, *Site 2* performed a highlighting operation $H = \mathbf{Hlt}[1, 3, [\langle 1, 3, \text{null}\rangle]]$ to highlight a region of three characters from position 1 in grey (i.e., characters b, c, and d). At *Site 1*, after the execution of E, the document content is changed to *bcde*. When the remote highlighting H arrives and is executed, characters c, d, and e will be highlighted in grey, which apparently violates H's intention to highlight characters b, c, and d in grey.

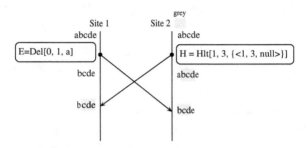

Figure 2.6: An example of intention violation

Highlighting operations have no impact on the document content, therefore they have no impact on insertion/deletion operations. On the contrary, insertion/deletion operations make changes to the document content, therefore they may have an impact on highlighting operations. The root of the problem in Figure 2.6 is that the deletion operation E has changed the document content on which the highlighting operation H was originally defined. Concurrent insertion/deletion operations may cause intention violation of highlighting operations. To preserve the intentions of highlighting operations in the presence of concurrent insertion/deletion operations, highlighting operations should include the effects of those concurrent insertion/deletion operations as follows

- For an insertion operation,
    1. if it is performed at the left side of a highlighting region covered by a highlighting operation, the highlighting region shifts to the right;

2. if it is performed within a highlighting region covered by a highlighting operation, the highlighting region expands; and

3. if it is performed at the right side of a highlighting region covered by a highlighting operation, it has no impact on the highlighting region.

- For a deletion operation,

   1. if it is performed at the left side of·a highlighting region covered by a highlighting operation,

      - if the deletion region covered by the deletion operation does not overlap with the highlighting region, the highlighting region shifts to the left;
      - otherwise the highlighting region is cut off from the left,

   2. if it is performed within a highlighting region covered by a highlighting operation,

      - if the deletion region completely falls into the highlighting region, the highlighting region shrinks;
      - otherwise the highlighting region is cut off from the right, and

   3. if it is performed at the right side of a highlighting region covered by a highlighting operation, it has no impact on the highlighting region.

Accordingly, transformation functions **IT_HI**(H, E) and **IT_HD**(H, E) are defined to inclusively transform a highlighting operation H against an insertion operation and a deletion operation E respectively, in such a way that the execution form of the highlighting operation H has taken into account the effect of the concurrent insertion/deletion operation E.

Procedure 2.3. *IT_HI(H, E)*
{   **if** P(E)$\leq$P(H)
   { P(H) += N(E);

```
    for (i=0; i<sizeof(OHL(H)); i++)
        OHL(H)[i].S += N(E);
} else if P(E)<P(H)+N(H)
{ N(H) += N(E);
    for (i=0; i<sizeof(OHL(H)); i++)
        if P(E)≤OHL(H)[i].S
            OHL(H)[i].S += N(E);
        else if P(E)≤OHL(H)[i].S+OHL(H)[i].L
            OHL(H)[i].L += N(E);
}
}
```

Procedure 2.4. *IT_HD(H, E)*

```
{ Transform-HD(P(H), N(H), E);
    for (i=0; i<sizeof(OHL(H)); i++)
        Transform-HD(OHL(H)[i].S, OHL(H)[i].L, E);
}
```

Procedure 2.5. *Transform-HD(P, L, E)*

```
{ if P(E)+N(E)≤P
    P -= N(E);
  else if P(E)<P and P(E)+N(E)<P+L
    L = P + L - P(E) - N(E);
  else if P(E)≥P and P(E)+N(E)≤P+L
    L -= N(E);
  else if P(E)≤P and P(E)+N(E)≥P+L
  { P = P(E);
    L = 0;
  } else if P(E)≥P and P(E)+N(E)≥P+L
```

L = P(E) - P;

}

So, in Figure 2.6, when the remote highlighting operation H arrives at *Site 1*, it should not be executed as-is. Instead, its execution form EH will be determined by transforming H against the concurrent editing operation E in such a way that $EH =$ **IT_HD**$(H, E) = $ **Hlt**$[0, 3, [\langle 0, 3, \text{null}\rangle]]$. Consequently, after the execution of EH, characters b, c, and d are highlighted in grey, which correctly preserves H's intention.

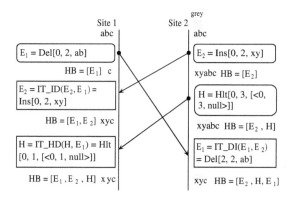

Figure 2.7: Another example of intention violation

Look at another example, as shown in Figure 2.7, where a document initially contained characters a, b, and c, replicated at two sites *Site 1* and *Site 2*. *Site 1* performed a deletion operation $E_1 = $ **Del**$[0, 2, \text{ab}]$ to delete 2 characters from position 0 (i.e., characters a and b). Concurrently, *Site 2* performed two operations $E_2 = $ **Ins**$[0, 2, \text{xy}]$ to insert characters x and y at position 0 (i.e., before character a) and $H = $ **Hlt**$[0, 3, [\langle 0, 3, \text{null}\rangle]]$ to highlight 3 characters from position 0 (i.e., characters x, y, and a). At *Site 1*, after the execution of E_1, characters a and b are removed and the document contained only character c. When the remote insertion operation E_2 arrives, because $E_2 \parallel E_1$, E_2 must be transformed against E_1 to include E_1's effect by performing $E_2 = \mathbf{IT\_ID}(E_2, E_1) = \mathbf{Ins}[0, 2, xy]$ [137]. After the execution of transformed E_2, characters x and y are inserted at position 0. When the remote highlighting operation H arrives, because $H \parallel E_1$ and $E_2 \rightarrow H$, H will be transformed against E_1 (not including E_2) by performing $H = \mathbf{IT\_HD}(H, E_1)$ $= \mathbf{Hlt}[0, 1, [\langle 0, 1, \text{null} \rangle]]$. When the transformed H is executed, only character x is highlighted, which apparently violates H's intention of highlighting both characters x and y.

The root of this problem is that concurrent insertion/deletion and highlighting operations may be generated on different document contents, resulting in their parameters being not directly comparable. As a result, simply applying IT_HI and IT_HD transformation functions to transform a highlighting operation against concurrent insertion/deletion operations may not produce correct results. In this example, the deletion operation E_1 was defined on the document content containing characters a, b, and c while the highlighting operation H was defined on the document content containing characters x, y, a, b, and c. Sun et $al.$ [137] have addressed similar issue in the transformation of insertion/deletion operations. To ensure the correctness of $\mathbf{IT}(O_a, O_b)$ in the event that O_a and O_b were not defined on the same document content, O_b should be transformed against other operations to ensure that O_b was defined on the document content same as that on which O_a was defined. The $GOTO$ (Generic Operational Transformation Optimized) [136] is introduced as follows:

Algorithm 2.2. $GOTO(O_{new}, HB): O'_{new}$

At site k, HB $= [E_1, \cdots, E_m]$ stores m executed insertion/deletion operations. When a new operation O_{new} is generated locally, it will be executed as-is and appended to HB, which becomes $[E_1, \cdots, E_m, O_{new}]$. When a remote operation O_{new} arrives,

1. Scan HB[1, m] from left to right to find the first operation that is concurrent with O_{new}. If no such operation is found, $O'_{new} = O_{new}$.

2. Otherwise, suppose E_k is found. Then scan HB$[k+1, m]$ to find operations causally before O_{new}. If no single such operation is found, O_{new}'s execution form is achieved by transforming O_{new} against operations in HB$[k, m]$, that is $O'_{new} = \textbf{LIT}(O_{new}, \text{HB}[k, m])$.

3. Otherwise, Let $[E_{C_1}, \cdots, E_{C_r}]$ be the list of operations in HB$[k+1, m]$, which are causally before O_{new}. The list of operations $[E_{C_1}, \cdots, E_{C_r}]$ are transformed and shifted (with the **LTranspose**(L) procedure) to the position before E_k by

   for (i=1; i<r; i++)

   LTranspose(HB$[k + i - 1, C_i]$);

   After that, operations that are causally before O_{new} are placed before E_k while operations that are concurrent with O_{new} are placed after E_k. O_{new}'s execution form O'_{new} is then achieved by transforming O_{new} against operations in HB$[k+r, m]$, that is $O'_{new} = \textbf{LIT}(O_{new}, \text{HB}[k+r, m])$.

The *LIT* function and the *LTranspose* procedure are defined as follows

Function 2.4. *LIT(O, L): O'*

{ **for** (i=0; i<**sizeof**(L); i++)

    IT(O, L[i]);

  return O;

}

Procedure 2.6. *LTranspose(L)*

{ **for** (k = **sizeof**(L); k > 1; k--)

  { /* transform */

   Transpose(L[k-1], L[k]);

   /* shift */

   O = L[k];

   L[k] = L[k-1];

```
    L[k-1] = O;
  }
}
```

Procedure 2.7. *Transpose(O_a, O_b)*

{ **ET**(O_b, O_a);

   IT(O_a, O_b);

}

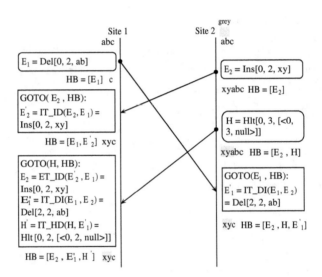

Figure 2.8: GOTO algorithm to solve the intention violation problem

So, in Figure 2.7, when the remote insertion operation E_2 arrives at *Site 1*, **GOTO**(E_2, HB) is executed to determine E_2's execution form E_2' as shown in Figure 2.8. Because E_1 is the only operation in HB and concurrent with E_2, $E_1' =$ **IT_ID**(E_2, E_1) = **Ins**[0, 2, xy]. After the execution of E_2', characters x and y are inserted at position 0. When the remote highlighting operation H arrives at *Site 1*, **GOTO**$(H$, HB$)$ is executed to determine H's execution form H' as follows: first, scan HB $= [E_1, E'_2]$ to find the first operation that is concurrent with H, which should be E_1. Second, scan $[E'_2]$ to find the first operation that is causally before H, which should be E'_2. Third, transform and shift E'_2 to the left of E_1 by **LTranspose**(HB[1, 2])). After that, HB $= [E_2, E'_1]$, where $E_2 = $ **ET_ID**$(E'_2, E_1) = $ **Ins**$[0, 2, xy]$ and $E'_1 = $ **IT_DI**$(E_1, E_2) = $ **Del**$[2, 2, ab]$. Finally, H's execution form H' is determined by transforming H against E'_1, that is $H' = $ **IT_HD**$(H, E'_1) = $ **Hlt**$[0, 2, [\langle 0, 2, \text{null}\rangle]]$. After the execution of H', characters x and y are highlighted, which correctly preserves H's intention.

2.3.4 A transformation control algorithm

Based on the *HOSE* algorithm for preserving convergence and the *GOTO* algorithm for preserving intention, a new transformation control algorithm named *PICOT* (Preserving Intention and Convergence by Operational Transformation) is devised to preserve both intention and convergence in the presence of insertion, deletion, and highlighting operations.

Algorithm 2.3. *PICOT(O_{new}, HB): EO_{new}*

At site k, $HB = [O_1, \cdots, O_m]$ stores m executed insertion/deletion/highlighting operations. When a new operation O_{new} is generated locally, it is executed as-is and then appended to HB, which becomes $[O_1, \cdots, O_m, O_{new}]$. When a remote operation O_{new} arrives,

- If O_{new} is an insertion/deletion operation,

  1. Scan HB[1, m] from left to right to find the first *insertion/deletion* operation that is concurrent with O_{new}. If no such operation is found, $EO_{new} = O_{new}$.

2. Otherwise, suppose O_k is found. Then scan HB$[k+1, m]$ to find **insertion** and **deletion** operations, which are causally before O_{new}. If no single such operation is found, O_{new}'s execution form is determined by transforming O_{new} against operations in HB$[k, m]$, that is $EO_{new}=$**LIT**$(O_{new}, $ HB$[k, m])$.

3. Otherwise, Let $[O_{E_1}, \cdots, O_{E_r}]$ ($1 \leq E_1, \cdots, E_r \leq$ m) be the list of **insertion/deletion** operations in HB$[k+1, $ m], which are causally before O_{new}. Operations in $[O_{E_1}, \cdots, O_{E_r}]$ are transformed and shifted to the position before O_k by

    for (i=1; i<r; i++)

        LTranspose(HB$[k + i$ -1, $E_i]$);

    After that, **insertion/deletion** operations causally before O_{new} are placed before O_k while **insertion/deletion** operations concurrent with O_{new} are placed after O_k. O_{new}'s execution form is then determined by transforming O_{new} against operations in HB$[k+r, $ m], that is, $EO_{new} = $ **LIT**$(O_{new}, $ HB$[k+r, $ m]).

4. Execute EO_{new} and append EO_{new} to *HB*.

- If O_{new} is a highlighting operation,

    1. Suppose $[O_{E_1}, \cdots, O_{E_l}]$ be the list of **insertion/deletion** operations in *HB*. Transform and shift the list of **insertion/deletion** operations $[O_{E_1}, \cdots, O_{E_l}]$ to the left side of *HB* by

        for (i=1; i<l; i++)

            LTranspose(HB$[i, E_i]$);

        After that, all insertion/deletion operations are at the left side of *HB* while all highlighting operations are at the right side of *HB*, which should look like $[O_{E_1}, \cdots, O_{E_l}, O_{H_1}, \cdots, O_{H_r}]$ where $[O_{E_1}, \cdots, O_{E_l}]$ ($1 \leq E_1, \cdots, E_l \leq$ m) are insertion/deletion operations and $[O_{H_1}, \cdots, O_{H_r}]$ ($1 \leq H_1,$

$\cdots$, $H_r \leq$ m and H_1, $\cdots$, $H_r \neq E_1$, $\cdots$, E_l) are highlighting operations. This is an ***essential*** step because it is after this step that all highlighting operations are ensured to be defined on the document content the same as that on which O_{new} was defined. As a result, the parameters of highlighting operations in *HB* are directly comparable with O_{new}'s parameters in doing *IT_EH* and *IT_HH* transformations.

2. To preserve O_{new}'s intention in the presence of concurrent insertion/deletion operations, O_{new}'s execution form is achieved by $O'_{new} = \mathbf{GOTO}(O_{new}, [O_{E_1}, \cdots, O_{E_l}])$. To further preserve convergence in the presence of concurrent highlighting operations, O_{new}'s execution form is further achieved by $EO_{new} = \mathbf{HOSE}(O'_{new}, [O_{H_1}, \cdots, O_{H_r}])$.

3. Execute EO_{new} and insert O'_{new} into HB at the position before O_{H_k} ($H_1 \leq H_k \leq H_r$), which then becomes $[O_{E_1}, \cdots, O_{E_l}, O_{H_1}, \cdots, O_{H_{k-1}}, O'_{new}, O_{H_k}, \cdots, O_{H_r}]$. O_{H_k} is the first highlighting operation that is totally after O_{new} in HB.

It should be mentioned that transforming an insertion/deletion operation against a highlighting operation does not have any impact on the insertion/deletion operation. Therefore, these transformation functions are void:

- **IT_IH** (E, H): Inclusively transforming an insertion operation E against a highlighting operation H.

- **IT_DH**(E, H): Inclusively transforming a deletion operation E against a highlighting operation H.

- **ET_IH** (E, H): Exclusively transforming an insertion operation E against a highlighting operation H.

- **ET_DH**(E, H): Exclusively transforming a deletion operation D against a highlighting operation H.

An example is used to to demonstrate how the *PICOT* algorithm works. Consider a document with characters *a*, *b*, *c*, *d*, and *e*, replicated at two sites *Site 1* and *Site 2* as shown in Figure 2.9. *Site 1* performed a deletion operation $E_1 = \mathbf{Del}[1, 1, b]$ to delete the character at position 1 (i.e., character *b*) and a highlighting operation $H_1 = \mathbf{Hlt}[0, 3, [\langle 0, 3, null \rangle]]$ to highlight 3 characters from position 0 (i.e., characters *a*, *c*, and *d*) in dark. Concurrently, *Site 2* performed a deletion operation $E_2 = \mathbf{Del}[3, 1, d]$ to delete the character at position 3 (i.e., character *d*) and a highlighting operation $H_2 = \mathbf{Hlt}[2, 2, [\langle 2, 2, null \rangle]]$ to highlight 2 characters from position 2 (i.e., characters *c* and *e*) in grey.

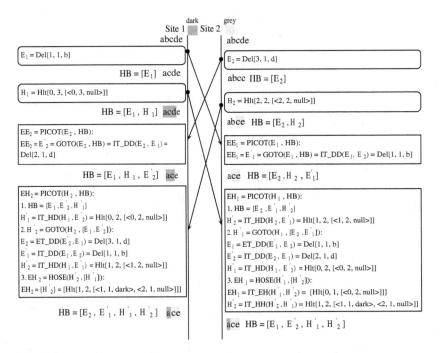

Figure 2.9: PICOT algorithm to preserve both intention and convergence

At *Site 1*, after the execution of E_1 and H_1, the document contains characters a, c, d, and e with characters a, c, and d highlighted in dark and $HB = [E_1, H_1]$. When the remote deletion operation E_2 arrives, $\mathbf{PICOT}(E_2, HB)$ is executed to determine E_2's execution form EE_2. Because E_1 is the only ***insertion/deletion*** operation in HB and it is concurrent with E_2, $E_2' = \mathbf{IT\_DD}(E_2, E_1) = \mathbf{Del}[2, 1, d]$. After the execution of $EE_2 = E_2'$, the character at position 2 (i.e., character d) is removed, and $HB = [E_1, H_1, E_2']$.

When the remote highlighting operation H_2 arrives, $\mathbf{PICOT}(H_2, HB)$ is executed to determine H_2's execution form EH_2 as follows. First, reorder HB to make all insertion/deletion operations at the left side and all highlighting operations at the right side. After that, $HB = [E_1, E_2', H_1']$ where $H_1' = \mathbf{IT\_HD}(H_1, E_2') = \mathbf{Hlt}[0, 2, [\langle 0, 2, null\rangle]]$. Second, H_2's execution form is first determined by $H_2' = \mathbf{GOTO}(H_2, [E_1, E_2'])$. After that, HB $= [E_2, E_1', H_1']$ where $E_2 = \mathbf{ET\_DD}(E_2', E_1) = \mathbf{Del}[3, 1, d]$ and $E_1' = \mathbf{IT\_DD}(E_1, E_2) = \mathbf{Del}[1, 1, b]$, and $H_2' = \mathbf{IT\_HD}(H_2, E_1') = \mathbf{Hlt}[1, 2, [\langle 1, 2, null\rangle]]$. H_2's execution form is further determined by $EH_2 = \mathbf{HOSE}(H_2', [H_1'])$. Because H_2' is totally after H_1', $EH_2 = [H_2']$. Finally, execute the highlighting operation in EH_2 and insert H_2' into HB at the position after H_1'. After that, characters c and e are highlighted in grey while character a remains highlighted in dark, $\mathbf{OHL}(H_2')$ is replaced with new *OHRs* $[\langle 1, 1, dark\rangle, \langle 2, 1, null\rangle]$, and HB $= [E_2, E_1', H_1', H_2']$.

At *Site 2*, after the execution of E_2 and H_2, the document contains characters a, b, c, and e with characters c and e highlighted in grey, and $HB = [E_2, H_2]$. When the remote deletion operation E_1 arrives, $\mathbf{PICOT}(E_1, HB)$ is executed to determine E_1's execution form EE_1. Because E_2 is the only insertion/deletion operation in HB and it is concurrent with E_1, $E_1' = \mathbf{IT\_DD}(E_1, E_2) = \mathbf{Del}[1, 1, b]$. After the execution of $EE_1 = E_1'$, the character at position 1 (i.e., character b) is removed, and $HB = [E_1, H_1, E_1']$.

When the remote highlighting operation H_1 arrives, $\mathbf{PICOT}(H_1, HB)$ is executed to determine H_1's execution form EH_1 as follows. First, reorder HB to make all insertion/deletion operations at the left side and all highlighting operations at the right side. After that, $HB = [E_2, E_1', H_2']$ where $H_2' = \textbf{IT\_HD}(H_2, E_1') = \textbf{Hlt}[1, 2, [\langle 1, 2, \text{null}\rangle]]$. Second, H_1's execution form is first determined by $H_1' = \textbf{GOTO}(H_1, [E_2, E_1'])$. After that, HB $= [E_1, E_2', H_2']$ where $E_1 = \textbf{ET\_DD}(E_1', E_2) = \textbf{Del}[1, 1, \text{b}]$ and $E_2' = \textbf{IT\_DD}(E_2, E_1) = \textbf{Del}[2, 1, \text{d}]$, and $H_1' = \textbf{IT\_HD}(H_1, E_2') = \textbf{Hlt}[0, 2, [\langle 0, 2, \text{null}\rangle]]$. H_1's execution form is further determined by $\textbf{HOSE}(H_1', [H_2'])$. Because H_1' is totally before H_2', $EH_1 = \textbf{IT\_EH}(H_1', H_2') = [\textbf{Hlt}[0, 1, [\langle 0, 2, \text{null}\rangle]]]$ and $H_2' = \textbf{IT\_HH}(H_2', H_1') = \textbf{Hlt}[1, 2, [\langle 1, 1, \text{dark}\rangle, \langle 2, 1, \text{null}\rangle]]$. Finally, execute the highlighting operation in EH_1 and insert H_1' into HB at the position before H_2'. After that, only character a is highlighted in dark while character c and e remain highlighted in grey, and HB $= [E_1, E_2', H_1', H_2']$.

If the highlighting operation H_2 were not moved to the position after E_1', as required by $\textbf{PICOT}(H_1, HB)$, the result would be wrong. In that case, $H_2 = \textbf{Hlt}[2, 2, [\langle 2, 2, \text{null}\rangle]]$ and $EH_1 = \textbf{IT\_EH}(H_1', H_2) = [\textbf{Hlt}[0, 2, [\langle 0, 2, \text{null}\rangle]]]$. Consequently, after the execution of the highlighting operation in EH_1, characters a and c would be highlighted in dark, which is wrong because H_1 should not overshadow the highlighting region covered by H_2. As mentioned in the $PICOT$ algorithm, not moving all highlighting operations after all insertion/deletion operations would result in the parameters of highlighting operations being not directly comparable because they were defined on different document contents. In this example, the result is wrong because H_1' was defined on the document that contains characters a, c, and e while H_2 was defined on the document that contains characters a, b, c, and e.

2.4   Flexible undo solution

Only one-step or chronological undo [131] of highlighting operations is available in single-user editors and there is no known solution for collaborative undo of highlighting operations in any multi-user collaborative editors. Neither one-step nor chronological collaborative undo of highlighting operations is suitable for focus-changing during a real-time collaborative editing session because the flow of changing focuses during a real-time discussion is not structured chronologically, which is subject to the nature of the discussion topic and the thinking style of every participant. By contrast, collaborative selective undo [8, 24, 103, 131] of highlighting operations is more suitable for focus-changing because it is able to support undo of any highlighting operation at any time. Existing solutions are about collaborative selective undo of insertion/deletion operations [103, 131] or object creation/removal operations [8, 24] and are not directly applicable to highlighting operations.

Generally speaking, to correctly undo a highlighting operation, the effect of the undone operation must be removed from the document while the effects of all other operations must be maintained. Chronological undo in single-user editing is easy to achieve because the operation to be undone must be the most recent one, which means all operations executed after that operation must all have been undone. Therefore, simply executing the inverse of that operation would remove its effect while the effects of all other operations are maintained. By contrast, it is non-trivial to achieve selective undo of highlighting operations because the current highlighting regions in the document can be different from those at the time when that operation was created. Consequently, simply executing the inverse of that operation could alter some highlighting regions covered by highlighting operations performed after that operation. In multi-user collaborative editing, the mixture of concurrent do and undo of insertion, deletion, and highlighting operations makes collaborative selective undo even more complicated.

In this thesis research, a flexible undo algorithm $SUIT$ (Selective Undo by Inclusive Transformation) is proposed to support selective undo of any insertion/deletion/highlighting operation at any time. To undo operation O in a history buffer HB, the algorithm is executed as follows: first, find O in HB. Second, make O's inverse operation $\overline{O}$. Third, determine $\overline{O}$'s execution form $E\overline{O}$ by transforming $\overline{O}$ with operations after O in HB. Fourth, execute $E\overline{O}$ to remove O's effect from the document. Finally, propagate the undo command carrying O's identifier $\mathbf{Id}(O)$ to remote sites if the undo is initiated locally. There are two main reasons for propagating $\mathbf{Id}(O)$ rather than $E\overline{O}$. One reason is that a remote site may have a different HB, therefore $E\overline{O}$ derived in terms of the local HB may not be applicable to the remote site. The other reason is that direct execution of $E\overline{O}$ at a remote site could alter the effect of concurrent operations at that site because the derivation of $E\overline{O}$ has no knowledge of those concurrent operations.

Algorithm 2.4. $SUIT(\mathbf{Id}(O),\ HB)\colon E\overline{O}$

At site k, HB[1, m] stores m executed operations. To undo the operation whose identifier is $\mathbf{Id}(O)$ in HB,

1. Find operation $O =$ HB[i] $(1 \le i \le m)$ with a matching of $\mathbf{Id}(O)$ in HB.

2. If $\mathbf{T}(O) = \mathbf{Ins}/\mathbf{Del}$, that is, O is an insertion/deletion operation, the $ANYUNDO$ algorithm [132] for selectively undoing any insertion/deletion operation in a HB can be directly applied to undoing O as follows

   (a) Make O's inverse operation by $\overline{O} = \mathbf{makeInverse}(O)$.

   (b) $\overline{O}$'s execution form $E\overline{O}$ is determined by transforming $\overline{O}$ with the list of operations in HB[i+1, m] by $E\overline{O} = \mathbf{LIT\_Transpose}(\overline{O}, \text{HB}[i+1, m])$.

3. If $\mathrm{T}(O) == \mathbf{Hlt}/\mathbf{Uhlt}$, that is, O is a highlighting or the inverse of a highlighting operation,

(a) Suppose $[O_{E_1}, \cdots, O_{E_t}]$ be the list of **insertion/deletion** operations in HB[i, m]. Transform and shift the list of operations to the left of HB[i] by

> **for** (k=1; k<t; k++)
>
>> **LTranspose**(HB[i+k-1, E_k]);

After that, there is no insertion/deletion operation after O in HB and HB[j] $= O$ $(i \leq j \leq m)$ with a matching of **Id**(O).

(b) Make O's inverse operation $\overline{O}$ by $\overline{O} = $ **makeInverse**(O).

(c) Derive $\overline{O}$'s execution form $E\overline{O}$ by $E\overline{O} = $ **transformDo**($\overline{O}$, HB[j+1, m]) (The *transformDo* function defined in the *HOSE* algorithm in Section 2.3).

4. Execute $E\overline{O}$.

5. Mark O and $\overline{O}$ as a do-undo pair.

6. Finally, propagate the undo command carrying **Id**(O) to remote sites if the undo is initiated locally.

In the *SUIT* algorithm, it is essential to transform and shift all insertion/deletion operations to the left side of the highlighting operation to be undone. The reason is that $EH_1 = $ **IT_EH**(H_1, H_2) transformation function is lossy. After transformation, highlighting regions covered by EH_1 are only some fragments of the original highlighting region covered by H_1. When highlighting operations in EH_1 are to be transformed against an insertion/deletion operation, the relation between highlighting regions covered by EH_1 and the effect region covered by the insertion/deletion operation does not correctly reflect the relation between the highlighting region covered by H_1 and the effect region covered by the insertion/deletion operation. Therefore the algorithm must prevent highlighting operations in EH_1 from being transformed against any insertion/deletion operation. An example will illustrate this point at a later stage.

Marking do-undo pair is another technical essential in the algorithm. For instance, if $HB = [O_1, \cdots, O_i, \cdots, O_m]$, when O_i is undone, HB will become $[O_1, \cdots, O_i^*, \cdots, O_m]$ where O_i^* is a do-undo pair. When O_i is redone, HB will become $[O_1, \cdots, O_i, \cdots, O_m]$. The main reasons for marking do-undo pair are as follows: first, it can save the memory for explicitly storing inverse operations and avoid the cost for timestamping inverse operations. Second, transforming an operation against a list of operations will skip those do-undo pairs, which can avoid some undo puzzles caused by the fact that transforming an operation O_a against another operation O_b and then its inverse operation $\overline{O_b}$ may not equal to transforming O_a against an I (identify) operation [132]. Finally, it can avoid defining and executing transformation functions IT_UH, IT_UU, IT_UI, and IT_UD for transforming the inverse of a highlighting operation against a highlighting operation, the inverse of another highlighting operation, and an insertion/deletion operation.

The **makeInverse**(O) function is defined to make the inverse of operation O. It is described as follows

Function 2.5. *makeInverse(O):* $\overline{O}$

{   switch $T(O)$

    { **case Hlt:** $\overline{O} =$ **Uhlt**$[P(O), N(O), OHL(O)]$;

          break;

      case Uhlt: $\overline{O} =$ **Hlt**$[P(O), N(O), OHL(O)]$;

          break;

      case Ins: $\overline{O} =$ **Del**$[P(O), N(O), S(O)]$;

          break;

      case Del: $\overline{O} =$ **Ins**$[P(O), N(O), S(O)]$;

          break;

  }

  return $\overline{O}$;

}

The **LIT_Transpose**(O, L) function returns O's execution form by inclusively transforming O against the list of operations in L. In the meantime, the list of operations in L are also transformed against O in order to include O' effect.

Function 2.6. *LIT_Transpose(O, L): EO*

{ for (i = 0; i < **sizeof**(L); i++)

{ TO = **IT**(L[i], O);

O = **IT**(O, L[i]);

L[i] = TO;

}

}

An example is used to illustrate how the *SUIT* algorithm works. As shown in Figure 2.10, a document initially contained characters a, b, c, d, and e. A highlighting operation H_1 = **Hlt**[0, 3, [⟨0, 3, null⟩]] was performed to highlight 3 characters from position 0 (i.e., characters a, b, and c) in dark. Then a highlighting operation H_2 = **Hlt**[2, 3, [⟨2, 1, dark⟩, ⟨3, 2, null⟩]] was performed to highlight 3 characters from position 2 (i.e., characters c, d, and e) in grey. Finally, an insertion operation E = **Ins**[2, 2, xy] was performed to insert 2 characters x and y at position 2 (i.e., between character c and d). Characters x and y inserted by E fall into H_1's highlighting region, so they were highlighted in dark. To selectively undo H_1 in HB = [H_1, H_2, E], as shown in Figure 2.10(A), if H_1's inverse operation $\overline{H_1}$ = **makeInverse**(H_1) = **Uhlt**[0, 3, [⟨0, 3, null⟩]] were executed as-is, characters a, b, and x would be dehighlighted, which is wrong because part of the highlighting region covered H_1 has not yet been removed (character y is still highlighted in dark). The reason is that $\overline{H_1}$'s did not take into account the effects of subsequent operations H_2 and E.

As shown in Figure 2.10(B), if $\overline{H_1}$'s execution form $E\overline{H_1}$ were determined by transforming $\overline{H_1}$ against the list of operations in [H_2, E] by $E\overline{H_1}$ = **transformDo**($\overline{H_1}$,

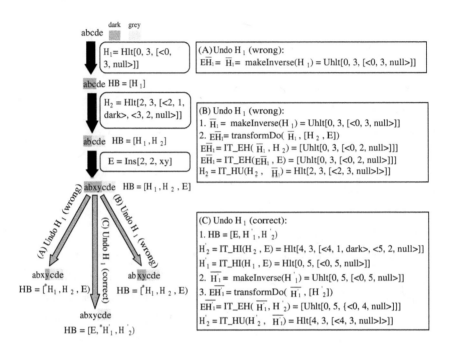

Figure 2.10: SUIT algorithm to selectively undo a highlighting operation

$[H_2, E])$ = $[\mathbf{Uhlt}[0, 3, [\langle 0, 2, null\rangle]]]$, the execution of the highlighting operation
in $E\overline{H_1}$ would dehighlight characters a and b, which is also wrong because part of
the highlighting region covered by H_1 has not yet been removed (character x and
y are still highlighted in dark). The reason is that after $E\overline{H_1} = \mathbf{IT\_EH}(\overline{H_1}, H_2)$,
the highlighting region covered by $E\overline{H_1}$ only contains characters a and b and it is
only a fragment of the highlighting region covered by $\overline{H_1}$. Consequently, when the
highlighting operation in $E\overline{H_1}$ is further transformed against the insertion operation
E, it is unable to know that characters x and y inserted by operation E were part of the
highlighting region covered by the highlighting region H_1 and should be dehighlighted

as well.

As shown in Figure 2.10(C), the **SUIT**(**Id**(H_1), HB) algorithm can be used to correctly undo H_1 as follows: first, find H_1 in HB with a matching of **Id**(H_1), which is HB[1]. Second, transform and shift the insertion operation E to the left side of H_1 in HB. After that, $HB = [E, H'_1, H'_2]$ where $H'_2 = $ **IT_HI**$(H_2, E) = $ **Hlt**[4, 3, [$\langle 4$, 1, dark$\rangle$, $\langle 5$, 2, null$\rangle$]] and $H'_1 = $ **IT_HI**$(H_1, E) = $ **Hlt**[0, 5, [$\langle 0$, 5, null$\rangle$]] and HB[2] = H'_1. Third, make H'_1's inverse operation by $\overline{H'_1} = $ **makeInverse**$(H'_1) = $ **Uhlt**[0, 5, [$\langle 0$, 5, null$\rangle$]]. Fourth, derive $\overline{H'_1}$'s execution form $E\overline{H'_1}$ by transforming $\overline{H'_1}$ with H'_2 with $E\overline{H'_1} = $ **transformDo**$(\overline{H'_1}$, HB[3]). After that, $E\overline{H'_1} = $ **IT_EH**$(\overline{H'_1}, H'_2) = $ [**Uhlt**[0, 5, [$\langle 0$, 4, null$\rangle$]]] and $H'_2 = IT_HU(H'_2, \overline{H'_1}) = $ **Hlt**[4, 3, [$\langle 4$, 3, null$\rangle$]]. Finally, execute the highlighting operation in $E\overline{H'_1}$ and mark H'_1 and $\overline{H'_1}$ as a do-undo pair in HB. After that, characters a, b, x, and y are dehighlighted while characters c, d, and e remain highlighted in grey and HB = [E, *H'_1, H'_2].

Furthermore, the *SUIT* algorithm is able to handle situations where the undo of a highlighting operation is mixed with a concurrent highlighting/insertion/deletion operation, or concurrent undo of a highlighting/insertion/deletion operation. Please refer to Appendix A - *More selective undo examples* for a detailed description on the examples illustrating those situations.

2.5 Conclusions and future work

In a highly interactive environment, group awareness has proven essential to improve the quality of real-time interaction. We contribute a collaborative highlighting technique for gesture communication, which is particularly effective in improving the quality of real-time interaction on text-based source code documents. Highlighting in single-user editors provides users with a mechanism for supporting non-real-time communication between the author and readers but collaborative highlighting in real-time collaborative editing systems is even more valuable because it can serve as a gestural communication tool for improving the quality of real-time interaction.

We emulate the representation of highlights on user interface used in single-user editors in collaborative editors in order to encourage users who are used to the single-user application to learn, use and adopt the multi-user collaborative version. We use colours to differentiate highlights performed by different users to provide group awareness support in multi-user environments. A significant contribution is the extension of the operational transformation technique, originally proposed for consistency maintenance in real-time collaborative editing, to support group awareness by means of collaborative highlighting. The contribution includes a package of operational transformation functions and transformation control algorithms for consistency maintenance and a flexible undo solution that has the capability of undoing any operation at any time.

Furthermore, the collaborative highlighting technique can be applied to handling *updating* operations that change attributes of characters, such as color-changing, font-changing, size-changing, italicizing, underlining, and so on. All technical solutions presented in this chapter have been implemented in the *REDUCE* real-time collaborative editing system to test the correctness of the collaborative highlighting technique and to demonstrate the feasibility and usefulness of the collaborative highlighting gesture communication tool. We are in the process of applying the collaborative highlighting technique to supporting other group awareness features such as collaborative font-changing, collaborative size-changing, collaborative italicizing, collaborative underlining, and so on. We are also investigating how to develop the collaborative highlighting technique into a generic approach, for handling consistency maintenance and flexible undo of general updating operations.

Chapter 3

Flexible operation-based merging

In the implementation phase of a collaborative programming process, unconstrained, syncretic, non-real-time collaborative editing of the same source code is needed for programmers to work on different components because they require little interaction with each other. As introduced in Chapter 1, merging is the core technical component in the *Copy-Modify-Merge* approach to support unconstrained, syncretic, non-real-time collaborative editing of the same document. In this chapter, we will review some representative merging techniques that have been used in various SCM systems and non-real-time collaborative editing systems, and present a novel flexible operation-based merging technique for non-real-time collaborative editing as well as version control. The proposed technique is efficient to be used in the Internet environment and has the capability of textually integrating all changes concurrently made by multiple users, and automatically detecting and resolving syntactic conflicts according to application-dependent user-specified policies.

3.1 Introduction

Merging is the process of integrating different pieces of work done in a concurrent way by multiple users on the same document, which may happen at two stages. As shown in Figure 3.1, initially, *Site 1* and *Site 2* checked out version R_0 of the shared document from the repository as working copies. The initial document state of the working copy is W_0^1 at *Site 1* and W_0^2 at *Site 2* respectively. The working copy at *Site 1* is developed from its initial state W_0^1 to state W_m^1 with a sequence of editing commands $[O_1^1, \cdots, O_m^1]$. Concurrently the working copy at *Site 2* is developed from its initial state W_0^2 to state W_n^2 with another sequence of editing commands $[O_1^2, \cdots, O_n^2]$.

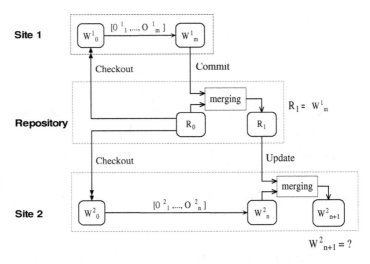

Figure 3.1: Merging may happen at two stages

First, merging may happen at the *committing* stage when the working copy W_m^1 at *Site 1* is committed into the repository to generate a new version R_1. Merging at this stage is called *commit merging*, where changes made between W_0^1 and W_m^1 are integrated into version R_0 to generate the new version R_1 in the repository. Second, merging may happen at the *updating* stage when the working copy W_n^2 at *Site 2* is updated by version R_1 from the repository. Merging at this stage is called *update merging*, where changes made between versions R_0 and R_1 are integrated into W_n^2 to generate a new working copy W_{n+1}^2 at *Site 2*.

Commit merging is easy to achieve and the merging result is deterministic. In Figure 3.1, by simply applying changes made between W_0^1 and W_m^1 to version R_0, the new version R_1 will be generated, which equals to W_m^1. However, update merging is difficult to achieve and the merging result is dependent on how the merging algorithm is designed [18]. In Figure 3.1, W_{n+1}^2 cannot be generated by simply applying changes made between R_0 and R_1 (i.e., the sequence of editing commands $[O_1^1, \cdots, O_m^1]$) to W_n^2 because the sequence of editing commands were defined on the document state W_0^1 and could not be applied to the document state $W_n^2 \neq W_0^1$.

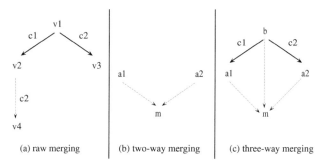

Figure 3.2: Types of update merging

Update merging is a challenging issue and various techniques have been devised to tackle this issue in the past years. These techniques can be can be classified as: *raw merging*, *two-way merging*, and *three-way merging* [28]. *Raw merging* simply applies a change in a different context. For example, in Figure 3.2(a), change **c2** was originally performed independent of change **c1** and is later combined with **c1** to produce the new version **v4**. As a matter of fact, a change may not be always possible to be applied in a different context. For example, **c2** may fail if it applies to a nonexistent object in **v2**, resulting in the inconsistency between **v4** and **v3**. Raw merging is supported by SCM systems like *SCCS* [112] and *COV* [83].

Two-way merging compares two alternative versions **a1** and **a2** and merges them into a single version **m**. It can merely detect differences between the two alternatives and displays them to the user who has to resolve the differences manually. Two-way merging is not practically useful because it does not have any automation in resolving differences but it is the basis of *three-way merging*. To reduce the number of decisions to be made by the user, *three-way merging* is able to automatically resolve some differences by referring to a common baseline. For example, in Figure 3.2(c), if a difference between alternatives **a1** and **a2** is detected, three-way merging will consult their common baseline **b**. If a change has been applied in only one version, this change will be incorporated into **m** automatically. Otherwise, a conflict is detected, which could be resolved manually or automatically. Three-way merging has been widely used in many notable *SCM* systems such as *CVS* [10, 56], *Subversion* [27], *ClearCase* [1], and *Continuus* [19, 34].

Conflicts are contradictory changes and their definition, detection, and resolution are application-dependent. In terms of the semantic level at which conflicts are defined, merging capabilities can be classified as *textual merging, syntactic merging,* and *semantic merging*. *Textual merging* is only applicable to plain text files and it attempts to generate a merged plain text file by integrating textual changes made in individual files. Textual merging is the primary and the only successful merging function supported by most *SCM* systems. Although an arbitrary text file is expected as the result of textual merging, theoretically the merged text file could have integrated all textual changes concurrently made in individual files if the textual merging algorithm is properly designed. In other words, textual merging should not impose any restrictions on changes to be integrated and the merged text file could integrate all textual changes. However, most textual merging algorithms do impose some unjustified restrictions for the sake of simplification, which have prevented changes from being completely integrated. For example, some textual merging algorithms do not allow changes made within the same line of a shared text file to be integrated. In this chapter, we will systematically exploit this issue and present a novel textual merging technique that is able to integrate all textual changes.

Syntactic merging exploits the context-free syntax of the documents to be merged and can guarantee a syntactically correct result after merging. Conflicts are defined in terms of the syntax of the documents to be merged. The more the syntax can be well-formulated, the more automatic the syntactic merging process would be. For text files, syntactic merging should be built on top of textual merging and in order to support syntactic merging with rich syntax, the underlying textual merging algorithm should be powerful enough to textually integrate all changes. Although syntactic merging has been studied for a long time, it has only been realized in a few research prototypes [18, 145], which are however too slow to be practically usable, at least for programming language [50]. In this chapter, we will present a flexible syntactic merging framework that uses a generic and flexible textual merging technique to support a range of application-dependent user-specified syntactic merging policies.

Semantic merging takes into account the semantics of the documents to be merged and performs sophisticated semantic analysis in order to detect conflicts between changes [11]. However, it is difficult to come up with a definition of semantic conflict that is neither too strong nor too weak while determinable [28]. Therefore, semantic conflict detection and resolution have to be partly automatic and partly manual with as much information as possible provided by the system. The semantic merging algorithms developed so far are applicable only to simple programming languages (not C or C++) [11, 13, 69] and it is still a long way for semantic merging to become practice.

The rest of the chapter is organized as follows. Major textual merging techniques and major issues to be tackled are reviewed in the following section. Then technical solutions to the major issues are presented accordingly, including a compression algorithm and a novel textual merging algorithm. The next section presents a flexible syntactic merging framework and a generic and flexible syntactic merging algorithm. Finally the chapter is concluded with a summary of major contributions and future work.

3.2   Textual merging

Three-way merging is the most effective textual merging technique and can detect conflicts, automatically merge non-conflicting changes, and solve conflicts automatically or provide useful information for users to solve conflicts manually. A key in three-way merging is the acquisition of differences between documents, which are referred to as *deltas*. Deltas play an essential role in detecting conflicting changes and merging non-conflicting changes. In principle, without considering syntax or semantics of documents to be merged, there should be no conflict at all in textual merging. The so-called conflict (we name it as false conflict for the simplicity of explanation) between two changes is simply a result of the limitation of existing merging algorithms that do not know how to integrate the two changes into a new version by means of the acquired deltas. Furthermore, occurrence of false conflicts is directly related to how deltas are represented. In terms of how deltas are acquired and represented, textual merging techniques can be classified as *state-based merging* and *operation-based merging*.

3.2.1   State-based merging technique

In state-based merging, deltas are derived by executing a text differentiation algorithm that compares two text files to generate the differences between them. The most reputable text differentiation algorithm is the **diff** (f_1, f_2) algorithm [71, 88], which compares the two text files f_1 and f_2 and generates an editing script (or difference report) with which one file can be transformed to the other. There are some font-end tools built upon the *diff* algorithm, such as the *spiff* [94] and *flexible diff* [96], which provide users with some necessary and useful flexibility to control how the *diff* algorithm is performed and how the generated editing scripts are reported. For example, a user can instruct *spiff* to ignore differences between floating point numbers that are below a user-specified threshold or ignore white spaces and comments in differentiating program source code. The *diff* algorithm and a variety of its font-end tools have been used in most *SCM* systems. Various state-based textual merging algorithms have been devised based on the deltas derived by text differentiation algorithms. A typical three-way state-based textual merging algorithm is **diff3**(f_1, f_b, f_2), which produces a merged text file based on text files f_1 and f_2 and their baseline file f_b by utilizing deltas derived by the *diff* algorithm. The *diff3* textual merging algorithm has been widely used in *SCM* systems such as *SCCS* [112], *RCS* [142] and *CVS* [10].

The representation of deltas

Deltas between two text files are represented as editing scripts and can be used to transform one file to the other. For example, if D_{12} is the editing scripts from text file f_1 to f_2, then applying these editing scripts to f_1 will transform f_1 to f_2. This transformation procedure is denoted as $f_2 = f_1 \circ D_{12}$ for the sake of explanation. Editing Scripts are described by three kinds of editing operations: *add* (*a*), *delete* (*d*), and *change* (*c*). An adding operation is denoted as **a**[SL, NoL, ToL] to represent adding *NoL* new lines of text *ToL* after line *SL*. A changing operation is denoted as **c**[SL, NoL, ToL] to represent replacing *NoL* lines starting from line *SL* with new lines of text *ToL*. A deletion operation is denoted as **d**[SL, NoL] to represent deleting *NoL* lines starting from line *SL*. In fact, a deletion operation can be represented by a changing operation **c**[SL, NoL, ToL] with empty *ToL*.

For example, as shown in Figure 3.3, an initial text file f_1 described four major topics on collaborative editing. File f_1 can be revised into a new file f_2 as follows: insert a new line "*- Concurrency Control*" as the first item; insert word "*Group*" before word "*Undo*"; and remove item "*- Workflow management*". Editing scripts D_{12} describing the deltas from f_1 to f_2 consists of a list of editing operations [O_1, O_2, O_3] where $O_1 = $ **d**[5, 1] or **c**[5, 1, ""] to delete the fifth line (i.e., the last line) "*- Workflow Management*", $O_2 = $ **c**[3, 1, "*- Group Undo*"] to replace the third line "*- Undo*" with the new line "*- Group Undo*", and $O_3 = $ **a**[1, 1, "*- Concurrency Control*"] to add a new line "*- Concurrency Control*" after the first line "*Topics on collaborative editing:*".

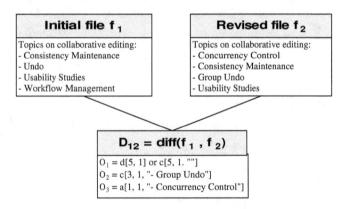

Figure 3.3: The representation of editing scripts

Editing scripts are line-based in the sense that if there is a single change within a line, the whole line is regarded as changed. In Figure 3.3, the line-based editing operations O_1 and O_3 have captured the real editing actions of inserting a new item and removing an existing item. However, the line-based editing operation O_2 does not capture the real editing action of inserting a word within an existing item. The line-based representation of editing scripts could be even more coarse-grained in the sense that if there is a change in every consecutive line, those consecutive lines as a whole, referred to as an *editing block*, are regarded as changed. For example, as shown in Figure 3.4, file f_1 has been revised into a new file f_2 by changing the word *"Studies"* in the item *"- Usability Studies"* from plural to singular *"Study"* in addition to those revisions made in Figure 3.3. Editing scripts in Figure 3.4 are significantly different from those in Figure 3.3. In particular, consecutive lines 3, 4, 5 constitute an editing block with editing operation $O_1 = \mathbf{d}[3, 3]$ or $\mathbf{d}[3, 3, ``"]$ to delete 3 lines starting from line 3, and $O_2 = \mathbf{a}[2, 2, ``- Group Undo\backslash n- Usability Study"]$ to insert two new lines after line 2. Apparently, editing operations O_1 and O_2 do not reflect the real editing actions performed by the user.

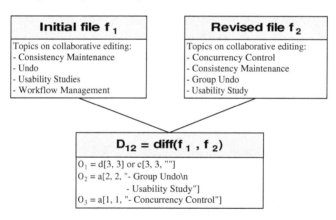

Figure 3.4: Coarse-grained representation of editing scripts

It is the coarse-granularity of derived editing scripts that causes the false conflict problem in state-based textual merging. In the *diff3* merging algorithm, a false conflict would occur if an editing block covered by an editing operation overlaps with another editing block covered by another editing operation and these two editing operations are contradictory in the sense they change the same line(s) to different values. For example, as shown in Figure 3.5, the baseline file f_b contains four items describing the topics on collaborative editing. It has been revised into file f_1 as follows: add word *"Group"* in the item *"- Undo"*; change word *"Studies"* to *"Study"* in the item *"- Usability Studies"*; and remove the last item *"- Workflow Management"*. Concurrently, it has also been revised into another file f_2 as follows: add a new item *"- Concurrency Control"* as the first item; add word *"Selective"* in the item *"- Undo"*; and remove the last item *"- Workflow Management"*.

Editing script D_{b1} contains editing operation $O_1^1 = \mathbf{c}[3, 2, $ *"- Group Undo\n- Usability Study"*] to represent deltas from f_b to f_1. Editing script D_{b2} contains editing operations $O_1^2 = \mathbf{d}[5, 1]$, $O_2^2 = \mathbf{c}[3, 1, $ *"- Selective Undo"*] and $O_3^2 = \mathbf{a}[1, 1, $ *"- Concurrency Control"*] to represent deltas from f_b to f_2. When f_2 is merged with f_1 to produce a merged text file f_m, the *diff3* algorithm will be executed as follows: first, the editing block covered by O_1^2 in D_{b2} contains the fifth line and the editing block covered by O_1^1 in D_{b1} contains the third, fourth, and fifth lines. These two editing blocks overlap but editing operations O_1^2 and O_1^1 are not contradictory because both intend to change the fifth line *"- Workflow Management"* to *""*. Therefore, the effect of O_1^2 is integrated into the merged file f_m: the item *"- Workflow Management"* is removed. Second, the editing block covered by O_2^2 in D_{b2} contains the third line and the editing block covered by O_1^1 in D_{b1} contains the third, fourth, and fifth lines. These two editing blocks overlap and editing operations O_1^2 and O_1^1 are contradictory because O_2^2 intends to change the third line to *"- Selective Undo"* while O_1^1 intends to change the same line to *"- Group Undo"*. As a result, it is a false conflict and the merging algorithm simply keeps both changes in the merged file f_m. Finally, editing block covered by O_3^2 in D_{b2} does not overlap with the editing block covered by O_1^1 in D_{b1}. Therefore, the effect of O_3^2 is integrated into the merged file f_m: a new item *"-

Concurrency Control" is added.

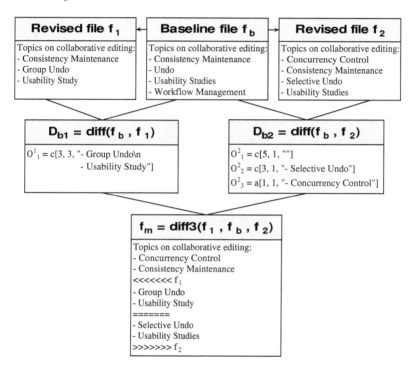

Figure 3.5: An example of three-way textual merging supported by diff3

The reason why text differentiation algorithms generate line-based editing scripts is that it is too time-consuming to generate fine-grained editing scripts. The text differentiation algorithm proposed by Hunt *et al.* [72] has a time complexity of $\Omega(m \times n)$ in terms of the string lengths m and n alone, and is even worse if taking into account how much the two strings are different. The algorithm proposed by Myers [93] is significantly improved if the two strings to be differentiated are not too different and it has been widely implemented as the *diff* utility in various *UNIX* systems and most *SCM* systems. The algorithm has a time complexity of $O(N \times D)$ if D is small, where N is the total lengths of the two strings and D is the size of the minimum editing script between the two strings. However, if D is large (e.g., for two strings that are completely different, $D = 2N$), its time complexity will be $O(N \lg N + D^2)$, even worse than the algorithm proposed by Hunt *et al.* [72]. Therefore, to make the algorithm efficient, the minimum editing script D between the two strings has to be small and the compromise is to compare the two strings line by line to derive line-based editing scripts instead of comparing them character by character to derive character-based editing scripts [142].

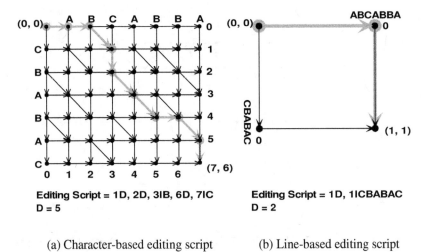

| (a) Character-based editing script | (b) Line-based editing script |

Figure 3.6: Character-based versus line-based editing script

For example, Figure 3.6(a) is the editing graph used in [93], where the source string is **ABCABBA** and the destination string is **CBABAC**. The editing graph has a vertex at each point in the grid (x,y) (x $\in$ [0, 7] and y $\in$ [0, 6]). The vertices of the editing graph are connected by horizontal, vertical, and diagonal edges to form a directed acyclic graph. *Horizontal edges* connect each vertex to its right neighbour (i.e., (x-1,y) → (x,y) corresponding to the deletion of character at position (x,0) for x ∈ [0, 7] and y ∈ [0, 6]). *Vertical edges* connect each vertex to the neighbour below it (i.e., (x,y-1) → (x,y) corresponding to the insertion of character at position (0,y) for x ∈ [0, 7] and y ∈ [0, 6]). If the character at position (x,0) is the same as the character at position (0,y), then there is a *diagonal edge* connecting vertex (x-1,y-1) to vertex (x,y), corresponding to keep that common character.

According to the text differentiation algorithm proposed by Myers [93], the size of the minimum editing script for transforming the source string **ABCABBA** to the destination string **CBABAC** is 5, if the editing script is character-based, which is significantly larger than the size of the corresponding minimum line-based editing script, which is 2. If deltas are derived in a more fine-grained way, they can certainly help merging algorithms reduce the chance of complaining false conflicts. However, even fine-grained editing scripts do not necessarily mean they have captured the real editing actions performed by the user. Consequently, they may mislead merging algorithms to produce a merging result undesirable to the user. For example, in Figure 3.6(a), the character-based editing script contains five editing operations: **1D** to delete the first character *A*, **2D** to delete the second character *B*, **3IB** to insert character *B* at position 3, **6D** to delete the sixth character *B*, and **7IC** to insert character *C* at position 7. But as shown in Figure 3.6(b), the real editing actions performed by the user could be **1D** to delete all seven characters and **1ICBABAC** to insert six new characters.

It should be pointed out that deltas are also important for storing versions in the repository in *SCM* systems. In the repository, versions are stored in such a way that the latest version is stored intact while old versions are stored as deltas, although the user interface completely hides this fact [124, 142]. Using deltas to represent versions in repository is a space-time tradeoff: deltas reduce the space consumption but increase access time. Statistics [142] show that the latest version is the one that is retrieved in 95 percent of all check-out cases, therefore it is significant to reduce access time by storing the latest version intact.

Merging process

A state-based merging process involves a working site, the repository site, and data transfers between them. Time spent at the working site is denoted as T_{wok}, time spent at the repository site is denoted as T_{rep}, and time spent for data transfers between the working site and the repository site is denoted as T_{com}. Another important measure is the system response time denoted as T_{res}, which is the time interval between when the user issues a merging command and the user re-gains the control of the system to issue other commands at a working site. T_{res} is very important in measuring the performance of a merging process because it is visible by users and has a substantial impact on users' evaluation on the system. T_{wok}, T_{rep}, and T_{com} are used to measure the consumption of computing cycles and network bandwidth, which may have direct or indirect impact on T_{res}.

Figure 3.7 shows the state-based commit merging process to merge the working copy W_m^1 at *Site 1* with version R_0 in the repository to generate a new version R_1. The process is described as follow:

1. *Site 1* sends a request to the repository, asking whether its working copy with baseline version number 0 is committable or not.

2. The repository processes the request and sends back the reply, telling whether the request is permitted or not.

3. If the request is not permitted, the merging process fails. Otherwise, *Site 1* spends time T_{wok} to compress the working copy with general file compression algorithms (it is optional), and to prepare for transferring the working copy. Counting for T_{res} ends at this step.

4. The working copy at *Site 1* takes time T_{com} to be transferred to the repository.

5. The repository spends time T_{rep} to merge W_0^1 with R_0 to generate a new version R_1. The repository first uncompresses *Site 1*'s working copy W_m^1 (it is optional), then executes the text differentiation algorithm $D = \mathbf{diff}(W_m^1, R_0)$ to derive the deltas D between W_m^1 and R_0, and finally generates the new version $R_1 = W_m^1$ and replaces R_0 with D.

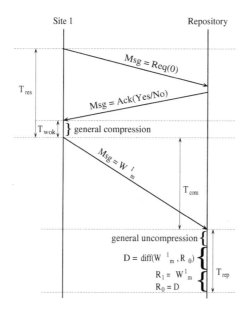

Figure 3.7: A state-based commit merging process

Figure 3.8 shows the state-based updating merging process to merge version R_1 with the working copy W_n^2 at *Site 2* to generate a new document state W_{n+1}^2. The process is described as follows:

1. *Site 2* sends a request to the repository site, carrying the baseline version number

0 for the working copy.

2. The repository takes time T_{rep} to process the request. It first retrieves version $R_0 = R_1 \circ D$, then compresses files R_0 and R_1 (optional), and finally transfers the two files to *Site 2*.

3. The two files take time T_{com} to arrive at *Site 2*.

4. *Site 2* spends time T_{wok} to merge version R_1 into the working copy. It first uncompresses files R_0 and R_1 (optional), then derives deltas D_1 (from W_n^2 to R_1) by $D_1 = \mathbf{diff}(W_n^2, R_1)$ and deltas D_2 (from R_0 to R_1) by $D_2 = \mathbf{diff}(R_0, R_1)$, and finally generates a new document state W_{n+1}^2 by executing $\mathbf{diff3}(W_n^2, R_0, R_1, D_1, D_2)$. Counting for the system response time T_{res} ends here.

As shown in Figure 3.7, in the commit merging process, T_{res} is short and independent of the files to be merged. It is good that users will not be discouraged by other delays involved in a commit merging process. T_{com} is dependent on the size of the working copy to be committed into the repository. Time for deriving deltas dominates T_{rep} at the repository site. By comparison, as shown in Figure 3.8, in the update merging process, T_{res} is determined by the whole merging process, which is mainly measured by T_{rep}, T_{com}, and T_{wok}. First, T_{rep} is dominated by the time spent on the retrieval of version R_0, which is dependent on the number of editing operations in the deltas D. Second, T_{com} is dependent on the total sizes of files R_0 and R_1. Finally, T_{wok} is dominated primarily by the derivation of deltas D_1 and D_2, and secondarily by the execution of merging algorithm to generate a new document state of the working copy. In general, T_{wok} is dependent on the total sizes of the three files W_n^2, R_0, and R_1, and how much these three files are different.

To sum, time spent on deltas related tasks, such as transferring files across the network, deriving deltas, performing deltas on one document to generate or retrieve another document, is significant in a state-based merging process. In particular, it has a fundamental impact on the system response in an update merging process. Responsiveness could be very poor under the circumstances that the files are large, network resources are scarce, and/or computation power of hosts is low.

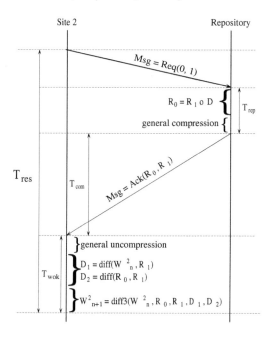

Figure 3.8: A state-based update merging process

3.2.2 Operation-based merging technique

Operation-based merging takes advantage of real change operations that were performed during development [84, 83]. It was originally proposed for object merging in object-oriented databases [84], object-based graphical applications [9], or calender applications. Operation-based merging takes two sequences of change operations and combines them into a single sequence by re-ordering, detecting both inconsistencies and conflicts. Therefore operation-based merging can in principle be applied to arbitrary object types whose data-type invariants are automatically respected, and be used to merge entire object systems in a variety of formats [84]. Moreover, because operation-based merging is based on the real change operations performed by users rather than artificial change operations derived by algorithms, the merged result is more likely to be consistent from the user's point of view, where many unnecessary false conflicts can be avoided, more syntax or semantics related conflicts can be detected, and more support can be provided for conflict resolution.

Operation-based merging is a general approach and state-based merging can be regarded as a restricted form of operation-based merging for the support of textual merging, which attempts to reconstruct change operations after the fact [84]. The reconstructed transformation is only one of many paths to transform a document from its initial state to its final state and it is hardly possible to coincide with the user's actual performed transformation. Furthermore, derived editing scripts in state-based merging are coarse-grained in the sense they are modifications to lines. By contrast, operation-based merging utilizes user's actual performed editing operations that are far more fine-grained in the sense that they can be modifications to arbitrary sequence of characters. As a result, operation-based merging has the potential to avoid false conflicts in textual merging, detect more syntax or semantics related conflicts in syntactic or semantic merging, and provide more support for conflict resolution.

The representation of deltas

To support operation-based merging, user-issued editing operations during the process of editing a text file must be physically saved in logs. The logged editing operations are actually the deltas in transforming the text file from its initial state to the final state. For example, in Figure 3.1 in Section 5.1, the list of operations $[O_1^1, \cdots, O_m^1]$ are the deltas in transforming the working copy at *Site 1* from its initial state W_0^1 to the final state W_m^1 while the list of operations $[O_1^2, \cdots, O_n^2]$ are the deltas in transforming the working copy at *Site 2* from its initial state W_0^2 to the final state W_n^2. To support textual merging, a text file can be treated as a sequence of characters and user-issued editing operations can be represented as insertion/deletion of a sequence of characters at certain positions in the file.

Following the same notations used in Chapter 2, an insertion/deletion operation is denoted as **Ins/Del**$[P, N, S]$ to insert/delete a string S of N characters at position P. It should be pointed out that unlike a deletion operation used in state-based merging, which does not keep the lines that have been removed, a deletion operation used in operation-based merging keeps the sequence of characters that has been deleted. The merit of this representation is that the inverse operations [132] can be directly used as backward deltas in operation-based merging while state-based merging has to derive forward and backward deltas separately [142]. For example, in Figure 3.7, $D =$ **diff**(W_m^1, R_0) is derived as backward deltas [142] in transforming version R_1 (equal to W_m^1) back to the old version R_0. But in Figure 3.8, $D_2 =$ **diff**(R_0, R_1) has to be derived to represent forward deltas [142] in transforming the old version R_0 to the new version R_1.

Furthermore, to support syntactic or semantic merging, editing operations in operation-based merging may be defined on the basis of the internal structure of the text file. For example, a book can be divided into chapters, sections, paragraphs, and lines, and an editing operation can be specified to insert a new paragraph after Paragraph x in Section y of Chapter z. Editing operations performed on tree-structured text documents such as XML or HTML files can be specified to add a new node to a subnode tree or excise an existing node from the tree [36]. Because the rules for syntactic merging or semantic merging are application-dependent, the representation of editing operations has to be dependent on the internal structure of the files used by certain applications.

Merging process

Figure 3.9 shows the operation-based commit merging process to merge the working copy W_m^1 at *Site 1* with version R_0 in the repository to generate a new version R_1. The process is described as follows:

1. *Site 1* sends a request to the repository, asking whether its working copy with baseline version number 0 is committable or not.

2. The repository processes the request and sends back the reply, telling whether the request is permitted or not.

3. If the request is not permitted, the merging process fails. Otherwise, *Site 1* spends time T_{wok} to compress the list of editing operations $[O_1^1, \cdots, O_m^1]$ with general file compression algorithms (optional), and to prepare for transferring the list of operations. Counting for T_{res} ends at this step.

4. The list of operations take time T_{com} to be transferred to the repository.

5. The repository site spends T_{rep} in merging the list of operations into version R_0 to generate a new version R_1. It first uncompresses the list of operations, then applies them to version R_0 to generate $R_1 = R_0 \circ [O_1^1, \cdots, O_m^1]$, and finally replace R_0 with the list of operations.

By comparing the state-based commit merging process shown in Figure 3.7 and the operation-based commit merging process shown in Figure 3.9, it can be concluded that T_{res}, T_{wok}, T_{com}, and T_{rep} in an operation-based commit merging process can be shorter than those in a corresponding state-based commit merging process if the size of the list of editing operations $[O_1^1, \cdots, O_m^1]$ is smaller than the size of the working copy W_m^1 and the number of operations in the list is in the same order of the number of operations in the derived deltas. In particular, T_{wok} and T_{res} can be shorter than those in state-based merging if the size of the list of operations $[O_1^1, \cdots, O_m^1]$ is smaller than the size of the working copy. T_{com} can be shorter than that in state-based merging if the size of the list of operations is smaller than the size of the working copy W_m^1. T_{rep} is mainly dominated by the time for applying the list of operations $[O_1^1, \cdots, O_m^1]$ to R_0 to generate R_1, and is dependent on the number of operations in the list. T_{rep} in an operation-based commit merging process can be shorter than that in state-based merging if the number of operations in the list is in the same order of the number of operations in the deltas derived by the *diff* algorithm.

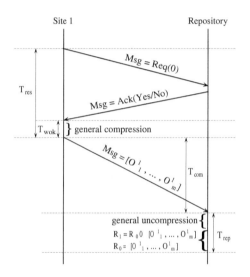

Figure 3.9: An operation-based commit merging process

Figure 3.10 shows the operation-based updating merging process to merge version R_1 into the working copy W_n^2 at *Site 2* to generate a new document state W_{n+1}^2. The process is described as follows:

1. *Site 2* sends a request to the repository site, carrying the baseline version number 0 for the working copy.

2. The repository site takes T_{rep} to compress of the list of operations $[O_1^1, \cdots, O_m^1]$

representing deltas between version R_0 and R_1 (optional), and to prepare for transferring the list of operations to *Site 2*.

3. The list of operations take T_{com} to be transferred to *Site 2*.

4. *Site 2* takes T_{wok} to merge the list operations into the working copy to generate a new document state W_{n+1}^2. It first uncompresses the list of operations (optional), then combines the list of operations with the local sequence of editing operations $[O_1^2, \cdots, O_n^2]$ into a single sequence, and finally applies the single sequence to W_n^2 to generate W_{n+1}^2.

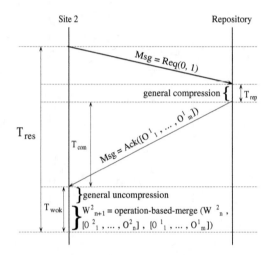

Figure 3.10: An operation-based update merging process

By comparing the state-based update merging process shown in Figure 3.8 and the operation-based update merging process shown in Figure 3.10, it can be concluded that T_{res}, T_{wok}, T_{com}, and T_{rep} in an operation-based update merging process are significantly shorter than those in the corresponding state-based update merging process if the size of the list of operations $[O_1^1, \cdots, O_m^1]$ is smaller than the total sizes of version R_0 and R_1, and the number of operations in the list $[O_1^1, \cdots, O_m^1]$ and the number of operations in the local log are in the same order of those derived deltas. In particular, T_{rep} is shorter than that in state-based merging because the repository does not need to retrieve version R_0. T_{com} can be shorter than that in state-based merging if the size of the list of operations is smaller than the total sizes of versions R_0 and R_1. T_{wok} is dominated by the time for combining the list of operations from the repository and operations in the local log into a single sequence, and applying the combined sequence to W_n^2 to generate W_{n+1}^2. T_{wok} in an operation-based merging process can be shorter than that in the corresponding state-based merging process if the number of operations in the list and the number of operations in the local log are in the same order of those derived deltas. Because T_{res} is mainly dominated by T_{wok}, T_{com}, and T_{rep}, T_{res} should be shorter than that in state-based merging if T_{wok}, T_{com}, and T_{rep} are all shorter respectively.

Challenging issues

Although operation-based merging has so many merits, it is very challenging to take advantage of these merits. The first challenging issue is how to log operations. There is no commonly used editor that provides the function of logging user-issued editing operations. It appears that the only way is to implement a log-enabled editor [121] that is capable of logging editing operations. While this approach is doable in practice, it is undesirable. First, it is non-trivial and very costly to design and implement an editor as sophisticated as existing ones such as Microsoft *Word* [17] or GNU *Emacs* [20]. Second, it is difficult to convince users to abandon their favourite editors and work with the unfamiliar log-enabled editor just for the sake of taking advantage of operation-based merging. Finally, existing *SCM* systems with the underlying state-based merging technology allow users to edit files with any editors. It is an endearing feature since different editors may be specially good at editing different kinds of documents and different users may have different tastes in choosing editors. It is unacceptable in reality if operation-based merging forces users to adopt the same specially designed log-enabled editor despite their different favourites and the diversity of documents to be edited.

One approach is to modify the source code of existing editors to make them capable of logging editing operations. *DistEdit* [76] adopted a similar technique to convert existing single-user editors such as *Emacs* and *Vi* into group editors. This approach only changes a small portion of the source code of existing single-user editors but does not change the appearance and functionality of existing single-user editors. Its limitations are as follows: first, many commonly used commercial editors such as Microsoft *Word* do not provide access to its source code. Therefore, those editors cannot be converted into group editors or made log-enabled in this approach. Second, group editors or log-enabled editors implemented in the *DistEdit* approach cannot adapt to the evolvement of the corresponding single-user editors. In other words, if a single-user editor is released with a new version, its group or log-enabled version has to be re-implemented to catch up with its new release.

Li *et al.* [81] addressed this issue by proposing the technique of transparent sharing of single-user editors to convert them into group editors without modifying the source code. The basic idea is to intercept and save edit-related events such as keyboard strokes and mouse down, up and movements, and to assemble them as meaningful editing operations via the programming interfaces provided by single-user editors and the operating systems in which editors are running if the programming interfaces are inadequate. This approach does not require modifying the source and therefore can be used to make existing editors capable of logging editing operations without touching their source code. Furthermore, group editors or log-enabled editors implemented in this approach can automatically adapt to new versions of their corresponding single-user editors without re-implementation. The same transparent approach has been applied to the design and implementation of *CoWord* [133], which is a real-time collaborative version of Microsoft *Word*.

The second challenging issue is how to control the *scale* of logs for an operation-based merging process to outperform the corresponding state-based merging process. The scale of a log consists of two aspects: the size of the log and the number of editing operations in the log. As discussed in operation-based merging processes, it is the scale of logs that determines whether an operation-based merging process outperforms a corresponding state-based merging process. Without proper control of the scale of a log, editing operations could be accumulated in a log so drastically that an operation-based merging process could become worse than in the corresponding state-based merging process. The last issue is how to devise an operation-based textual merging algorithm that takes two sequences of editing operations and combines them into a single sequence with which changes made in one version can be all integrated into another version without complaining false conflicts.

3.3 A log compression algorithm

When a group of people do non-real-time collaborative editing or team software development, individuals are usually assigned with different tasks. To fulfill her/his own task, an individual participant makes her/his own time and progress schedules to make her/his changes to the shared resources available to others. The work performed by an individual participant tends to last hours, days, or even weeks till it is mature enough to be made publicly available. During the long development period, editing operations performed by an individual participant are accumulated in a log that could grow to an undesirable scale. An experiment that supports this point will be described in a later section.

3.3.1 Related work

Munson and Dewan [92] expressed their argument with the technique of operation-based merging from the perspective of long editing histories: the longer and the more fine-grained the history, the more tedious and time-consuming operation-based merging becomes. Petersen *et al.* [100] addressed the issue of write-log management in *Bayou*'s anti-entropy protocol for the propagation of write operations between weakly consistency storage replicas. If a replica does not discard any write operation from its write-log, the write-log could grow dramatically. In practice, it is unreasonable to assume that replicas can store ever-growing logs of write operations. For replicas to effectively manage the storage resources of their write-logs, *Bayou* allows each replica to independently decide when and how aggressively to prune a prefix of its write-log subject to the constraint that only stable writes can get discarded. An important consequence of this approach is that a replica may discard write operations that have not been propagated to other replicas, leading to inconsistency. *Bayou*'s answer to this question is to transfer the full database state from one replica to the other if the two replicas are far from consistent. However, this approach is not applicable to the reduction of log sizes in operation-based merging for non-real-time collaborative editing or version control since it sometimes needs to transfer a full, large document over the network, which is exactly what operation-based merging wants to avoid.

Lippe [84] proposed the concept of redundant operations in operation-based merging. An operation is redundant if its effect has been completely removed or overwritten by later operations. Examples of redundant operations are operations on objects that are removed later on, and update operations whose effects are overwritten by later update operations. Redundant operations may frequently occur in some applications where a user often explores alternative solutions by backtracking, and consequently, modifications related to a previous solution become redundant. Although the objective of removing redundant operations is to remove unnecessary conflicts and to speed up conflict detection [84], the scale of a log is reduced if redundant operations in the log have been removed. Although the definition of redundant operations and the technique for removing redundant operation proposed by Lippe [84] are not directly applicable to the logs for operation-based textual merging where editing operations are performed on a sequence of characters instead of independent objects, the concept of redundant operations is one source of inspiration for the following novel log compression algorithm.

3.3.2 Definitions

The following definitions are used to describe the relationship between any two operations in a log. Given any editing operation $O = \textbf{Ins/Del}[P, N, S]$, $\textbf{P}(O)$ denotes O's position parameter, $\textbf{N}(O)$ denotes O's length parameter, $\textbf{S}(O)$ denotes O's text parameter, and $\textbf{T}(O) =$ denotes O's type parameter. Given an initial document state S_0 and a log L storing a sequence of editing operations $[O_1, \cdots, O_n]$ performed on S_0, the document state before the execution of O_1 is S_0, and the document state after the execution of operation O_i $(1 \leq i \leq n)$ is denoted as $S_i = S_0 \circ [O_1, \cdots, O_i]$. Therefore $CT_{O_1} = S_0$, $CT_{O_i} = S_{i-1} = S_0 \circ [O_1, \cdots, O_{i-1}]$ $(1 < i \leq n)$, and $O_{i-1} \mapsto O_i$ $(1 < i \leq n)$.

Definition 3.1. Operation overlapping relation "$\oplus$"

Given two operations O_a and O_b where $O_a \mapsto O_b$, O_a and O_b are *overlapping*, denoted as $O_a \oplus O_b$, **iff** one of following conditions holds:

1. $\textbf{T}(O_a) = \textbf{T}(O_b) = Ins$, and $\textbf{P}(O_a) < \textbf{P}(O_b) < \textbf{P}(O_a) + \textbf{N}(O_a)$.

2. $\textbf{T}(O_a) = \textbf{T}(O_b) = Del$, and $\textbf{P}(O_b) < \textbf{P}(O_a) < \textbf{P}(O_b) + \textbf{N}(O_b)$.

3. $\textbf{T}(O_a) = Ins$ and $\textbf{T}(O_b) = Del$, and $\textbf{P}(O_a) \leq \textbf{P}(O_b) < \textbf{P}(O_a) + \textbf{N}(O_a)$ or $\textbf{P}(O_b) \leq \textbf{P}(O_a) < \textbf{P}(O_b) + \textbf{N}(O_b)$.

Two operations O_a and O_b are overlapping if their effect regions are overlapping. First, if an insertion operation O_b inserts a string that falls into the effect region of a previous insertion operation O_a, then O_a and O_b are overlapping. Second, if a deletion operation O_a deletes a range that falls into the effect region of a later deletion operation O_b, then O_a and O_b are overlapping. Third, if an insertion operation O_a inserts a string which or part of which falls into the effect region of a later deletion operation O_b, then O_a and O_b are overlapping. Finally, under no circumstance could an insertion operation overlap with a previous deletion operation because there is no way for a string to be inserted into a nonexistent string (i.e., a string that has already been deleted). For example, as shown in Figure 3.11, a document is initially empty and finally contains characters c and z after five editing operations $[O_1, \cdots, O_5]$ have been performed. Operation $O_1 = \mathbf{Ins}[0, 3, abc]$ inserted 3 characters a, b, and c at position 0 and operation $O_2 = \mathbf{Ins}[2, 2, xy]$ inserted 2 characters x and y at position 2 (i.e., after character b). We have $O_1 \oplus O_2$ because the string xy inserted by O_2 falls into the string abc inserted by O_1. This relation can be further confirmed by Definition 3.1(1): $O_1 \mapsto O_2$, $\mathbf{T}(O_1) = \mathbf{T}(O_2) = Ins$, and $(\mathbf{P}(O_1){=}0) < (\mathbf{P}(O_2){=}2) < (\mathbf{P}(O_1){+}\mathbf{N}(O_1){=}0{+}3{=}3)$.

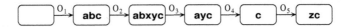

Figure 3.11: A log for illustrating relationships between operations

Then operation $O_3 = \mathbf{Del}[1, 2, bx]$ deleted 2 characters b and x at position 1 (i.e., after character a). We have $O_2 \oplus O_3$ because the string bx deleted by O_2 includes character x that is part of the string xy inserted by O_2. This relation can be further confirmed by Definition 3.1(3): $O_2 \mapsto O_3$, $\mathbf{T}(O_2) = Ins$ and $\mathbf{T}(O_3) = Del$, and $(\mathbf{P}(O_3){=}1) < (\mathbf{P}(O_2){=}2) < (\mathbf{P}(O_3){+}\mathbf{N}(O_3){=}1{+}2{=}3)$. Operation $O_4 = \mathbf{Del}[0, 2, ay]$ deleted 2 characters a and y at position 0. We have $O_3 \oplus O_4$ because the string bx deleted by O_3 falls into string ay deleted by O_4. This relation can be further confirmed by Definition 3.1(2): $O_3 \mapsto O_4$, $\mathbf{T}(O_3) = \mathbf{T}(O_4) = Del$, and $(\mathbf{P}(O_4)=0) <$ $(\mathbf{P}(O_3)=1) < (\mathbf{P}(O_4)+\mathbf{N}(O_4)=0+2=2)$. Finally, operation $O_5 = \mathbf{Ins}[0, 1, z]$ inserted one character z at position 0. O_5 could not overlap with O_4 according to Definition 3.1.

Definition 3.2. Operation adjacent relation "⊖"

Given two operations O_a and O_b where $O_a \mapsto O_b$, O_a and O_b are *adjacent*, denoted as $O_a \ominus O_b$, *iff* one of the following conditions holds:

1. $\mathbf{T}(O_a) = \mathbf{T}(O_b) = Ins$, and $\mathbf{P}(O_b) = \mathbf{P}(O_a)$ or $\mathbf{P}(O_b) = \mathbf{P}(O_a)+\mathbf{N}(O_a)$.

2. $\mathbf{T}(O_a) = \mathbf{T}(O_b) = Del$, and $\mathbf{P}(O_a) = \mathbf{P}(O_b)+\mathbf{N}(O_b)$ or $\mathbf{P}(O_a) = \mathbf{P}(O_b)$.

The same type of two operations are adjacent if their effect regions are adjacent. If an insertion operation O_b inserts a string that is adjacent to the string inserted by a previous insertion operation O_a, then O_a and O_b are adjacent. If a deletion operation O_b deletes a range that is adjacent to the range deleted by a previous deletion operation O_a, then O_a and O_b are adjacent. For instance, in the example shown in Figure 3.11, if O_2 was changed to $\mathbf{Ins}[0, 2, xy]$ to insert 2 characters x and y at position 0, it would be $O_1 \ominus O_2$ because the string xy inserted by O_2 is left adjacent to the string abc inserted by O_1. This relation can be further confirmed by Definition 3.2(1): $O_1 \mapsto O_2$, $\mathbf{T}(O_1) = \mathbf{T}(O_2) = Ins$, and $(P(O_2)=0) = P(O_1)=0)$. Similarly, if O_4 was changed to $\mathbf{Del}[0, 1, a]$ to delete the character a at position 0, it would be $O_3 \ominus O_4$ because the character a deleted by O_4 is left adjacent to the string bx deleted by O_3. This relation can be further confirmed by Definition 3.2(2): $O_3 \mapsto O_4$, $\mathbf{T}(O_3) = \mathbf{T}(O_4) = Del$, and $(P(O_3)=1) = (\mathbf{P}(O_4)+\mathbf{N}(O_4)=0+1=1)$.

Definition 3.3. Operation disjointed relation "⊙"

Given two operations O_a and O_b, O_a and O_b are *disjointed*, denoted as $O_a \odot O_b$, *iff* neither $O_a \oplus O_b$ nor $O_a \ominus O_b$.

Two operations are disjointed if their effect regions are neither overlapping nor adjacent. The following example shows the relations between any pair of neighbouring editing operations in a log. As shown in Figure 3.12, a document initially contained three characters x, y, and z, which was developed to the state containing characters x, c, 1, 2, and 3 by a sequence of five editing operations saved in the log $L = [O_1, O_2, O_3, O_4, O_5]$. Operation $O_1 = \textbf{Ins}[3, 1, c]$ inserted one character c at position 3 (i.e., after character z) and operation $O_2 = \textbf{Ins}[3, 2, ab]$ inserted 2 characters a and b also at position 3. It must be $O_1 \ominus O_2$ according to Definition 3.2(1): $O_1 \mapsto O_2$, $\textbf{T}(O_1) = \textbf{T}(O_2) = Ins$, and $(\textbf{P}(O_2)=3) = (\textbf{P}(O_1)=3)$. Then operation $O_3 = \textbf{Del}[2, 2, za]$ deleted 2 characters z and a at position 2 (i.e., after character y). It must be $O_2 \oplus O_3$ according to Definition 3.1(3): $O_2 \mapsto O_3$, $\textbf{T}(O_2) = Ins$ and $\textbf{T}(O_3) = Del$, and $(\textbf{P}(O_3)=2) < (\textbf{P}(O_2)=3) < (\textbf{P}(O_3)+\textbf{N}(O_3)=2+2=4)$. Operation $O_4 = \textbf{Del}[1, 2, yb]$ deleted 2 characters y and b at position 1 (i.e., after character x). It must be $O_3 \oplus O_4$ according to Definition 3.1(2): $O_3 \mapsto O_4$, $\textbf{T}(O_3) = \textbf{T}(O_4) = Del$, and $(\textbf{P}(O_4)=1) < (\textbf{P}(O_3)=2) < (\textbf{P}(O_4)+\textbf{N}(O_4)=1+2=3)$. Finally, operation $O_5 = \textbf{Ins}[2, 3, 123]$ inserted 3 characters 1, 2, and 3 at position 2 (i.e., after character c). It must be $O_4 \odot O_5$ according to Definition 3.3: neither $O_4 \oplus O_5$ nor $O_4 \ominus O_5$.

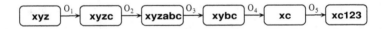

Figure 3.12: A log for illustrating relationships between neighbouring operations

3.3.3   Operational merging technique

Two adjacent operations can be merged into one operation by concatenating their effect regions. In this way, the number of operations in the log can be reduced by one. The same type of two overlapping operations can be merged into one operation by combining their effect regions. In this way, the number of operations in the log can be reduced by one. Different types of two overlapping operations can be merged in such a way that the overlapping region is removed from both operations. In this way, the size of the log can be reduced and the number of operations in the log could be reduced by one or two if the effect region of one operation totally falls into the effect region of the other operation or the effect regions of the two operations are completely overlapping. The technique of merging adjacent and overlapping operations is called *operational merging* technique, which can be used to reduce the scale of a log by reducing the size of the log and the number of operations in the log.

The **OM**(O_a, O_b) function for merging operations O_a and O_b where $O_a \mapsto O_b$ is defined as follows:

Function 3.1. *OM(O_a, O_b): (O'_a, O'_b)*

    1. Precondition for input parameters: $O_a \mapsto O_b$

    2. Postcondition for output: $O'_a \odot O'_b$

{ if T(O_a) == *Ins* **and T**(O_b) == *Ins*

    return OM_II(O_a, O_b);

  else if T(O_a) == *Ins* **and T**(O_b) == *Del*

    return OM_ID(O_a, O_b);

  else if T(O_a) == *Del* **and T**(O_b) == *Del*

    return OM_DD(O_a, O_b);

  else

    return (O_a, O_b);

}

The **OM_II**(O_a, O_b) function is defined to merge two insertion operations O_a and O_b where $O_a \mapsto O_b$. If $O_a \odot O_b$, they will not be merged in any way and returned as-is. If $O_a \oplus O_b$ or $O_a \ominus O_b$, O_a and O_b will be merged into a single insertion operation O'_a that integrates the effect regions covered by both O_a and O_b. In the example shown in Figure 3.12, because $O_1 \ominus O_2$, O_1 and O_2 can be merged by **OM_II**(O_1, O_2) = (O'_1, I) where $O'_1 = $ **Ins**[3, 3, abc].

Function 3.2. $OM\_II(O_a, O_b)$: (O'_a, O'_b)

{ //$O_a \oplus O_b$ or $O_a \ominus O_b$

    if $\mathbf{P}(O_b) \geq \mathbf{P}(O_a)$ and $\mathbf{P}(O_b) \leq \mathbf{P}(O_a)+\mathbf{N}(O_a)$

    { $head = \mathbf{substr}(\mathbf{S}(O_a), 0, \mathbf{P}(O_b)\text{-}\mathbf{P}(O_a))$;

     $tail = \mathbf{substr}(\mathbf{S}(O_a), \mathbf{P}(O_b)\text{-}\mathbf{P}(O_a), \mathbf{N}(O_a))$;

     $\mathbf{T}(O'_a) = Ins$;

     $\mathbf{P}(O'_a) = \mathbf{P}(O_a)$;

     $\mathbf{N}(O'_a) = \mathbf{N}(O_a)+\mathbf{N}(O_b)$;

     $\mathbf{S}(O'_a) = head + \mathbf{S}(O_b) + tail$;

     return (O'_a, I); //I is an identity

    } **else** //$O_a \odot O_b$

     return (O_a, O_b);

}

The **OM_DD**(O_a, O_b) function is defined to merge two deletion operations O_a and O_b where $O_a \mapsto O_b$. If $O_a \odot O_b$, they will not be merged in any way and returned as-is. If $O_a \oplus O_b$ or $O_a \ominus O_b$, O_a and O_b will be merged into a single deletion operation O'_a that integrates the effect regions covered by both O_a and O_b. In the example shown in Figure 3.12, because $O_3 \oplus O_4$, O_3 and O_4 will be merged by **OM_DD**(O_3, O_4) = (O'_3, I) where $O'_3 = \mathbf{Del}[1, 4, yzab]$.

Function 3.3. $OM\_DD(O_a, O_b)$: (O'_a, O'_b)

{ //$O_a \oplus O_b$ or $O_a \ominus O_b$

    if $\mathbf{P}(O_a) \geq \mathbf{P}(O_b)$ and $\mathbf{P}(O_a) \leq \mathbf{P}(O_b)+\mathbf{N}(O_b)$

    { $head = \mathbf{substr}(\mathbf{S}(O_b), 0, \mathbf{P}(O_a)\text{-}\mathbf{P}(O_b))$;

     $tail = \mathbf{substr}(\mathbf{S}(O_b), \mathbf{P}(O_a)\text{-}\mathbf{P}(O_b), \mathbf{N}(O_b))$;

     $\mathbf{T}(O'_a) = Del$;

     $\mathbf{P}(O'_a) = \mathbf{P}(O_b)$;

     $\mathbf{N}(O'_a) = \mathbf{N}(O_a)+\mathbf{N}(O_b)$;

$\mathbf{S}(O'_a) = head + \mathbf{S}(O_a) + tail;$

$\mathbf{return}\ (O'_a,\ I);\ //I$ is an identity

$\}$ $\mathbf{else}$ $//O_a \odot O_b$

$\mathbf{return}\ (O_a,\ O_b);$

$\}$

The $\mathbf{OM\_ID}(O_a, O_b)$ function is defined to merge an insertion operation O_a and a deletion operation O_b where $O_a \mapsto O_b$. If $O_a \odot O_b$, they will not be merged in any way and return as-is. If $O_a \oplus O_b$, the overlapping region will be removed from both O_a and O_b in such a way that the common substring ST inserted by O_a but later deleted by O_b is eliminated from both O_a and O_b. In particular,

- If $\mathbf{S}(O_a) = \mathbf{S}(O_b)$, then $ST = \mathbf{S}(O_a) = \mathbf{S}(O_b)$, and O_a and O_b must have completely counteracted against each other. Therefore, both O_a and O_b are redundant operations [84] and can be safely removed from the log. So $\mathbf{OM\_ID}(O_a, O_b) = (I, I)$ where I is an identity.

- If $S(O_a)$ is a substring of $S(O_b)$, then $ST = S(O_a)$, and O_a must have totally been overwritten by O_b. Therefore, O_a is a redundant operation [84] and can be safely removed from the log. So $\mathbf{OM\_ID}(O_a, O_b) = (I, O'_b)$ where $\mathbf{T}(O'_b)$ $= Del$, $\mathbf{P}(O'_b) = \mathbf{P}(O_b)$, $\mathbf{N}(O'_b) = \mathbf{N}(O_b) - \mathbf{N}(O_a)$, and $\mathbf{S}(O'_b)$ is achieved by removing the substring $\mathbf{S}(O_a)$ from $\mathbf{S}(O_b)$.

- If $S(O_b)$ is a substring of $S(O_a)$, then $ST = S(O_b)$, and O_b must have counteracted only part of O_a's effect and nothing else has been deleted by O_b. Therefore, O_b is a redundant operation [84] and can be safely removed from the log. So, $\mathbf{OM\_ID}(O_a, O_b) = (O'_a, I)$ where $\mathbf{T}(O'_a) = Ins$, $\mathbf{P}(O'_a) = \mathbf{P}(O_a)$, $\mathbf{N}(O'_a) = \mathbf{N}(O_a) - \mathbf{N}(O_b)$, and $\mathbf{S}(O'_a)$ is achieved by removing the substring $\mathbf{S}(O_b)$ from $\mathbf{S}(O_a)$.

- Otherwise ST is the common substring in both $\mathbf{S}(O_a)$ and $\mathbf{S}(O_b)$, and O_a and O_b must have partially counteracted against each other. In other words, part of the string inserted by O_a has been deleted by O_b, but O_b have also deleted other characters that were not inserted by O_a. Therefore, none of O_a and O_b is a redundant operation [84] but both of them can be condensed in such a way that ST is eliminated from both O_a and O_b. So $\mathbf{OM\_ID}(O_a, O_b) = (O'_a, O'_b)$ where $\mathbf{T}(O'_a) = Ins$, $\mathbf{P}(O'_a) = \mathbf{P}(O_a)$, $\mathbf{N}(O'_a) = \mathbf{N}(O_a) - \mathbf{Length}(ST)$, $\mathbf{S}(O'_a)$ is achieved by removing the substring ST from $\mathbf{S}(O_a)$, $\mathbf{T}(O'_b) = Del$, $\mathbf{P}(O'_b) = \mathbf{P}(O_b)$, $\mathbf{N}(O'_b) = \mathbf{N}(O_b) - \mathbf{Length}(ST)$, and $\mathbf{S}(O'_b)$ is achieved by removing the substring ST from $\mathbf{S}(O_b)$.

The $\mathbf{OM\_ID}(O_a, O_b)$ function is the most effective operational merging function for reducing the scale of a log, which can dramatically reduce the size of a log and the number of operations in the log by removing redundant operations or redundant information in operations. In the example shown in Figure 3.12, because $O_2 \oplus O_3$, O_2 and O_3 will be merged by $\mathbf{OM\_ID}(O_2, O_3) = (O'_2, O'_3)$ where $O'_2 = \mathbf{Ins}[3, 1, b]$ and $O'_3 = \mathbf{Del}[2, 1, z]$.

Function 3.4. $OM\_ID(O_a, O_b): (O'_a, O'_b)$

$\{$ //$\mathbf{S}(O_a)$ is a substring of $\mathbf{S}(O_b)$ or $\mathbf{S}(O_a) = \mathbf{S}(O_b)$

  if $\mathbf{P}(O_b) \leq \mathbf{P}(O_a)$ and $\mathbf{P}(O_b)+\mathbf{N}(O_b) \geq \mathbf{P}(O_a)+\mathbf{N}(O_a)$

  //$\mathbf{S}(O_a) = \mathbf{S}(O_b)$

  if $\mathbf{P}(O_b) == \mathbf{P}(O_a)$ and $\mathbf{P}(O_b)+\mathbf{N}(O_b) == \mathbf{P}(O_a)+\mathbf{N}(O_a)$

    return (I, I);

  //$\mathbf{S}(O_a)$ is a substring of $\mathbf{S}(O_b)$

  else

    $\{$ $head = \mathbf{substr}(\mathbf{S}(O_b), 0, \mathbf{P}(O_a)-\mathbf{P}(O_b))$;

      $tail = \mathbf{substr}(\mathbf{S}(O_b), \mathbf{P}(O_a)+\mathbf{N}(O_a)-\mathbf{P}(O_b), \mathbf{N}(O_b))$;

      $\mathbf{T}(O'_b) = Del$;

      $\mathbf{P}(O'_b) = \mathbf{P}(O_b)$;

      $\mathbf{N}(O'_b) = \mathbf{N}(O_b) - \mathbf{N}(O_a)$;

$\mathbf{S}(O'_b) = head + tail;$

return $(I, O'_b);$

}

//$\mathbf{S}(O_b)$ is a substring of $\mathbf{S}(O_a)$

else if $\mathbf{P}(O_b) \geq \mathbf{P}(O_a)$ **and** $\mathbf{P}(O_b)+\mathbf{N}(O_b) \leq \mathbf{P}(O_a)+\mathbf{N}(O_a)$

{ $head = \mathbf{substr}(\mathbf{S}(O_a), 0, \mathbf{P}(O_b)\text{-}\mathbf{P}(O_a));$

$tail = \mathbf{substr}(\mathbf{S}(O_a), \mathbf{P}(O_b)+\mathbf{N}(O_b)\text{-}\mathbf{P}(O_a), \mathbf{N}(O_a));$

$\mathbf{T}(O'_a) = Ins;$

$\mathbf{P}(O'_a) = \mathbf{P}(O_a);$

$\mathbf{N}(O'_a) = \mathbf{N}(O_a) - \mathbf{N}(O_b);$

$\mathbf{S}(O'_a) = head + tail;$

return $(O'_a, I);$

}

//One case that $\mathbf{S}(O_a)$ and $\mathbf{S}(O_b)$ partially overlap

else if $\mathbf{P}(O_b) > \mathbf{P}(O_a)$ **and** $\mathbf{P}(O_b)+\mathbf{N}(O_b) > \mathbf{P}(O_a)+\mathbf{N}(O_a)$

{ $\mathbf{T}(O'_a) = Ins;$

$\mathbf{P}(O'_a) = \mathbf{P}(O_a);$

$\mathbf{N}(O'_a) = \mathbf{P}(O_b) - \mathbf{P}(O_a);$

$\mathbf{S}(O'_a) = \mathbf{substr}(\mathbf{S}(O_a), 0, \mathbf{P}(O_b)\text{-}\mathbf{P}(O_a));$

$\mathbf{T}(O'_b) = Del;$

$\mathbf{P}(O'_b) = \mathbf{P}(O_b);$

$\mathbf{N}(O'_b) = \mathbf{P}(O_b) + \mathbf{N}(O_b) - \mathbf{P}(O_a) - \mathbf{N}(O_a);$

$\mathbf{S}(O'_b) = \mathbf{substr}(\mathbf{S}(O_b), \mathbf{P}(O_a)+\mathbf{N}(O_a)\text{-}\mathbf{P}(O_b), \mathbf{N}(O_b));$

return $(O'_a, O'_b);$

}

//Another case that $S(O_a)$ and $S(O_b)$ partially overlap

else if $P(O_b) < P(O_a)$ **and** $P(O_b)+N(O_b) < P(O_a)+N(O_a)$

{ $T(O'_a) = Ins$;

$P(O'_a) = P(O_a)$;

$N(O'_a) = P(O_a) + N(O_a) - P(O_b) - N(O_b)$;

$S(O'_a) = \mathbf{substr}(S(O_a), P(O_b)+N(O_b)-P(O_a), N(O_a))$;

$T(O'_b) = Del$;

$P(O'_b) = P(O_b)$;

$N(O'_b) = P(O_a) - P(O_b)$;

$S(O'_b) = \mathbf{substr}(S(O_b), 0, P(O_a)-P(O_b))$;

return (O'_a, O'_b);

}

//$O_a \odot O_b$

else

return (O_a, O_b);

}

3.3.4 The compression algorithm

By applying operational merging to the neighbouring operations in log $L = [O_1, O_2, O_3, O_4, O_5]$, L can be compressed step by step as shown in Figure 3.13.

1. $O_1 \ominus O_2$, which can be merged by $\mathbf{OM\_II}(O_1, O_2) = (O_1^1, I)$ where $O_1^1 = \mathbf{Ins}[3, 3, abc]$. After that, $L = [O_1^1, O_3, O_4, O_5]$.

2. $O_1^1 \oplus O_3$, which can be merged by $\mathbf{OM\_ID}(O_1^1, O_3) = (O_1^2, O_3^1)$ where $O_1^2 = \mathbf{Ins}[3, 2, bc]$ and $O_3^1 = \mathbf{Del}[2, 1, z]$. After that, $L = [O_1^2, O_3^1, O_4, O_5]$.

3. $O_3^1 \oplus O_4$, which can be merged by $\mathbf{OM\_DD}(O_3^1, O_4) = (O_3^2, I)$ where $O_3^2 =$

Del[1, 3, yzb]. After that, $L = [O_1^2, O_3^2, O_5]$.

4. $O_1^2 \oplus O_3^2$, which can be merged by **OM_ID**$(O_1^2, O_3^2) = (O_1^3, O_3^3)$ where $O_1^3 =$ **Ins**[3, 1, c] and $O_3^3 =$ **Del**[1, 2, yz]. After that, $L = [O_1^3, O_3^3, O_5]$.

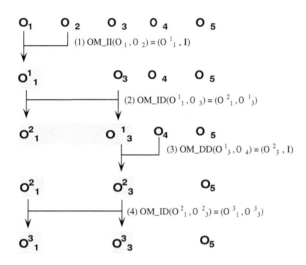

Figure 3.13: Log L is compressed by applying operational merging

Because $O_1^3 \odot O_3^3$ and $O_3^3 \odot O_5$, log L could not be further compressed by applying operational merging on neighbouring operations. The number of operations in L has been reduced from 5 to 3, achieving a 40 percent reduction. The size of a log is the total sizes of individual operations measured in bytes. For an operation $O =$ **Ins/Del**[P, N, S], one byte is used to describe O's type parameter **T**$(O) = Ins/Del$, four bytes are used to describe O's position parameter **P**$(O) = P$, four bytes are used to describe O's length parameter **N**$(O) = N$, and each character is allocated with one byte for O's text parameter **S**$(O) = S$. For $O_5 =$ **Ins**[2, 3, 123], its size is $1 + 4 + 4 + 3 = 12$ bytes. So for $L = [O_1, O_2, O_3, O_4, O_5]$, its size is $10 + 11 + 11 + 11 + 12$

$= 65$ bytes. After L has been compressed to $[O_1^3, O_3^3, O_5]$, its size is $10 + 11 + 12 = 33$, achieving a 49 percent reduction. The question is whether there is any room for L to be further compressed by applying operational merging. In other words, for all operations in the compressed L, are there any that are still overlapping or adjacent? The following definition helps clarify this issue:

Definition 3.4. Maximal compression

Given a log L, L_Γ denotes its *maximally compressed* form, where given any two operations O_i and O_j, it must be $O_i \odot O_j$.

For the example shown in Figure 3.13, $L = [O_1, \cdots, O_5]$ and its compressed form $L_c = [O_1^3, O_3^3, O_5]$. According to Definition 3.4, given $O_1^3 \odot O_3^3$ and $O_3^3 \odot O_5$, it is up to the relation between O_1^3 and O_5 to determine whether L_c is a L_Γ. The final state of the document contains characters x, c, 1, 2, and 3 and the string *123* inserted by operation O_5 is right adjacent to the character c inserted by operation O_1^3. Therefore we have $O_1^3 \ominus O_5$. But these two operations could not be merged by applying **OM_II**(O_1^3, O_5). The root of the problem is that $OM(O_a, O_b)$ requires the precondition of $O_a \mapsto O_b$ in order to determine whether O_a and O_b are overlapping or adjacent. But this condition is violated in **OM_II**(O_1^3, O_5). In $L_c = [O_1^3, O_3^3, O_5]$, it does not hold $O_1^3 \mapsto O_5$ because $O_1^3 \mapsto O_3^3 \mapsto O_5$. Consequently, **OM_II**(O_1^3, O_5) cannot detect $O_1^3 \ominus O_5$ by directly comparing their parameters: $(\mathbf{P}(O_5)=2) \neq (\mathbf{P}(O_1^3)=3)$ and $(\mathbf{P}(O_5)=2) \neq (\mathbf{P}(O_1^3)+\mathbf{N}(O_1^3)=3+1=4)$.

On the one hand, for any operation L[i] in log L $(1 \leq i \leq |L|)$, L[i] can be overlapping or adjacent not only with its left neighbour L[i-1] or right neighbour L[i+1], but also with any operation L[j] $(j \neq i)$. On the other hand, the operational merging function **OM**(L[i], L[j]) or **OM**(L[j], L[i]) requires L[i] $\mapsto$ L[j] or L[j] $\mapsto$ L[i] to detect whether L[i] and L[j] are overlapping or adjacent. This precondition is met if $j = i\text{-}1$ or $j = i+1$, but how to meet this precondition if $j \neq i\text{-}1$ and $j \neq i+1$? We propose a solution to solve this problem by changing the contextual preceding relations between operations in a log with the operational transformation technique [136]. In exclusion transformation function $O'_a = \mathbf{ET}(O_a, O_b)$, the precondition is $O_b \mapsto O_a$ and the postcondition is $O'_a \sqcup O_b$. In inclusion transformation function $O'_a = \mathbf{IT}(O_a, O_b)$, the precondition is $O_a \sqcup O_b$ and the postcondition is $O_b \mapsto O'_a$. Therefore the $\mathbf{Transpose}(O_a, O_b) = (O'_b, O'_a)$ function in Chapter 2 can be used to swap the context preceding relation between O_a and O_b. The precondition of the function is $O_a \mapsto O_b$ and the postcondition is $O'_b \mapsto O'_a$. Furthermore, the $\mathbf{LTranspose}(L)$ procedure can be used to transpose the last operation in log L to the beginning and make the last operation contextually preceding the first operation in L.

For $L_c = [O_1^3, O_3^3, O_5]$, after applying $\mathbf{LTranspose}(L_c[1, 2])$, we get $L_c = [O_3^{3'}, O_1^{3'}, O_5]$ where $O_3^{3'} = \mathbf{ET\_DI}(O_3^3, O_1^3) = \mathbf{Del}[1, 2, yz]$ and $O_1^{3'} = \mathbf{IT\_ID}(O_1^3, O_3^{3'}) = \mathbf{Ins}[1, 1, c]$, and $O_3^{3'} \mapsto O_1^{3'} \mapsto O_5$. Since $(\mathbf{P}(O_5)=2) = (\mathbf{P}(O_1^{3'})+\mathbf{N}(O_1^{3'})=1+1=2)$, according to Definition 3.2, $O_1^{3'} \ominus O_5$ and they can be merged by applying $\mathbf{OM\_II}(O_1^{3'}, O_5) = (O_1^{4'}, I)$ where $O_1^{4'} = \mathbf{Ins}[1, 4, c123]$. After that, $L_c = [O_3^{3'}, O_1^{4'}]$ is a L_Γ because $O_3^{3'} \odot O_1^{4'}$. The number of operations in L_c is 2, achieving a 60 percent reduction. The size of L_c is $11 + 17 = 28$ bytes, achieving a 57 percent reduction.

The proposed log compression algorithm, named as *COMET* (Compression by Operational MErging and Operational Transformation), scans log L from right to left, and repeatedly merges and transposes every operation in L with its left neighbour by means of operational merging and operational transformation until it has reached the beginning of L or has been eliminated (i.e., become an identify operation I). If an operation reached the beginning of L, it must be disjointed with all other operations in L, and this operation is then removed from L and appended to the compressed log L_c. Figure 3.14 depicts how the *COMET* compression algorithm works to compress a log L with three operations O_1, O_2, and O_3. In step (1), $O_2 \mapsto O_3$, so they are merged by $\mathbf{OM}(O_2, O_3)$. If O_3 has not been eliminated this step, it is then transposed to the left of O_2 by $\mathbf{LTranspose}(L[2, 3])$. In step (2), $O_1 \mapsto O_3^1$, so they are merged by $\mathbf{OM}(O_1,\ O_3^1)$. If O_3^1 has not been eliminated in this step, it is then transposed to the left of O_1 by $\mathbf{LTranspose}(L[1,\ 2])$. Now O_3^2 has reached the beginning of L, therefore it is removed from L and appended to L_c. In step (3), $O_1^1 \mapsto O_2^1$, so they are merged by $\mathbf{OM}(O_1^1,\ O_2^1)$. If O_2^1 has not been eliminated in this step, it is then transposed to the left of O_1 by $\mathbf{LTranspose}(L[1,\ 2])$. After reaching the beginning of L, O_2^2 is removed from L and appended to L_c. Finally, in step (4), since O_1^2 is the last operation in L, it is removed from L and appended to L_c. After that, L is empty and $L_c = [O_3^2,\ O_2^2,\ O_1^2]$.

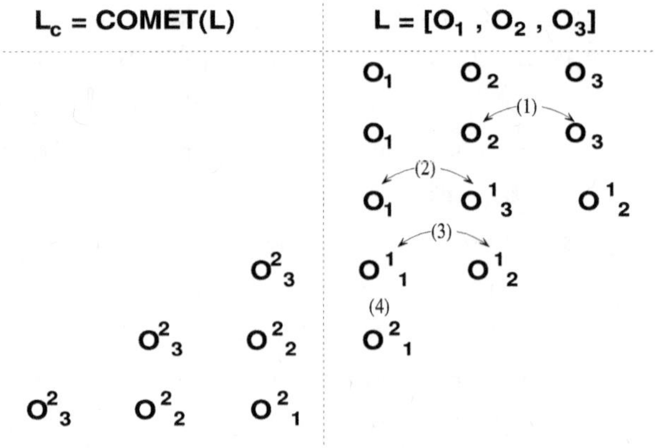

Figure 3.14: The depiction of COMET compression algorithm: $L_c = \text{COMET(L)}$

The *COMET* compression algorithm is defined as follows.

Algorithm 3.1. *COMET(L): L_c*

```
{   Lc = COMEType(L, Any);
    return Lc;

}
```

Function **COMEType**(L, T) is defined to merge operations with type T with all other operations in log L. In particular, if $\mathbf{T} = \mathbf{Ins}$, the function will merge all insertion operations with the rest of operations in L. If $\mathbf{T} = \mathbf{Del}$, the function will merge all deletion operations with the rest of operations in L. If $\mathbf{T} = \mathbf{Any}$, the function will merge all operations with the rest of operations in L.

Function 3.5. *COMEType(L, T): L_c*

{ **while** ($i = \mathbf{lastIndex}(L, T)) > 0$)

  { **if** ($i == 1$) //Only the first operation in L is with type T

    { **Append**(L_c, L[i]);

    Remove(L, i);

    break; //out of the while loop

    } **else**

    { **for** ($j = i$ - 1; $j > 0$; $j - -$)

      { (L'_j, L'_i) = **OM**(L[j], L[i]);

      if ($L'_j == L'_i == I$) //L[j] and L[i] completely counteract against each other

      { **Remove**(L, i);

      Remove(L, j);

      break; //out of the for loop

      } **else if** ($L'_j == I$)//L[j] is completely masked by L[i]

      { L[i] = L'_i;

      Remove(L, j);

      $i = i$ - 1;

      } **else if** ($L'_i == I$)//L[i] is eliminated in merging with L[j]

      { L[j] = L'_j;

      Remove(L, i);

      break; //out of the for loop

      } **else**//L[j] and L[j] are partially overlapping

```
    { L[j] = L'_j;
      L[i] = L'_i;
      LTranspose(L[j, i]);
      i = i - 1;
    }
  }
  if (i == 1)//L[i] has reached the beginning of L
  { Append(L_c, L[i]);
    Remove(L, i);
  }
 }
}
}
```

Function **lastIndex**(L, T) is defined to return the index of the last operation with type T in L. If the function returns 0, then there is no operation with type T in L.

Function 3.6. *lastIndex(L, T):* $0 \leq i \leq |L|$

```
{  for (i = |L|; i > 0; i − −)
       if (T(L[i]) == T)
           break;
    return i;
}
```

For the example in Figure 3.12, log $L = [O_1, O_2, O_3, O_4, O_5]$ can be compressed to L_c by **COMET**(L) as follows:

1. The last operation in L is O_5. Because $O_4 \mapsto O_5$ and $O_4 \odot O_5$, **OM**(O_4, O_5) will return them as-is. When they are swapped by **LTranspose**(L[4, 5]), $L = [O_1, O_2, O_3, O_5^1, O_4^1]$ where $O_5^1 = $ **ET_ID**$(O_5, O_4) = $ **Ins**[4, 3, 123] and $O_4^1 = $ **IT_DI**$(O_4, O_5^1) = $ **Del**[1, 2, yb].

2. Because $O_3 \mapsto O_5^1$ and $O_3 \odot O_5^1$, $\mathbf{OM}(O_3, O_5^1)$ will return them as-is. When they are swapped by $\mathbf{LTranspose}(L[3, 4])$, $L = [O_1, O_2, O_5^2, O_3^1, O_4^1]$ where $O_5^2 = \mathbf{ET\_ID}(O_5^1, O_3) = \mathbf{Ins}[6, 3, 123]$ and $O_3^1 = \mathbf{IT\_DI}(O_3, O_5^2) = \mathbf{Del}[2, 2, za]$.

3. Because $O_2 \mapsto O_5^2$ and $O_2 \odot O_5^2$, $\mathbf{OM}(O_2, O_5^2)$ will return them as-is. When they are swapped by $\mathbf{LTranspose}(L[2, 3])$, $L = [O_1, O_5^3, O_2^1, O_3^1, O_4^1]$ where $O_5^3 = \mathbf{ET\_II}(O_5^2, O_2) = \mathbf{Ins}[4, 3, 123]$ and $O_2^1 = \mathbf{IT\_II}(O_2, O_5^3) = \mathbf{Ins}[3, 2, ab]$.

4. Because $O_1 \mapsto O_5^3$ and $O_1 \ominus O_5^3$, O_5^3 will be merged into O_1 by $\mathbf{OM}(O_1, O_5^3) = \mathbf{OM\_II}(O_1, O_5^3) = (O_1^1, I)$ where $O_1^1 = \mathbf{Ins}[3, 4, c123]$. After that, O_5^3 is removed from L and L becomes $[O_1^1, O_2^1, O_3^1, O_4^1]$.

5. The last operation in L is O_4^1. Because $O_3^1 \mapsto O_4^1$ and $O_3^1 \oplus O_4^1$, O_4^1 will be merged into O_3^1 by $\mathbf{OM}(O_3^1, O_4^1) = \mathbf{OM\_DD}(O_3^1, O_4^1) = (O_3^2, I)$ where $O_3^2 = \mathbf{Del}[1, 4, yzab]$. After that, O_4^1 is removed from L and L becomes $[O_1^1, O_2^1, O_3^2]$.

6. The last operation in L is O_3^2. Because $O_2^1 \mapsto O_3^2$ and $O_2^1 \oplus O_3^2$, O_2^1 will be merged into O_3^2 by $\mathbf{OM}(O_2^1, O_3^2) = \mathbf{OM\_ID}(O_2^1, O_3^2) = (I, O_3^3)$ where $O_3^3 = \mathbf{Del}[1, 2, yz]$. After that, O_2^1 is removed from L and L becomes $[O_1^1, O_3^3]$.

7. The last operation in L is O_3^3. Because $O_1^1 \mapsto O_3^3$ and $O_1^1 \odot O_3^3$, $\mathbf{OM}(O_1^1, O_3^3)$ will return them as-is. When they are swapped by $LTranspose(L[1, 2]) = (O_3^4, O_1^2)$ where $O_3^4 = \mathbf{ET\_DI}(O_3^3, O_1^1) = \mathbf{Del}[1, 2, yz]$ and $O_1^2 = \mathbf{IT\_ID}(O_1^1, O_3^4) = \mathbf{Ins}[1, 4, c123]$, O_3^4 reaches the beginning of L and is removed from L and appended to L_c. After that, $L = [O_1^2]$ and $L_c = [O_3^4]$.

8. O_1^2 is the last and the only operation in L, so it is removed from L and appended to L_c. After that, L is empty and $L_c = [O_3^4, O_1^2]$. Apparently $L_c = \mathbf{COMET}(L) = L_\Gamma$ because $O_3^4 \odot O_1^2$.

The question is whether the *COMET* compression algorithm always achieves maximal compression. In other words, given any log L, if $L_c = \mathbf{COMET}(L)$, does it always hold that L_c is a L_Γ? Look at the example in Figure 3.15, where a document initially contained one character y and was then developed to the state containing two characters x and z by three operations. Those three operations have been saved in log $L = [O_1, O_2, O_3]$, where $O_1 = \textbf{Ins}[1, 1, z]$ was to insert one character z at position 1 (i.e., after character y), $O_2 = \textbf{Del}[0, 1, y]$ was to delete one character at position 0 (i.e., character y), and $O_3 = \textbf{Ins}[0, 1, x]$ was to insert one character x at position 0.

Figure 3.15: A log for illustrating interrelations between operations

Log L can be compressed to L_c by $\textbf{COMET}(L)$ as follows.

1. The last operation in L is O_3. Because $O_2 \mapsto O_3$ and $O_2 \odot O_3$, $\textbf{OM}(O_2, O_3)$ will return them as-is. When they are swapped by $\textbf{LTranspose}(L[2, 3]) = (O_3^1, O_2^1)$ where $O_3^1 = \textbf{ET\_ID}(O_3, O_2) = \textbf{Ins}[0, 1, x]$ and $O_2^1 = \textbf{IT\_DI}(O_2, O_3^1) = \textbf{Del}[1, 1, y]$, $L = [O_1, O_3^1, O_2^1]$.

2. Because $O_1 \mapsto O_3^1$ and $O_1 \odot O_3^1$, $\textbf{OM}(O_1, O_3^1)$ will return them as-is. When they are swapped by $\textbf{LTranspose}(L[1, 2]) = (O_3^2, O_1^1)$ where $O_3^2 = \textbf{ET\_II}(O_1, O_3^1) = \textbf{Ins}[0, 1, x]$ and $O_1^1 = \textbf{IT\_II}(O_1, O_3^2) = \textbf{Ins}[2, 1, z]$, O_3^2 reaches the beginning of L. So, O_3^2 is removed from L and appended to L_c. After that, $L = [O_1^1, O_2^1]$ and $L_c = [O_3^2]$.

3. The last operation in L is O_2^1. Because $O_1^1 \mapsto O_2^1$ and $O_1^1 \odot O_2^1$, $\textbf{OM}(O_1^1, O_2^1)$ will return them as-is. When they are swapped by $\textbf{LTranspose}(L[1, 2]) = (O_2^2, O_1^2)$ where $O_2^2 = \textbf{ET\_DI}(O_2^1, O_1^1) = \textbf{Del}[1, 1, y]$ and $O_1^2 = \textbf{IT\_ID}(O_1^1, O_2^2) = \textbf{Ins}[1, 1, z]$, O_2^2 reaches the beginning of L. So, O_2^2 is removed from L and appended to L_c. After that, $L = [O_1^2]$ and $L_c = [O_3^2, O_2^2]$.

4. O_1^2 is the last and the only operation in L. So, it is removed from L and appended to L_c. After that, L is empty and $L_c = [O_3^2, O_2^2, O_1^2]$.

In this example, L_c has the same size and number of operations as L does, which means L was not compressed by the *COMET* algorithm at all. Is this because L is already a L_Γ? The answer is no. It is obvious that $O_1 \ominus O_3$ because the character z inserted by O_1 is right adjacent the character x inserted by O_3. The reason why O_1 and O_3 were not merged is that the current *COMET* compression algorithm has missed crucial interrelations between insertion and deletion operations.

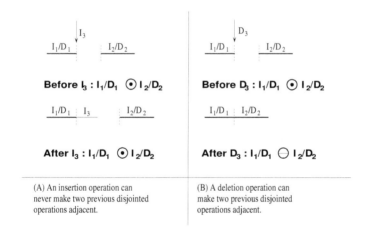

(A) An insertion operation can never make two previous disjointed operations adjacent.

(B) A deletion operation can make two previous disjointed operations adjacent.

Figure 3.16: Interrelations between operations

A later insertion operation can never create new adjacent relations among previous operations. As shown in Figure 3.16(A), operation I_2 (an insertion operation) or D_2 (a deletion operation) is disjointed with a previous operation I_1/D_1 at the time of execution. If a new insertion operation I_3 inserts a sequence of characters, for instance between the effect regions covered by I_1/D_1 and I_2/D_2, it can never make I_2/D_2 adjacent with I_1/D_1. In contrast, a later deletion operation could create new adjacent relations among previous operations. As shown in Figure 3.16(B), operation I_2/D_2 is disjointed with a previous operation I_1/D_1 at the time of execution. If a new deletion operation D_3 is performed to delete all characters between the effect regions covered by I_1/D_1 and I_2/D_2, I_2/D_2 becomes adjacent with I_1/D_1. Nevertheless, without the execution of D_3, I_1/D_1 and I_2/D_2 would still be disjointed and could not be merged.

Therefore, for the example shown in Figure 3.15, in step (2) of **COMET**(L), $L = [O_1, O_3^1, O_2^1]$ where O_1 and O_3^1 are insertion operations and O_2^1 is a deletion operation. Without taking into account the effect of the later deletion operation O_2^1, it would be $O_1 \odot O_3^1$ because O_1 was to insert character z after character y while O_3^1 was to insert character x before character y. In other words, if character y were not deleted by the later operation O_2^1, it would be impossible for character z inserted by O_1 to be adjacent with character x inserted by O_3^1. Therefore, the solution to this problem is to transpose all deletion operations to the left side of all insertion operations. This solution can effectively detect new overlapping relations created by deletion operations. For instance, in step (2) of **COMET**(L) where $L = [O_1, O_3^1, O_2^1]$, if the deletion operation O_2^1 were transposed to the beginning of L by **LTranspose**$(L[1, 3])$, L would become $[O_2^2, O_1^1, O_3^2]$ where $O_2^2 = $ **Del**$[0, 1, y]$, $O_1^1 = $ **Ins**$[0, 1, z]$, and $O_3^2 = $ **Ins**$[0, 1, x]$. After that, it can be detected that $O_1^1 \ominus O_3^2$ and those two operations can be merged by **OM**$(O_1^1, O_3^2) = $ **OM_II**$(O_1^1, O_3^2) = (O_1^2, I)$ where $O_1^2 = $ **Ins**$[0, 2, xz]$.

Therefore, the *COMET* compression algorithm is modified to first merge all deletion operations with other operations and then merge insertion operations with the rest of the operations. In this way, insertion operations must have already taken into account the effects of all deletion operations. Therefore, the algorithm can merge insertion operations whose adjacent relations are created by later deletion operations. As a result, a compressed log $L_c = \textbf{COMET}(L)$ must look like: $[D_1, \cdots, D_r, I_1, \cdots, I_s]$ where D_i $(1 \le i \le r)$ is a deletion operation and I_j $(1 \le j \le s)$ is an insertion operation. The modified *COMET* algorithm is as follows:

Algorithm 3.2. *COMET(L): L_c*

{ $L_c = \textbf{COMEType}(L, \textit{Del})$;

   $L_c += \textbf{COMEType}(L, \textit{Ins})$;

   return L_c;

}

   To compress the log L in Figure 3.15, $L_c = \textbf{COMET}(L)$ will be executed as follows.

1. The last deletion operation in L is O_2. Because $O_1 \mapsto O_2$ and $O_1 \odot O_2$, $\textbf{OM}(O_1, O_2)$ will return them as-is. When they are swapped by $\textbf{LTranspose}(L[1, 2]) = (O_2^1, O_1^1)$ where $O_2^1 = \textbf{ET\_DI}(O_2, O_1) = \textbf{Del}[0, 1, y]$ and $O_1^1 = \textbf{IT\_ID}(O_1, O_2^1) = \textbf{Ins}[0, 1, z]$, O_2^1 reaches the beginning of L. So O_2^1 is removed from L and appended to L_c. After that, L becomes $[O_1^1, O_3]$ and $L_c = [O_2^1]$.

2. The last insertion operation in L is O_3. Because $O_1^1 \mapsto O_3$ and $O_1^1 \ominus O_3$, O_3 will be merged into O_1^1 by $\textbf{OM}(O_1^1, O_3) = \textbf{OM\_II}(O_1^1, O_3) = (O_1^2, I)$ where $O_1^2 = \textbf{Ins}[0, 2, xz]$. After that, $L = [O_1^2]$.

3. The last and the only insertion operation in L is O_1^2. So, O_1^2 is removed from L and appended to L_c. After that, L is empty and $L_c = [O_2^1, O_1^2]$. $L_c = \textbf{COMET}(L) = [O_2^1, O_1^2]$ must be a L_Γ because $O_2^1 \odot O_1^2$.

   The modified *COMET* algorithm is able to achieve maximal compression, which is formally established in the following theorem:

Theorem 3.1. *Given a log L, if $L_c = \textbf{COMET}(L)$, then L_c must be a L_Γ.*

Proof: refer to Appendix B - *Formal proofs of theorems and properties* for the formal proof of the theorem.

Theorem 3.1 describes the completeness property of the $COMET$ compression algorithm in the sense that it is able to achieve maximal compression. This property is important to keep the scale of a log small so that an operation-based merging process can outperform the corresponding state-based merging process. An experiment has been carried out to support this point. Given a log $L = [O_1, \cdots, O_n]$ storing a list of user-issued operations for transforming a document from its initial state to the final state, $L_c = \mathbf{COMET}(L) = [EO_1, \cdots, EO_m]$ ($m \leq n$) is a L_Γ, where EO_i ($1 \leq i \leq m$) is referred to as an *effective operation*. A list of effective operations is the minimal list of essential operations in transforming the document from its initial state to the final state while preserving the intentions of user-issued editing operations.

3.3.5 Discussions on the COMET compression algorithm

A list of effective operations is equivalent in effect to a list of editing scripts derived by text differentiation algorithms. A list of effective operations is one alternative list of editing scripts used to transform a document from its initial state to its final state, while a list of editing scripts derived by text differentiation algorithms is the shortest list of editing scripts used to transform the document from the same initial state to the same final state. The difference between the two lists is that the former list preserves the intentions of user-issued actions while the latter list attempts to reconstruct actions after the fact and has little chance to preserve the intentions of user-issued actions. For the sake of comparison, both effective operations and editing scripts are represented as character-based.

For the example in 3.12, the document initially contained a string *xyz* and was transformed to another string *xc123* by a list of user-issued editing operations stored in log $L = [O_1, O_2, O_3, O_4, O_5]$. When L is compressed, $L_c = \mathbf{COMET}(L) = [O_3^4,$

O_1^2] where $O_3^4 = \textbf{Del}[1, 2, \text{yz}]$ and $O_1^2 = \textbf{Ins}[1, 4, \text{c123}]$ are effective operations. If effective operations are represented as character-based, then $L_c = [EO_1, EO_2, EO_3, EO_4, EO_5, EO_6]$ where $EO_1 = \textbf{Del}[1, 1, \text{y}]$, $EO_2 = \textbf{Del}[1, 1, \text{z}]$, $EO_3 = \textbf{Ins}[1, 1, \text{c}]$, $EO_4 = \textbf{Ins}[2, 1, 1]$, $EO_5 = \textbf{Ins}[3, 1, 2]$, and $EO_6 = \textbf{Ins}[4, 1, 3]$. The editing graph for transforming string xyz to string $xc123$ is shown in Figure 3.17.

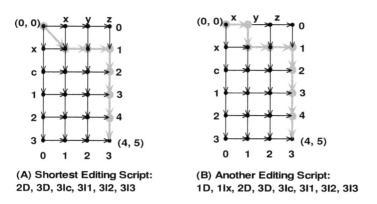

(A) Shortest Editing Script:
2D, 3D, 3Ic, 3I1, 3I2, 3I3

(B) Another Editing Script:
1D, 1Ix, 2D, 3D, 3Ic, 3I1, 3I2, 3I3

Figure 3.17: Editing graph transforming string xyz to string xc123

According to the text differentiation algorithm presented in [93], the shortest editing script for transforming string xyz to string $xc123$ contains five editing operations shown in Figure 3.17(A): **2D**(delete character y), **3D**(delete character z), **3Ic**(insert character c), **3I1**(insert character 1), **3I2**(insert character 2), and **3I3**(insert character 3). In this example, the list of shortest editing scripts derived by the text differentiation algorithm accidentally coincides with the list of effective operations $[EO_1, EO_2, EO_3, EO_4, EO_5, EO_6]$. As pointed out, the list of effective operations and the list of shortest editing scripts are two of many alternative paths in transforming a document from its initial state to the final state. These two paths may not necessarily be the same because the user may not necessarily choose the shortest path to transform a document from its initial state to the final final state. For example, in Figure 3.17(B), the user may choose another path that is different from the shortest path in Figure 3.17(A) to transform string *xyz* to string *xc123*. That path consists of the following list of effective operations: **1D**(delete character x), **1Ix**(insert character x), **2D**(delete character y), **3D**(delete character z), **3Ic**(insert character c), **3I1**(insert character 1), **3I2**(insert character 2), and **3I3**(insert character 3).

Nevertheless, the scale of a list of effective operations is comparable to that of the shortest list of editing scripts derived by text differentiation algorithms with both the size of the list and the number of operations within the list a complexity of $\mathbf{O}(m+n)$ where m is the size of the source string and n is the size of the destination string. For the example in Figure 3.17, the upper bound of the number of operations is $3 + 5 = 8$ and the upper bound of the size is $3 + 5 = 8$ bytes if deletion/insertion of a character is represented by one byte. As stressed in Section 3.2, reducing the scale of logs to the same order of the scale of editing scripts derived by text differentiation algorithm is important for an operation-based merging process to outperform the corresponding state-based merging process.

It should be highlighted that the execution of the log compression algorithm does not necessarily contribute to the times of an operation-based merging process because the compression algorithm can be executed progressively during editing. For instance, it can be executed in the background periodically or with some predefined thresholds during editing. On the contrary, the execution of text differentiation algorithms directly contributes to the times of a state-based merging process because they have to be executed at the time of merging in order to derive correct deltas for state-based textual merging algorithms to use.

Generally speaking, the *COMET* compression algorithm is able to compress a log more significantly if operations in the log are more localized because in this case

operations are more likely to be overlapping or adjacent. In reality, if a user writes
a chapter for a book, or a component for a software system, it is very likely that
editing operations performed by the user are localized. In this case, compression is
essential because massive editing operations may be generated and the scale of the
log storing these operations can become very large. Furthermore many operations in
the log can be redundant in the sense that they do not contribute to the final state
of the document at all. Many others can be partially redundant in the sense that
their effects are only partially reflected in the final state of the document. This is
because constructing a document from scratch requires a lot of try-and-failures and
alternative explorations. As a result, the log can be compressed by the *COMET*
algorithm very significantly in this case. By contrast, if a user revises a chapter in
a book or a component in a software system, it is less likely that editing operations
performed by the user are localized. In this case, compression is less essential because
relatively small number of editing operations will be generated during the revision
process. These small number of operations are scattered across the document and
most of them have contributed their effects or partial effects to the final document.
As a result, the log will be compressed by the *COMET* algorithm less significantly in
this case.

3.4   An operation-based textual merging algorithm

As mentioned before, operation-based merging was originally proposed for object
merging in object-oriented databases [84], object-based graphical applications [9],
or calender applications. Operation-based merging algorithms devised for those applications usually take two sequences of operations and combines them into a single sequence by means of re-ordering and the rules of re-ordering are very much
application-dependent.

3.4.1 Related work

In the *GINA* system [9], if two authors of a document begin with the same version and create different versions by executing different editing commands, the command history that are associated objects forms a two-branched tree, with each author's actions form one branch of the tree. The merging of the two authors' changes is performed by taking one of the branches and applying it at the end of the other branch in the way of redoing one author's changes on the other author's version of objects. Because editing commands are associated with objects, if an editing command targeted at an object conflicts with another editing command targeted at the same object, the authors will be notified and will have to choose which changes to keep. They may choose to undo the affected editing command from the first branch and redo the one from the second branch, or simply not redo the one from the second branch. This approach is suitable for merging documents with independent objects such as graphic objects, object-oriented database objects, relational database entries, and spreadsheet cells. If two editing commands are targeting at the same object but with conflicting changes, only one change will be kept. Sun and Chen [23, 135] proposed the multiversioning technique for documents with independent objects, which internally keeps both conflicting changes as two separate versions and externally presents different views to different users.

The *IceCube* approach [75] is a general-purpose log-based reconciliation approach parameterized by object and application semantics. The merging of two authors' changes is performed by first combining two logs of operations into a single merged log in which operations are re-ordered in such a way that conflicts are minimized by observing object and application semantics and user intentions, and then replaying operations in the merged log against the initial state to yield a reconciled common final state. *Bayou* [45, 100] adopts a similar approach but uses predefined orders like the temporal order to merge two logs while the ordering of the reconciled log in

129

IceCube is computed flexibly by allowing the application programmer to express constraints and dependencies between operations, and by exploring orderings that satisfy these constraints and dependencies. This approach is particularly suitable for applications that are mostly concerned with the essential order in which actions should be performed, such as calender applications, transaction-based scheduling systems [101], and file synchronization systems [45, 100].

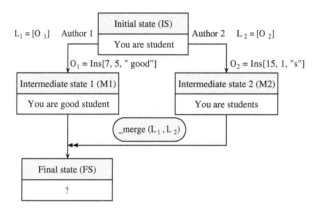

Figure 3.18: Operation-based merging algorithm

However, operation-based merging algorithms based on re-ordering are not suitable for supporting textual merging for non-real-time collaborative editing or version control. As shown in Figure 3.18, the initial state of a document (**IS**) contains a line: *You are student.* User *Author 1* developed the document to the intermediate state 1 (**M1**) with editing operation O_1 that has been stored in the log L_1, while user *Author 2* developed the document to the intermediate state 2 (**M2**) with editing operation O_2 that has been stored in the log L_2. $O_1 = \mathbf{Ins}[7, 5, \text{``}good\text{''}]$ was to insert a whitespace and word *good* at position 7, which transformed the document to the state containing a line: *You are good student.* $O_2 = \mathbf{Ins}[15, 1, \text{``}s\text{''}]$ was to insert a character s at position 15, which transformed the document to the state containing a line: *You are students.*

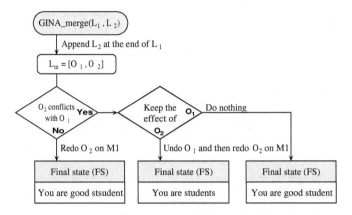

Figure 3.19: Operation-based merging algorithm based on the GINA approach

As shown in Figure 3.19, operation-based merging based on the *GINA* approach would execute **GINA_merge** (L_1, L_2) merging algorithm to merge the change made by *Author 2* into *Author 1*'s version of the document as follows: first combines the two sequences L_1 and L_2 into a single sequence L_m by appending L_2 at the end of L_1, and then checks whether O_2 conflicts with O_1. If they do not conflict, O_2 is redone on *Author 1*'s version of the document (viz., **M1**), and the final state would contain a line: *You are good stsudent*, which does not correctly incorporate the change made by *Author 2*. If they conflict in terms of targeting at the same line object, the authors will be provided with two choices of keeping the change made either by *Author 1* or by *Author 2* and the algorithm is unable to keep both changes.

By comparison, operation-based merging based on the *IceCube* approach would attempt to find a rational ordering between O_1 and O_2 to be presented in the merged log L_m, and applies operations in L_m on the initial document state to yield a reconciled final document state. As shown in Figure 3.20, if O_1 is ordered before O_2 in the reconciled log L_m^1, replaying O_1 and then O_2 sequentially on **IS** would yield a final state containing a line: *You are good stsudent*, which does not correctly incorporate the change made by *Author 2*. If O_2 is ordered before O_1 in the reconciled log L_m^2, replaying O_2 and then O_1 sequentially on **IS** would yield a final state containing a line: *You are good students*, which have correctly incorporated both changes made by *Author 1* and *Author 2*. However, there is no guarantee that such a rational ordering in which the final state can correctly incorporate all changes is always possible to be found, particularly when changes made by different authors are overlapping. Moreover, exploring all possible orderings suffers from a combinational explosion when the number of changes are enormous.

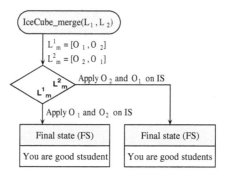

Figure 3.20: Operation-based merging algorithm based on the IceCube approach

3.4.2 An operation-based textual merging algorithm

If two authors of a document begin with the same version and create different versions by executing different editing operations, to correctly merge changes made by one author into the other's version of the document, operations generated by one author should be redone on the other author's version in such a way that the intentions of those operations are correctly preserved. In the above example, to redo the change made by *Author 2* on *Author 1*'s version of the document (viz., **M1**), character *s* should be inserted at the end of the word *student* not in the word. In fact, this issue is the same in nature to the intention violation problem in real-time collaborative editing [137].

Therefore, operational transformation technique can be used to support operation-based textual merging. In Figure 3.18, to redo operation O_2 on **M1**, O_2 should be inclusively transformed against O_1 before execution. That is, O_2's execution form EO_2 should be derived by $\textbf{IT\_II}(O_2, O_1) = \textbf{Ins}[20, 1, \text{``}s\text{''}]$. Execution of EO_2 on **M1** would yield a final state containing a line: *You are good students*, which has correctly incorporated the change made by *Author 2*. The operation-based textual merging algorithm $\textbf{OT\_merge}(L_1, L_2)$ is defined to first transform the list of operations in L_2 with the list of operations in L_1, and then execute transformed operations in L_2 sequentially on **M1**. It is described as follows:

Algorithm 3.3. *OT_merge(L_1, L_2)*

{ $(L_1', L_2') = \textbf{SLOT}(L_1, L_2)$;

  for $(i = 1; i \leq \textbf{sizeof}(L_2'); i{+}{+})$

      execute(L_2'[i]);

}

The $\textbf{SLOT}(L_1, L_2)$ (Symmetric Linear Operation Transformation) transformation control algorithm is defined to symmetrically transform two sequences of operations L_1 and L_2. The algorithm has a linear time complexity and is described as follows:

Function 3.7. *SLOT(L_1, L_2): (L_1', L_2')*

{ **for** $(i = 1; i \leq \textbf{sizeof}(L_2); i{+}{+})$

    for $(j = 1; j \leq \textbf{sizeof}(L_1); j{+}{+})$

      $(L_2'[i], L_1'[j]) = \textbf{SIT}(L_2[i], L_1[j])$;

return (L'_1, L'_2);

}

The **SIT**(O_a, O_b) (Symmetric Inclusive Transformation) function is defined to inclusively transform two operations O_a and O_b against each other. It is described as follows:

Function 3.8. $SIT(O_a, O_b)$: (O'_a, O'_b)

{ $O'_a = $ **IT**(O_a, O_b);

$O'_b = $ **IT**(O_b, O_a);

return (O'_a, O'_b);

}

Given a log L storing user-issued editing operations, operations in L must have been sorted in their causal order from left to right. That is, given any two operations L[i] and L[i+1] $(1 \leq i \leq |L|\text{-}1)$ in L, it must be L[i] $\rightarrow$ L[i+1] and L[i] $\mapsto$ L[i+1]. If L has been compressed by the *COMET* algorithm, according to the definition of the algorithm, it must still be L[i] $\mapsto$ L[i+1] although it could be either L[i] $\rightarrow$ L[i+1] or L[i+1] $\rightarrow$ L[i]. As a result, before **SLOT**(L_1, L_2), it must be L_1[j] $\mapsto$ L_1[j+1] $(1 \leq j \leq |L_1|\text{-}1)$ and L_2[i] $\mapsto$ L_2[i+1] $(1 \leq i \leq |L_2|\text{-}1)$. Furthermore, because two authors begin with the same version of a document and create different versions by executing different editing operations stored in two logs L_1 and L_2, it must be that L_1[1] $\sqcup$ L_2[1] and that operations in L_1 and L_2 are mutually concurrent in the sense that L_1[j] $\parallel$ L_2[i] $(1 \leq j \leq |L_1|\text{-}1, 1 \leq i \leq |L_2|\text{-}1)$.

After **SLOT**$(L_1, L_2) = (L'_1, L'_2)$, L'_2 stores the execution forms of operations in L_2. These operations have taken into account the effects of all operations in L_1. As a result, it must be L_1[1] $\mapsto \cdots \mapsto L_1$[$|L_1|$] $\mapsto L'_2$[1] $\mapsto \cdots \mapsto L'_2$[$|L'_2|$]. Consequently, operations in L'_2 can be executed on **M1** to merge changes made by *Author 2* into *Author 1*'s version of the document (i.e., **M1**); the merged final document state would be $FS_1 = $ **M1** $\circ L'_2$. On the other hand, L'_1 stores the execution forms of operations in L_1. These operations have taken into account the effects of all operations in L_2. As a result, it must be $L_2[1] \mapsto \cdots \mapsto L_2[|L_2|] \mapsto L_1'[1] \mapsto \cdots \mapsto L_1'[|L_1'|]$. Therefore, operations in L_1' can be executed on **M2** to merge changes made by *Author 1* into *Author 2*'s version of the document (i.e., **M2**); the merged final document state would be $FS_2 = \mathbf{M2} \circ L_1'$.

In order to maintain consistency in non-real-time collaborative editing, merging changes made by *Author 2* into *Author 1*'s version of the document should yield the same merged final version as that achieved by merging changes made by *Author 1* into *Author 2*'s version of the document. That is to say, the **SLOT**(L_1, L_2) algorithm should ensure $FS_1 = FS_2$ to maintain consistency. Because $FS_1 = \mathbf{M1} \circ L_2' = \mathbf{IS} \circ L_1 \circ L_2'$ and $FS_2 = \mathbf{M2} \circ L_1' = \mathbf{IS} \circ L_2 \circ L_1'$, it must be proven that $L_1 \circ L_2' \equiv L_2 \circ L_1'$ in order to prove $FS_1 = FS_2$. The formal proof is in the next section.

3.4.3   Discussions on the SLOT control algorithm

Compared with transformation control algorithms such as *dOPT* [46], *adOPTed* [109], *GOT* [137], and *GOTO* [136] proposed for real-time collaborative editing, *SLOT* is more efficient in the sense it is has a linear time complexity. In addition, it is also much simpler in the sense that it does not need any exclusion transformation, which is a significant merit in practice because it is difficult to define exclusion transformation functions that always meet the reversibility property (Property 1.3) due to the information loss in inclusion transformations [137].

Furthermore, the *SLOT* algorithm has avoided transformation property 2 (Property 1.2) that imposes a condition that the transformation of an operation against a pair of operations is independent of the order in which the pair of operations are transformed against each other. In practice, it is difficult to verify *TP2*; if *TP2* is violated, convergence may not be guaranteed. The reason why the *SLOT* algorithm can avoid *TP2* is that under no circumstance could an operation be transformed with the same pair of operations in different orders. Given any two logs L_1 and L_2, operations in L_1 and L_2 need to be transformed with each other by $\textbf{SLOT}(L_1, L_2)$ only once to maintain consistency. For example, in Figure 3.18, to merge changes made by *Author 2* into *Author 1*'s version of document (i.e., **M1**) and to merge changes made by *Author 1* into *Author 2*'s version of document (i.e., **M2**), $\textbf{SLOT}(L_1, L_2) = (L'_1, L'_2)$ will be executed only once. Then the two authors' versions of the document will be convergent after applying operations in L'_2 on **M1** and applying operations in L'_1 on **M2**.

The following theorem is established to prove that the $SLOT$ transformation control algorithm is able to maintain convergence:

Theorem 3.2. *Given any two logs L_1 and L_2, if $\textbf{SLOT}(L_1, L_2) = (L'_1, L'_2)$, then $L_1 \circ L'_2 \equiv L_2 \circ L'_1$.*

Proof: Suppose log L_1 contains a list of m editing operations $[D_1, \cdots, D_m]$. If log L_2 is empty, then $\textbf{SLOT}(L_1, L_2) = (L_1, [\,])$. The theorem apparently holds because $L_1 \circ [\,] \equiv [\,] \circ L_1$. Otherwise, suppose L_2 contains a list of n editing operations $[O_1, \cdots, O_n]$, then it must be $L'_1 = [D_1^n, \cdots, D_m^n]$ where D_i^n $(1 \leq i \leq m)$ is the transformed form of D_i that has inclusively transformed against all n editing operations in L_2 and $L'_2 = [O_1^m, \cdots, O_n^m]$ where O_j^m $(1 \leq j \leq n)$ is the transformed form of O_j that has inclusively transformed against all m operations in L_1.

According to the definition of the $SLOT$ transformation control algorithm, suppose $D_i^0 = D_i$ $(1 \leq i \leq m)$ and $O_j^0 = O_j$ $(1 \leq j \leq n)$, then $D_i^k = \textbf{IT}(D_i^{k-1}, O_k^{i-1})$ where $1 \leq i \leq m$, $1 \leq k \leq n$, and D_i^k is the transformed form of D_i that has inclusively transformed against the first k operations in L_2. $O_j^l = \textbf{IT}(O_j^{l-1}, D_l^{j-1})$ where $1 \leq j \leq n$, $1 \leq l \leq m$, and O_j^l is the transformed form of O_j that has inclusively transformed against the first l operations in L_1. Then we have: $L_2 \circ L'_1 \equiv [O_1, \cdots, O_n] \circ [D_1^n, \cdots, D_m^n] \equiv O_1 \circ \cdots \circ \underline{O_n \circ D_1^n} \circ \cdots \circ D_m^n \equiv \cdots \circ \underline{O_n \circ IT(D_1^{n-1}, O_n)} \circ \cdots$ (by $SLOT$) $\equiv \cdots \circ \underline{D_1^{n-1} \circ IT(O_n, D_1^{n-1})} \circ \cdots$ (by $TP1$) $\equiv \cdots \circ \underline{D_1^{n-1} \circ O_n^1} \circ \cdots$ (by $SLOT$) $\equiv O_1 \circ \cdots O_{n-1} \circ D_1^{n-1} \circ \underline{O_n^1 \circ D_2^n} \circ \cdots \circ D_m^n \equiv \cdots \circ \underline{O_n^1 \circ IT(D_2^{n-1}, O_n^1)}$

$\circ \cdots$ (by $SLOT$) $\equiv \cdots \circ D_2^{n-1} \circ IT(O_n^1, D_2^{n-1}) \circ \cdots$ (by $TP1$) $\equiv \cdots \circ D_2^{n-1} \circ O_n^2 \circ$
$\cdots$ (by $SLOT$) $\equiv \cdots \cdots \equiv O_1 \circ \cdots \circ O_{n-1} \circ D_1^{n-1} \circ D_2^{n-1} \cdots \circ D_m^{n-1} \circ O_n^m \equiv \cdots$
$\circ O_{n-1} \circ IT(D_1^{n-2}, O_{n-1}) \circ \cdots$ (by $SLOT$) $\equiv \cdots \circ D_1^{n-2} \circ IT(O_{n-1}, D_1^{n-2}) \circ \cdots$ (by
$TP1$) $\equiv \cdots \circ D_1^{n-2} \circ O_{n-1}^1 \circ \cdots$ (by $SLOT$) $\equiv O_1 \circ \cdots O_{n-2} \circ D_1^{n-2} \circ O_{n-1}^1 \circ D_2^{n-1}$
$\circ \cdots \circ D_m^{n-1} \circ O_n^m \equiv \cdots \cdots \equiv O_1 \circ \cdots \circ O_{n-2} \circ D_1^{n-2} \circ D_2^{n-2} \cdots \circ D_m^{n-2} \circ O_{n-1}^m$
$\circ O_n^m \equiv \cdots \cdots \equiv D_1^0 \circ D_2^0 \circ \cdots \circ D_m^0 \circ O_1^m \circ O_2^m \circ \cdots O_n^m \equiv D_1 \circ D_2 \circ \cdots \circ D_m$
$\circ O_1^m \circ O_2^m \circ \cdots O_n^m \equiv [D_1, \ldots, D_m] \circ [O_1^m, \cdots, O_n^m] \equiv L_1 \circ L_2'$. The theorem is
hereby proven.

In the event of log compression by the $COMET$ algorithm, we need to consider its effect on maintaining convergence by the $SLOT$ algorithm. If logs L_1 and L_2 are not compressed, we have proven $L_1 \circ L_2' \equiv L_2 \circ L_1'$ where $(L_1', L_2') = \mathbf{SLOT}(L_1, L_2)$. If L_1 was not compressed at the time of transformation but L_1' was compressed into $L_{1_c}' = \mathbf{COMET}(L_1')$ before being merged into $Author$ 2's version of document (i.e., $\mathbf{M2}$), in order to maintain convergence, it should be $L_1 \circ L_2' \equiv L_2 \circ L_{1_c}'$. Because $L_1 \circ L_2' \equiv L_2 \circ L_1'$ has been proven, we will prove $L_1 \circ L_2' \equiv L_2 \circ L_{1_c}'$ by proving $L_1' \equiv L_{1_c}'$. The following transpose property (TPP) and operational merging property (OMP) are important to prove the above theorem:

Property 3.1. *Transpose Property 1(TPP)*

Given any two operations O_a and O_b, where $O_a \mapsto O_b$, if $\mathbf{Transpose}(O_a, O_b) = (O_b', O_a')$, then $[O_a, O_b] \equiv [O_b', O_a']$.

This property has been described and proven by Sun [132].

Property 3.2. *Operational Merging Property (OMP)*

Given any two operations O_a and O_b, where $O_a \mapsto O_b$, if $\mathbf{OM}(O_a, O_b) = (O_a', O_b')$, then $[O_a, O_b] \equiv [O_a', O_b']$.

Proof: refer to Appendix B - *Formal proofs of theorems and properties* for the formal proof of the property.

Finally, according to the definition of the $COMET$ compression algorithm, and TPP and OMP properties, we have the following theorem:

Theorem 3.3. *Given a log L, if* **COMET***(L) = L_c, then $L \equiv L_c$.*

Proof: According to the definition of the *COMET* algorithm, L_c is obtained by repeatedly applying the *OM* function followed by the *Transpose* function on L. First, suppose L_c is obtained by applying the *OM* function followed by the *Transpose* function one time. Let $L = [O_1, \cdots, O_{i-1}, O_i, O_{i+1}, O_{i+2}, \cdots, O_n]$, and $L_c = [O_1, \cdots, O_{i-1}, O''_{i+1}, O''_i, O_{i+2}, \cdots, O_n]$ where **OM**$(O_i, O_{i+1}) = (O'_i, O'_{i+1})$ and **Transpose**$(O'_i, O'_{i+1}) = (O''_{i+1}, O''_i)$. Suppose $CT_{O_1} = S$, the theorem is true because:

1. $S' = S \circ L[1,\ i\text{-}1] = S \circ L_c[1,\ i\text{-}1]$ (by $L[1,\ i\text{-}1] = L_c[1,\ i\text{-}1]$);

2. $S'' = S' \circ L[i,\ i\text{+}1] = S' \circ L_c[i,\ i\text{+}1]$ (by *OMP* and *TPP*);

3. $S''' = S'' \circ L[i\text{+}2,\ n] = S'' \circ L_c[i\text{+}2,\ n]$ (by $L[i\text{+}2,\ n] = L_c[i\text{+}2,\ n]$).

It can be easily shown by an introduction argument that the theorem is true if L_c is obtained by applying the *OM* function followed by the *Transpose* function on L any number of times.

3.5 Syntactic merging

Syntactic merging exploits the context-free syntax of the versions to be merged in order to achieve a syntactically correct result after merging [18]. For text files, textual merging is the foundation of syntactic merging and should be powerful enough to textually integrate all changes in order to support rich syntactic merging. In this section, we will present a flexible syntactic merging framework and a flexible syntactic merging algorithm that is based on the operation-based textual merging algorithm described in the previous section.

Look at the example shown in Figure 3.21. The initial state of a document (**IS**) contained a line: *You are student.* User *Author 1* developed the document to the intermediate state 1 (**M1**) by performing editing operation O_1 that is stored in log

L_1, while user *Author 2* developed the document to the intermediate state 2 (**M2**) by performing editing operation O_2 that is stored in log L_2. Operation $O_1 = \mathbf{Ins}[7, 2, \text{ "}a\text{"}]$ was to insert an article for the word *student* to make it singular and transformed the document to the state: *You are a student*. Operation $O_2 = \mathbf{Ins}[15, 1, \text{ "}s\text{"}]$ was to insert a character s at the end of the word *student* to make it plural and transformed the document to the state: *You are students*.

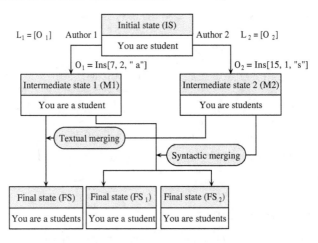

Figure 3.21: Syntactic merging versus textual merging

After textually merging the change made by *Author 2* into *Author 1*'s version of the document with the operation-based textual merging algorithm **OT_merge**(L_1, L_2), the merged final state of the document is: *You are a students*. However, it is not always desirable to textually merge all changes. In this example, the phrase *You are a students* is not syntactically correct according to English spelling and grammar checking syntax. Therefore syntactic merging is more desirable to control the merging behavior according to the context-free syntax of the documents to be merged. So, in this example, to syntactically merge the change made by *Author 2* into *Author 1*'s version of the document with English spelling and grammar syntax, the merged final state of the document could be either *You are a student* or *You are students*.

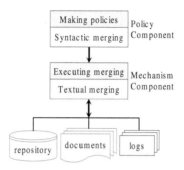

Figure 3.22: A flexible syntactic merging framework

3.5.1 A flexible syntactic merging framework

We propose a flexible syntactic merging framework that separates syntactic merging policies from the underlying textual merging mechanism. As shown in Figure 3.22, this framework consists of a policy component and a mechanism component. The policy component makes a wide range of document specific syntactic merging policies and the mechanism component is flexible and generic enough to perform textual merging according to the policy specified by the policy component. For example, if the shared document is an article, the syntactic merging policies could specify a set of English spelling and grammar checking rules. If the shared document is a software program, the syntactic merging policies could specify the programming language's syntax parsing rules. If changes to the shared document by different users have been well coordinated beforehand [28], for example, the work is properly divided in the way that different participants play different roles, it is possible that syntactic conflicts are completely avoided. For instance, two authors are jointly revising a scientific paper, one correcting spelling/grammar errors while the other adding references. Their changes made to the same paper could be as close as adjacent characters. But these changes do not cause any syntactic conflicts.

Syntactic merging policy

A syntactic merging policy can be specified as a set of SMR (Syntactic Merging Rules). Based on SMR, a function **Syntactic-Conflict** (SMR, O_r, O_l, CT) can be defined to determine whether two concurrent changes O_r and O_l syntactically conflict. On one extreme, the function could automatically return *true/false* without human intervention if SMR has been well formulated. For instance, in Figure 3.21, O_1 and O_2 were made concurrently by two users, both aiming to make the sentence *"You are student"* grammatically correct. O_1 makes the word *"student"* singular by inserting an article *"a"* while O_2 made the word *"student"* plural by inserting character *"s"*. If the SMR specifies grammar checking rules, *Syntactic-Conflict* $(SMR, O_2, O_1, $ *"You are student"*$)$ can automatically return *true* because incorporating both O_2 and O_1 to *"You are student"* would lead to the result *"You are a students"*, which is syntactically incorrect according to SMR. Automatic detection of syntactic conflicts is the most desirable way. However, it is not always achievable.

On the other extreme, the detection of syntactic conflicts could be completely manual if SMR cannot be formulated in any way. As a result, it is completely up to the user to determine what changes made by another user should be merged into her/his copy, possibly with consultation with that user. Manual detection of syntactic conflicts is the most general way for all kinds of documents. But it is the least desirable way. In many cases, the detection of syntactic conflicts should be a combination of both automatic and manual efforts. In other words, some syntactic conflicts can be automatically detected while some others may have to be detected by users.

Furthermore, the formulation of *SMR* is difficult, particularly for syntax-rich documents. Therefore the formulation of *SMR* itself deserves a lot of research but it is beyond the scope of this thesis work. An example of the **Syntactic-Conflict** (*SMR*, O_r, O_l, *CT*) function is given in Appendix C - *Sample code*. That function emulates the state-based merging behavior in the way that concurrent changes made within the same line or in adjacent lines are regarded as syntactically conflicting.

3.5.2 Syntactic merging algorithm

The mechanism component performs textual merging according to **SMR** specified by the policy component. Some critical issues have been identified in the mechanism component. First, an essential precondition for the **Syntactic-Conflict** (*SMR*, O_r, O_l, *CT*) function to make correct judgement is that $O_r \sqcup O_l$ and $CT_{O_r} = CT_{O_l} = CT$. An example is given below to show how the function returns a wrong judgement when the precondition is violated. As shown in Figure 3.23, a document initially contained a line *You are a students*. *Author 1* performed an operation $O_1 = $ **Del**[7, 2, " *a* "] to delete the article for the word *students* while *Author 2* sequentially performed two operations O_2 and O_3. $O_2 = $ **Ins**[7, 1, "\n"] inserted a *newline* character "\n" at position 7, and split the document into two lines: *You are* and *a students*. Then O_3 = **Del**[18, 1, "s"] deleted the character at position 18 (i.e., character *s* at the end of the word of *students*).

If *SMR* specifies that operations performed in the same line syntactically conflict, then *Syntactic-Conflict* function would return *true* for O_1 and O_2 because they were both performed in the first line, but would return *false* for O_1 and O_3 because O_1 was performed in the first line while O_3 was performed in the second line. The judgement for O_1 and O_3 is obviously wrong because O_1 and O_3 were targeting at the same line containing the phrase *a students*. The root of the problem is that the precondition of $O_1 \sqcup O_3$ is violated. O_1 was defined when the document contained only one line *You are a students* while O_3 was defined when the document contained two lines *You are* and *a students*. The operational transformation technique can be used to ensure the precondition.

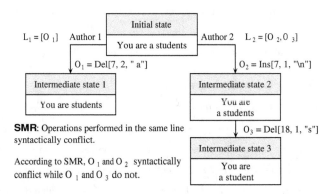

Figure 3.23: Syntactic-Conflict function returns wrong judgement

Second, it is essential to ensure that operations performed by one author can be correctly redone on another author's version of the document. Suppose two authors *Author 1* and *Author 2* begin with the same version and create different versions by executing different editing operations that are stored in logs L_1 and L_2 respectively. In order to merge changes made by *Author 2* into *Author 1*'s version of the document, operations in L_2 that do not syntactically conflict with any operation in L_1 must be redone, but may not be re-doable as-is. If operation $L_2[i]$ ($1 \leq i \leq |L_2|$) syntactically conflicts with operation $L_1[j]$ ($1 \leq j \leq |L_1|$), there are two alternative choices. One is to keep $L_2[i]$'s effect by first undoing $L_1[j]$ and then redoing $L_2[i]$. In this choice, a selective undo solution is needed to eliminate $L_1[i]$'s effect while keeping the effects of all other operations in L_1.

The other choice is to keep $L_1[j]$'s effect by ignoring $L_2[i]$. Nevertheless, operations following $L_2[i]$ (i.e., the list of operations $L_2[i+1, |L_2|]$), and not syntactically conflicting with any operation in L_1 must still be re-doable. This is quite different from the concept of transaction [48, 101] used in database systems, where the failure of one operation would fail all subsequent operations and consequently the entire transaction. The question here is how to redo these operations in the event that $L_2[i]$ cannot be redone. More precisely, given a log $L = [O_1, \cdots, O_n]$, if an operation O_k $(1 < k < n)$ cannot be executed, it cannot be simply ignored by executing O_{k+1} right after O_{k-1} because O_{k+1} was defined on the document state after the execution of O_k and cannot be executed as-is on the document state before the execution of O_k. In principle, in order to ignore O_k, operations $O_{k+1}, \cdots, O_n$ must be transformed to such forms that $O_{k-1} \mapsto O_{k+1}$, and $O_j \mapsto O_{j+1}$ $(k+1 \leq j < n)$.

The following example illustrates the above points. As shown in Figure 3.24, the initial state (IS) of a document contained a sentence: *You are student.* *Author 1* developed it to state $(M2)$ by executing two operations O_1^1 and O_2^1 that are stored in log L_1. $O_1^1 = \mathbf{Ins}[7, 2, \text{ "} a \text{"}]$ inserted an article for the word *student* to make it singular and $O_2^1 = \mathbf{Ins}[18, 1, \text{ "."}]$ added a full stop mark. *Author 2* developed it to state $(M4)$ by executing two operations O_1^2 and O_2^2 that are stored in log L_2. $O_1^2 = \mathbf{Ins}[15, 1, \text{ "} s \text{"}]$ inseredt character s at the end of the word *student* to make it plural and $O_2^2 = \mathbf{Ins}[8, 5, \text{ "} good \text{ "}]$ inserted an adjective *good* for the word *student*. To syntactically merge changes made by *Author 2* into *Author 1*'s version of the document (i.e., $M2$), it must be checked whether and how operations O_1^2 and O_2^2 are to be redone on $M2$. Operation O_1^2 conflicts with operation O_1^1 according to English spelling and grammar checking. If the solution is to keep O_1^1's effect by ignoring O_1^2, O_1^2's subsequent operation O_2^2 should still be redone because it does not conflict with any operation in L_1. As a result, after the execution of EO_2^2 (O_2^2's execution form), the final state of the document $(FS1)$ would be a sentence: *You are a good student.*, where the effects of O_1^1, O_2^1, and O_2^2 have been integrated. If the solution is to keep O_1^2's effect, O_1^1 must be first undone from $M2$ by executing $E\overline{O_1^1}$ ($\overline{O_1^1}$'s execution form), then O_1^2 and O_2^2 are redone by executing EO_1^2 (O_1^2's execution form) and EO_2^2 (O_2^2's execution form). As a result, the final state of the document would be a sentence: *You are good students.*, where the effects of O_1^2, O_2^1, and O_2^2 have been integrated while O_1^1's effect has been eliminated.

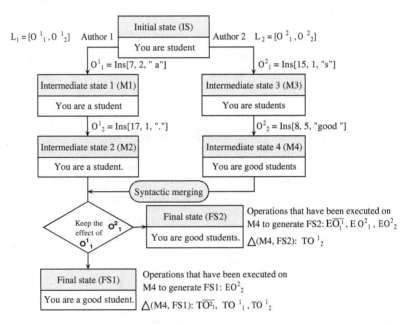

Figure 3.24: How to redo operations

Finally, representation of deltas between the version to be merged and the merged new version is important for supporting version control. In Figure 3.24, deltas between state **IS** and state **M2** are O_1^1 and O_2^1 (i.e., $\Delta(IS, M2) = [O_1^1, O_2^1]$) and deltas between state **IS** and state **M4** are O_1^2 and O_2^2 (i.e., $\Delta(IS, M4) = [O_1^2, O_2^2]$). After *Author 2*'s version of the document *M4* has been syntactically merged into *Author 1*'s version of the document *M2*, the final state *FS1/FS2* representing a merged new version is generated. Then what are the deltas between the version to be merged (i.e., *M4*) and the merged new version (i.e., *FS1/FS2*)? These deltas are essential for storing the new version *FS1/FS2* in the repository for version control

As we know, state-based merging relies on executing text differentiation algorithms on the two versions to derive the deltas, such as $\Delta(M4, FS1/FS1) = \mathbf{diff}(M4, FS1/FS1)$. However, the syntactic merging algorithm based on the operation-based textual merging should have the capability of deriving deltas between the version to be merged and the merged new version without requiring the execution of text differentiation algorithms. In Figure 3.24, *M4* includes the effects of operations O_1^2 and O_2^2 while *FS2* includes the effects of O_2^1, O_1^2, and O_2^2, therefore it should be $\Delta(M4, FS2) = TO_2^1$ where TO_2^1 is a transformed form of O_2^1. Similarly, *FS1* includes the effects of O_1^1, O_2^1, and O_2^2, therefore it should be $\Delta(M4, FS1) = [T\overline{O_1^2}, TO_1^1, TO_2^1]$ where $T\overline{O_1^2}$, TO_1^1, and TO_2^1 are transformed forms of $\overline{O_1^2}$, O_1^1, and O_2^1 respectively. In sum, the mechanism component in the syntactic merging framework should define the *Syntactic-Conflict* function according to *SMR* passed from the policy component, and a syntactic merging algorithm to determine the execution forms of those operations that can be redone, and derive the deltas between the version to be merged and the merged new version.

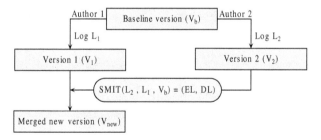

Figure 3.25: The setting of SMIT syntactic merging algorithm

As shown in Figure 3.25, *Author 1* and *Author 2* begin with the same baseline version V_b and create different versions V_1 and V_2 by executing different editing operations that have been stored in logs L_1 and L_2 respectively. The **SMIT**(L_2, L_1, V_b) (Syntactic Merging by Inclusion Transformation) algorithm is defined to syntactically merge changes made between V_b to V_2 by *Author 2* into *Author 1*'s version V_1 in order to generate a merged new version V_{new}. The algorithm is described as follows:

Algorithm 3.4. *SMIT(L_2, L_1, V_b): (EL, DL)*

Inputs:

1. L_2: The log storing operations made between V_b to V_2

2. L_1: The log storing operations made between V_b to V_1

3. V_b: The baseline version for both V_1 and V_2

Outputs:

1. EL: The list of operations to be executed on V_1 to generate V_{new}

2. DL: The list of operations representing the deltas between version V_2 and V_{new}

{ $CT_2 = V_b$; //initial context for V_2

    for ($i = 1$; $i \leq$ **sizeof**(L_2); $i{+}{+}$)

    { $CT_1 = CT_2$; //initial context for V_1

      $L_1\text{-}copy = L_1$; //L_1's copy

      $L_2^i\text{-}copy = L_2[i]$; //$L_2[i]$'s copy

      for ($j = 1$; $j \leq$ **sizeof**(L_1); $j{+}{+}$)

      { **if Syntactic-Conflict** (SMR, $L_2[i]$, $L_1[j]$, CT_1)

        { **if** the solution is to keep $L_1[j]$'s effect

          { $L_1 = L_1\text{-}copy$; //recover L_1's previous state

           $L_2[i] = L_2^i\text{-}copy$; //recover $L_2[i]$'s previous state

           $T\overline{O_i^2} = $ **UndoOperation**(i, L_2); //Undo $L_2[i]$

           $DL \mathrel{+}= T\overline{O_i^2}$; //append $T\overline{O_i^2}$ into DL

= type>147

$i = i - 1;$

break;

} **else if** to keep $L_2[i]$'s effect

{ $\overline{EO_j^1} = $ **UndoOperation**(j, L_1); //Undo $L_1[j]$

$EL \mathrel{+}= \overline{EO_j^1}$; //append $\overline{EO_j^1}$ into EL

$j = j - 1;$

}

} **else**

{ $CT_1 = CT_1 \circ L_1[j]$; //update V_1' context

SIT$(L_2[i], L_1[j])$; //transform $L_2[i]$ and $L_1[j]$ with each other

}

}

//$L_2[i]$ can be redone

if $j > $ **sizeof**(L_1)

{ $EL \mathrel{+}= L_2[i]$;

$CT_2 = CT_2 \circ L_2^i\text{-}copy$; //update V_2' context

}

}

$DL \mathrel{+}= L_1$; //append operations in L_1 into DL

//execute operations in EL on V_1 to generate V_{new}

for $(k = 1; k \leq$ **sizeof**$(EL); k{+}{+})$

execute $EL[k]$;

return (EL, DL);

}

The **UndoOperation**(k, L) function returns the execution form of $\overline{L[k]}$ for undoing the kth operation in log L, and removes the kth operation from the log.

Function 3.9. *UndoOperation(k, L):* $\overline{O_k}'$

{ $\overline{O_k}$ = **makeInverse**(L[k]); //defined in Chapter 2

     for $(i = k + 1; i \leq$ **sizeof**$(L); i{+}{+})$ //determine $\overline{O_k}$'s execution form

       SIT$(\overline{O_k},$ L[i]);

     remove L[k]; //remove the kth operation from L

     return $\overline{O_k}$; //return $\overline{O_k}$'s execution form

}

For the example in Figure 3.24, the syntactic merging algorithm **SMIT**$(L_2, L_1,$ *IS*) can be executed to syntactically merge changes made between state *IS* and state *M4* into *Author 1*'s version of the document *M2* with *SMR* specifying a set of English spelling and grammar checking rules. The algorithm will be executed as follows:

1. The initial context for *Author 2*: $CT_2 = IS = $ *You are student*

2. $i{=}1, L_2[1] = O_1^2 = Ins[15, 1,$ *"s"*$]$

    (a) The initial context for *Author 1*: $CT_1 = IS = $ *You are student*

    (b) $L_2^1\text{-}copy = O_1^2 = $ **Ins**$[15, 1,$ *"s"*$]$ and $L_1\text{-}copy = [O_1^1, O_2^1]$ where $O_1^1 = $ **Ins**$[7,$ 2, *" a"*$]$ and $O_2^1 = $ **Ins**$[17, 1,$ *"."*$]$

    (c) $j{=}1, L_1[1] = O_1^1 = Ins[7, 2,$ *" a"*$]$, **Syntactic-Conflict**$(SMR, L_2[1], L_1[1],$ $CT_1{=}You\ are\ student) = true$

       • If the user chooses to keep $L_1[1]$'s effect,

           i. $L_2[1] = L_2^1\text{-}copy = O_1^2 = Ins[15, 1,$ *"s"*$]$ and $L_1 = L_1\text{-}copy = [O_1^1,$ $O_2^1]$ where $O_1^1 = $ **Ins**$[7, 2,$ *" a"*$]$ and $O_2^1 = $ **Ins**$[17, 1,$ *"."*$]$

           ii. $T\overline{O_1^2} = $ **UndoOperation**$(1, L_2)$: $T\overline{O_1^2} = $ **IT_DI**$(\overline{O_1^2}, O_2^2) = $ **Del**$[20,$ 1, *"s"*$]$ and $L_2 = [O_2^{2\prime}]$ where $O_2^{2\prime} = $ **IT_ID**$(O_2^2, \overline{O_1^2}) = $ **Ins**$[8, 5,$ *"good "*$]$.

           iii. $DL = [T\overline{O_1^2}]$

           iv. Goto 6

       • If the user chooses to keep $L_2[1]$'s effect,

    i. $E\overline{O_1^1} = \textbf{UndoOperation}(1, L_1)$: $E\overline{O_1^1} = \textbf{IT\_DI}(\overline{O_1^1}, O_2^1) = \textbf{Del}[7,$
      2, " a "] and $L_1 = [O_2^{1'}]$ where $O_2^{1'} = \textbf{IT\_ID}(O_2^1, \overline{O_1^1}) = \textbf{Ins}[15, 1,$
      "."]

    ii. $EL = [E\overline{O_1^1}]$

(d) $j=1$, $L_1[1] = O_2^{1'} = \textbf{Ins}[15, 1,$ "."], **Syntactic-Conflict**(SMR, $L_2[1]$, $L_1[1]$, $CT_1=You\ are\ student$) = *false*

    i. $CT_1 = CT_1 \circ L_1[1] = You\ are\ student.$

    ii. **SIT**($L_2[1]$, $L_1[1]$): $L_2[1] = O_1^{2'} = \textbf{IT\_II}(O_1^2, O_2^{1'}) = \textbf{Ins}[15, 1,$ "s"] and $L_1[1] = O_2^{1''} = \textbf{IT\_II}(O_2^{1'}, O_1^2) = \textbf{Ins}[16, 1,$ "."]

(e) $j=2 > |L_1|=1$, $EL = [E\overline{O_1^1}, L_2[1]] = [E\overline{O_1^1}, O_1^{2'}]$, $CT_2 = CT_2 \circ L_2^1\text{-}copy = You\ are\ students$

3. $i=2$, $L_2[2] = O_2^2 = \textbf{Ins}[8, 5,$ "$good$ "]

(a) $CT_1 = CT_2 = You\ are\ students$

(b) $L_2^2\text{-}copy = O_2^2 = \textbf{Ins}[8, 5,$ "$good$ "] and $L_1\text{-}copy = [O_2^{1''}]$

(c) $j=1$, $L_1[1] = O_2^{1''} = \textbf{Ins}[16, 1,$ "."], **Syntactic-Conflict**(SMR, $L_2[1]$, $L_1[1]$, $CT_1=You\ are\ students$) = *false*

    i. $CT_1 = CT_1 \circ L_1[1] = You\ are\ students.$

    ii. **SIT**($L_2[2]$, $L_1[1]$): $L_2[2] = O_2^{2'} = \textbf{IT\_II}(O_2^2, O_2^{1''}) = \textbf{Ins}[8, 5,$ "$good$ "] and $L_1[1] = O_2^{1'''} = \textbf{IT\_II}(O_2^{1''}, O_2^2) = \textbf{Ins}[21, 1,$ "."]

(d) $j=2 > |L_1|=1$, $EL = [E\overline{O_1^1}, O_1^{2'}, L_2[2]] = [E\overline{O_1^1}, O_1^{2'}, O_2^{2'}]$, $CT_2 = CT_2 \circ L_2^2\text{-}copy = You\ are\ good\ students$

4. $i=3 > |L_2|=2$, $DL = [L_1[1]] = [O_2^{1'''}]$ where $O_2^{1'''} = \textbf{Ins}[21, 1,$ "."]

5. $FS2 = M2 \circ EL = M2 \circ [E\overline{O_1^1},\ O_1^{2'},\ O_2^{2'}] = $ *You are good students.*, where $E\overline{O_1^1}$ $= \mathbf{Del}[7, 2,\ ``a"]$, $O_1^{2'} = \mathbf{Ins}[15, 1,\ ``s"]$, and $O_2^{2'} = \mathbf{Ins}[8, 5, ``good\ "]$. $\Delta(M4,$ $FS2) = DL = [O_2^{1'''}\ ]$ where $O_2^{1'''} = \mathbf{Ins}[21, 1,\ ``."]$.

6. $i=1$, $L_2[1] = O_2^{2'} = \mathbf{Ins}[8, 5,\ ``good\ "]$

   (a) $CT_1 = CT_2 = $ *You are student*

   (b) $L_2^1\text{-copy} = O_2^{2'} = \mathbf{Ins}[8, 5,\ ``good\ "]$ and $L_1\text{-copy} = [O_1^1,\ O_2^1]$ where $O_1^1 = \mathbf{Ins}[7, 2,\ ``a"]$ and $O_2^1 = \mathbf{Ins}[17, 1,\ ``."]$

   (c) $j=1$, $L_1[1] = O_1^1 = \mathbf{Ins}[7, 2,\ ``a"]$, $\mathbf{Syntactic\text{-}Conflict}(SMR, L_2[1], L_1[1],$ $CT_1 = $ *You are student*$) = $ *false*

       i. $CT_1 = CT_1 \circ L_1[1] = $ *You are a student*

       ii. $\mathbf{SIT}(L_2[1], L_1[1])$: $L_2[1] = O_2^{2''} = \mathbf{IT\_II}(O_2^{2'}, O_1^1) = \mathbf{Ins}[10, 5,\ ``good\ "]$ and $L_1[1] = O_1^{1'} = \mathbf{IT\_II}(O_1^1, O_2^{2'}) = \mathbf{Ins}[7, 2,\ ``a"]$

   (d) $j=2$, $L_1[2] = O_2^1 = \mathbf{Ins}[17, 1,\ ``."]$, $\mathbf{Syntactic\text{-}Conflict}(SMR, L_2[1], L_1[2],$ $CT_1 = $ *You are a student*$) = $ *false*

       i. $CT_1 = CT_1 \circ L_1[2] = $ *You are a student.*

       ii. $\mathbf{SIT}(L_2[1], L_1[2])$: $L_2[1] = O_2^{2'''} = \mathbf{IT\_II}(O_2^{2''}, O_2^1) = \mathbf{Ins}[8, 5,\ ``good\ "]$ and $L_1[2] = O_2^{1'} = \mathbf{IT\_II}(O_2^1, O_2^{2''}) = \mathbf{Ins}[22, 2,\ ``."]$

   (e) $j=3 > |L_1|=2$, $EL = [L_2[1]] = [O_2^{2'''}]$, $CT_2 = CT_2 \circ L_2^1\text{-copy} = $ *You are good student*

7. $i=2 > |L_2|=1$, $DL = [T\overline{O_1^2}, L_1[1], L_1[2]] = [T\overline{O_1^2}, O_1^{1'}, O_2^{1'}]$.

8. $FS1 = M2 \circ EL = M2 \circ O_2^{2'''} = $ *You are a good student.*, where $O_2^{2'''} = \mathbf{Ins}[8, 5,\ ``good\ "]$. $\Delta(M4, FS1) = DL = [T\overline{O_1^2}, O_1^{1'}, O_2^{1'}]$ where $T\overline{O_1^2} = \mathbf{Del}[20, 1, ``s"]$, $O_1^{1'} = \mathbf{Ins}[7, 2,\ ``a"]$, and $O_2^{1'} = \mathbf{Ins}[22, 2,\ ``."]$.

3.5.3 Version control

According to the convention of storing versions in the repository where the latest version is stored in its entirety while other versions can be stored as deltas [142], different states of the document in Figure 3.24 are stored as versions in the repository as follows: the initial state IS was first imported into the repository as the starting version 1.1 and was stored in its entirety. That is, the repository containing version 1.1 should look like *1.1: You are student.* *Author 1* and *Author 2* both checked out version 1.1 as the baseline version $V_b = 1.1$, and developed it into two different states $M2$ and $M4$ by executing different editing operations that have been stored in logs L_1 and L_2 respectively.

When *Author 2* committed $M4$ into the repository to generate a new version 1.2, the latest version 1.2 will be stored in its entirety while the previous version 1.1 will be stored as deltas. That is, the repository containing version 1.2 and version 1.1 should look like *1.2: You are good students 1.1: O_1^2 O_2^2.* When *Author 1* updated $M2$ with version 1.2 generated by *Author 2*, the syntactic merging algorithm **SMIT**$([O_1^2, O_2^2], L_1, V_b)$ will be executed to return two lists of operations EL and DL. A new state $FS1/FS2$ will be generated by executing the list of operations in EL on $M2$. After that, *Author 1*'s baseline version V_b is updated to version 1.2, and deltas between the new baseline version V_b and the generated new state $FS1/FS2$ are the list of operations in DL. In particular, $FS1 = M2 \circ O_2^{2'''} =$ *You are a good student.* and $\Delta(V_b, FS1) = [T\overline{O_1^2}, O_1^{1'}, O_2^{1'}]$, $FS2 = M2 \circ [E\overline{O_1^1}, O_1^{2'}, O_2^{2'}]$ and $\Delta(V_b, FS2) = [O_2^{1'''}]$. When *Author 1* committed $FS1/FS2$ into the repository to generate a new version 1.3, the latest version 1.3 will be stored in its entirely while previous versions 1.2 and 1.1 will be stored as deltas. That is, the repository containing version 1.3, 1.2 and 1.1 should look like *1.3: You are a good student. 1.2: $T\overline{O_1^2}$ $O_1^{1'}$ $O_2^{1'}$ 1.1: O_1^2 O_2^2* or *1.3: You are good students. 1.2: $O_2^{1'''}$ 1.1: O_1^2 O_2^2.*

Suppose the repository contains: *1.3: You are a good student. 1.2: $T\overline{O_1^2}$ $O_1^{1'}$ $O_2^{1'}$*

1.1: $O_1^2\, O_2^2$. To check out the latest version 1.3, the text *You are a good student.* will be retrieved straightforward. To check out a previous version, the inverse operations of those operations will be executed sequentially on the latest version to retrieve the text. For instance, to checkout version 1.2, *1.2 = 1.3* $\circ\ [\overline{O^{1'}_2},\ \overline{O^{1'}_1},\ \overline{TO^2_1}] =$ *You are good students*, where $\overline{O^{1'}_2} = \mathbf{Del}[22,\ 2,\ "."]$, $\overline{O^{1'}_1} = \mathbf{Del}[7,\ 2,\ "\,a\,"]$, and $\overline{TO^2_1} = \mathbf{Ins}[20,\ 1,\ "s"]$. Similarly, to check out version 1.1, *1.1 = 1.3* $\circ\ [\overline{O^{1'}_2},\ \overline{O^{1'}_1},\ \overline{TO^2_1},\ \overline{O^2_2},\ \overline{O^2_1}] =$ *You are student*, where $\overline{O^2_2} = \mathbf{Del}[8,\ 5,\ "good\ "]$ and $\overline{O^2_1} = \mathbf{Del}[15,\ 1,\ "s"]$.

3.6 System design and implementation

The flexible operation-based merging technique has been implemented in a web-based flexible version control environment *FORCE* for the purpose of testing the correctness, demonstrating the feasibility, and providing a vehicle to explore system design and implementation issues and do a usability study. *FORCE* is a web-based source code editor with integrated version control support, which is able to support non-real-time collaborative editing and version control of the same document by means of the flexible operation-based merging technique presented in previous sections. As version control has been identified as a very desirable feature for editors [77], it is getting more and more common to integrate version control support into existing single-user editors. For example, *RCS* [142], *CVS* [56], and *SCCS* [112] have been integrated into popular text editor *Emacs* [20], and *CVS* [56] has been integrated into Sun's *Netbeans* Java integrated development environment [16]. Microsoft *Word 2000* [17] also has built-in preliminary version support. We implement a text editor in the *FORCE* environment, which is able to log editing operations for supporting flexible operation-based merging.

3.6.1 System configuration

The system configuration of *FORCE* is shown in Figure 3.26. The *FORCE* server is a Linux server that accommodates a web server, a *FORCE SCM* server implemented as a Java application, and a *FORCE* repository based on *Linux* file system. The *FORCE SCM* server manages the *FORCE* repository and communicates with *FORCE SCM* clients for supporting non-real-time collaborative editing and version control.

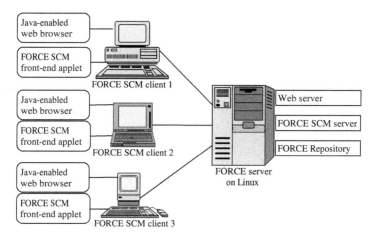

Figure 3.26: System configuration of FORCE

Each *FORCE SCM* client has a front-end tool implemented as a Java applet running inside a Java-enabled web browser at a collaborating site. As shown in Figure 3.27, the *FORCE SCM* front-end applet is a text editor with which users issue editing operations to edit a document. Those editing operations are saved in logs to support non-real-time collaborative editing of a shared document and version control of evolving documents, by means of the flexible operation-based merging technique. Users are able to issue version control commands from the interface of the editor, such as *import*: import a file to the repository to generate an initial version; *checkout*:

checkout a version from the repository; *commit*: commit a working copy into the repository to generate a new version; and *update*: update a working copy with a version from the repository.

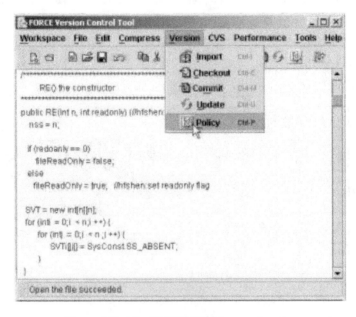

Figure 3.27: The FORCE SCM front-end applet

A log storing editing operations performed by a user can be compressed by the *COMET* log compression algorithm presented in Section 3.14. As shown in Figure 3.28(a), a log can be periodically compressed by specifying a time interval or manually compressed by issuing the *compress* command. After each compression, the log scale will become minimal in the sense that all operations in the log are disjointed. The operation-based textual merging algorithm *OT_merge* presented in Section 3.4, and the operation-based syntactic merging algorithm *SMIT* presented in Section 3.5 have been implemented to support update merging when a user issues the *update* version control command.

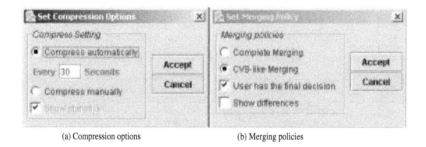

(a) Compression options   (b) Merging policies

Figure 3.28: Compression options and merging policies

As shown in Figure 3.28(b), if the merging policy is set to *Complete Merging*, the *OT_merge* textual merging algorithm will be executed to textually integrate all changes. By comparison, if the merging policy is set to *CVS-like Merging*, the *SMIT* syntactic merging algorithm will be executed to emulate the state-based merging effect (i.e., changes made in the same line by different users are syntactically conflicting) with the *Syntactic-Conflict* function defined in Appendix C. With the *CVS-like Merging* policy, if the option *User has the final decision* is checked, when a syntactic conflict is detected, it will be reported on the user interface with detailed information with which the user will give a final decision on whether the conflict stands or not. This feature is very useful in practice because with sufficient information users have the most profound knowledge in determining conflicts, but it is difficult for systems based on state-based merging technique to offer this feature.

3.6.2 A flexible operation-based merging experiment

An experiment was carried out to measure the performance of the *COMET* log compression algorithm and the efficiency difference between operation-based merging and state-based merging with *FORCE*. As shown in Figure 3.27, a Java class file *RE.java* for the *NICE* system has been edited and vision controlled by *FORCE*. The file initially contained 28 variable definitions and 69 empty method definitions with a size of 14,623 bytes, which was imported into the repository as the initial version *V 1.0*.

Log scale before compression		Log scale after compression		Compression rate	
Size (bytes)	Number of operations	Size (bytes)	Number of operations	Size (%)	Number of operations(%)
62408	3830	24461	80	60.80%	97.91%

Figure 3.29: Log compression after the construction period

After having been coded for more than two weeks in realizing those empty methods with the *FORCE* front-end editor, *RE.java* was increased to 30,140 bytes with the log accumulating 3,830 editing operations with the size of 62,408 bytes. As shown in Figure 3.29, when the log is compressed by the *COMET* compression algorithm, its size is reduced to 24,461 bytes with the compression rate of 60.80%, containing only 80 effective operations with the compression rate of 97.91%. Results shown in Figure 3.29 have coincided with the estimation on the performance of the *COMET* algorithm. To some extent, the results suggest that the more localized operations are, the higher the compression rate would be, because in the construction period for realizing empty methods in *RE.java*, operations were highly localized in constructing individual methods.

RE.java was committed into the repository to generate a new version *V 1.1*. Figure 3.30 shows the performance differences among state-based commit merging, operation-based commit merging without compression, and operation-based commit merging with compression in terms of: the response time T_{res}, the time T_{wok} spent on the working site, the time T_{com} spent on the communication between the working site and the repository, and time T_{rep} spent on the repository. It should be pointed out that all measures might look longer than expected because the working site was a relatively old machine with Pentium Celeron 333Hz CPU and 64M RAM, the connection between the working site and the *FORCE* server was a 56k dialup network, and both the *FORCE SCM* front-end and *FORCE SCM* server were implemented with the interpretive Java language. However, these numbers should have no problem in reflecting performance differences between state-based merging and operation-based merging since these performance numbers were collected at the same time and with the same hardware and software configurations.

	State-based merging	Operation-based merging without compression	Operation-based merging with compression
T_{res} (msec)	741	841	631
T_{wok} (msec)	9	13	7
T_{com} (msec)	2384 (30140bytes)	4937 (62408bytes)	1935(24461bytes)
T_{rep} (msec)	89	43	6

Figure 3.30: Performance differences of commit merging after construction period

From Figure 3.30, it can be seen that T_{res} and T_{wok} are almost the same for state-based merging and operation-based merging. T_{com} in operation-based merging without log compression is more than double that in state-based merging because the uncompressed log (62,408 bytes) is more than double the file itself (30,140 bytes) in size. In contrast, T_{com} in operation-based merging with log compression is slightly shorter than that in state-based merging. In state-based merging, the *FORCE SCM* server took $T_{rep} = 89$ miniseconds, mainly for executing the text differentiation algorithm to derive deltas between *V 1.1* and *V 1.0*. In contrast, in operation-based merging without compression, the *FORCE SCM* server only took half that time to apply 3,830 editing operations on *V 1.0* to generate *V 1.1*. More significantly, the *FORCE SCM* server only took $T_{rep} = 6$ miniseconds to apply 80 editing operations on *V 1.0* to generate *V 1.1*.

	State-based merging	Operation-based merging without compression	Operation-based merging with compression
T_{res} (msec)	17046	17635	2521
T_{wok} (msec)	13480	11446	210
T_{com} (msec)	3188 (44763bytes)	5756 (62408bytes)	1934(24461bytes)
T_{rep} (msec)	78	13	7

Figure 3.31: Performance difference of update merging after construction period

If a working copy of *V 1.0* was updated with *V 1.1* from the repository to generate a new document state the same as *V 1.1*, Figure 3.31 shows the performance differences among state-based update merging, operation-based update merging without compression, and operation-based update merging with compression in terms of T_{res}, T_{wok}, T_{com}, and T_{rep}. It can be seen from Figure 3.31 that state-based merging and operation-based merging without compression have similar performances in terms of T_{res} and T_{wok}. But T_{com} in operation-based merging without compression is nearly double than that in state-based merging due to its large log size while T_{rep} in state-based merging is significantly longer than that in operation-based merging, owing to the time needed for applying reverse deltas on *V 1.1* to retrieve *V 1.0*. However, operation-based merging with compression is significantly better than the other two in terms of any measure.

After having been debugged for more than one week in order to find and fix bugs within the source code file *RE.java*, the size of *RE.java* became 30,310 bytes. Although the file size is only slightly different, 587 operations have been accumulated in the log with a size of 10,500 bytes. As shown in Figure 3.32, when the log is compressed by the *COMET* compression algorithm, its size is reduced to 7,107 bytes with the compression rate of 32.31%, containing 243 effective operations with the compression rate of 58.60%.

Log scale before compression		Log scale after compression		Compssion rate	
Size (bytes)	Number of operations	Size (bytes)	Number of operations	Size (%)	Number of operations(%)
10500	587	7107	243	32.31%	58.60%

Figure 3.32: Log compression after the debugging period

Results shown in Figure 3.32 have also coincided with the estimation on the performance of the *COMET* algorithm from another perspective. To some extent, the results suggest that the less localized operations are, the lower the compression rate would be. In the debugging period for finding and fixing bugs in *RE.java*, operations were fewer than those in the construction period. But these operations were less localized in the sense that they were dispersed in various parts of the file, resulting in the log compressed not so significantly compared with that after the construction period.

	State-based merging	Operation-based merging without compression	Operation-based merging with compression
T_{res} (msec)	621	691	601
T_{wok} (msec)	15	6	3
T_{com} (msec)	3415 (30310bytes)	1185 (10500bytes)	815(7107bytes)
T_{rep} (msec)	80	33	14

Figure 3.33: Performance differences of commit merging after the debugging period

Finally, the debugged *RE.java* was committed into the repository to generate a new version V 1.2. It can be seen from Figure 3.33 that T_{res} and T_{wok} are pretty much the same for state-based merging and operation-based merging. But T_{com} and T_{rep} in operation-based merging (with and without compression) are both significantly shorter than those in state-based merging owing to the small size of the log and the small number of operations in the log.

	State-based merging	Operation-based merging without compression	Operation-based merging with compression
T_{res} (msec)	28399	4928	1963
T_{wok} (msec)	21732	3375	751
T_{com} (msec)	6332 (60450bytes)	1197 (10500bytes)	909(7107bytes)
T_{rep} (msec)	25	6	3

Figure 3.34: Performance differences of update merging after the debugging period

If a working copy of V 1.1 was updated with V 1.2 from the repository to generate a new document state same as V 1.2, it can be seen from Figure 3.34 that all measures in operation-based merging (with and without compression) are significantly shorter than those in state-based merging. It can be concluded from Figure 3.33 and Figure 3.34 that operation-based merging can be significantly more efficient than state-based merging if the log size is smaller than the file size itself, and it may not be so significant to improve the efficiency of an operation-based merging process by compressing a small scale log.

3.7 Conclusions and future work

Copy-Modify-Merge is a major technique to support non-real-time collaborative editing where merging is the core technical component. Merging can be used to support unconstrained, syncretic, non-real-time collaborative editing of the same source code file, and maintain consistency among different working copies. Textual merging has been studied for decades; the state-based merging is the most commonly used technique. Operation-based merging is an alternative technique and it is able to overcome some crucial drawbacks in the state-based merging technique such as low-efficiency and the possibility of complaining false conflicts.

To apply operation-based merging technique to textual merging, an operation-based textual merging algorithm based on the operational transformation technology has been proposed and it is capable of textually merging all changes made by different users. To make operation-based merging viable and more efficient than state-based merging in practice, logs for storing editing operations performed by users should be kept small. Therefore a log compression algorithm has been proposed for operation-based merging and it is able to maximally compress a log, in the sense that the size of the log as well as the number of operations within the log have both been minimized. Based on the operation-based textual merging, we further proposed a flexible syntactic merging framework that uses a generic and flexible textual merging mechanism to support a range of document dependent user-specified syntactic merging policies. Issues in the generic and flexible textual merging mechanism have been systematically studied and a flexible syntactic merging algorithm has been devised accordingly.

All proposed algorithms have been implemented in the *FORCE* flexible version control environment for the purpose of testing the correctness, demonstrating the feasibility, and providing a vehicle to explore system design and implementation issues and do a usability study. An experiment has been carried out to measure the performance of the *COMET* log compression algorithm and the efficiency differences between operation-based merging and state-based merging by using the system. The experiment results have confirmed those estimations made about the performance of the log compression algorithm and the performance of operation-based merging. One future work is to investigate how to extend the techniques proposed for supporting textual merging and syntactic merging to the support of semantic merging. Another future work is to systematically perform statistics study on the log compression algorithm. Moreover, it is also interesting to investigate how to extend the flexible operation-based merging technique to the configuration with multiple distributed repositories in the Internet environment.

Chapter 4

Flexible notification

In the implementation phase of a collaborative programming process, programmers who are working on the same component in a source code sometimes need to collaboratively edit the same component with frequent interaction or sometimes independently edit different parts of the same component for isolated functions with little interaction. Therefore, as specified in Section 1.3 of Chapter 1, an essential requirement of collaborative editing for supporting collaborative programming is that smooth, and flexible switching between real-time and non-real-time collaborative editing should be supported. Since notification is a common feature in both real-time and non-real-time collaborative systems, we propose a flexible notification framework that can be used to unify real-time and non-real-time collaborative systems, and a flexible notification technique that can be used to design a flexible collaborative editing system that is able to support unconstrained, responsive, real-time collaborative editing; unconstrained, syncretic, non-real-time collaborative editing, and smooth, flexible switching between real-time and non-real-time collaborative editing.

4.1 Introduction

Notification is an essential feature in collaborative systems, which determines when, what, and how changes made by one user are propagated, applied, and reflected on other users' interfaces. It is this feature that distinguishes collaborative systems from traditional multi-user systems, such as database management systems [48] and timesharing operating systems, where a user is normally not notified of the actions performed by other users [46].

Notification plays an important role in determining a system's capability and flexibility in supporting different kinds of collaborative work. If a system has adopted a notification strategy that *frequently* propagates one user's actions to others, then this system is capable of supporting *real-time (synchronous)* collaborative work, where multiple users can collaborate at *the same time*. In contrast, if a system has adopted a notification strategy that *infrequently* propagates one user's actions to others, then this system is more suitable for supporting *non-real-time (asynchronous)* collaborative work, where multiple users have to collaborate at *different times*. Usually, one collaborative system uses only one notification strategy, and existing collaborative systems have been classified to be either real-time or non-real-time. If notification is flexible enough to support multiple notification strategies, it is possible for the collaborative system to support both real-time and non-real-time collaborative work.

In past years, various notification strategies have been designed for different collaborative systems to meet their special collaboration needs. For example, the *REDUCE* editor [137] has focused on achieving high responsiveness and adopted a simple notification strategy: operations performed on the shared document by one user is immediately and automatically propagated to other users and reflected on other users' interfaces as soon as possible [82]. In the Internet-based real-time chatting tool *ICQ* [73], a message is sent as soon as the user hits the *Send* button and reflected on other users' interfaces on arrival. In the *SCM* system *CVS* [10, 56], a user can edit the copied document as long as s/he wishes. Changes made on the shared document by one user is not made available to others until the user manually issues the *commit* command, and updates made by other users are not integrated into the local copy unless the user manually issues the *update* command. In all these collaborative systems, the design of notification components has been ad hoc, and techniques used for supporting notification have been application-dependent. Little research has been done on generic aspects of notification to provide an integrated and unified view of existing notification strategies, and to provide a guideline for the design of new notification strategies.

In collaborative applications, notification can be used to support exchanging messages. For example, messaging systems like *Email* or *ICQ* [73] use notification to support message exchange. Notification can also be used to support concurrency control in order to maintain consistency of shared artifacts. For example, *REDUCE* [137] uses propagation of operations [82] and operational transformation [136] as the concurrency control mechanism to maintain consistency among replicated copies, and *CVS* [10, 56] uses propagation of working documents and version and merging [18, 84, 92, 124] as the concurrency control mechanism to maintain consistency among replicated copies. In addition, notification can be used to support other features such as group awareness. For example, *ICQ* [73] uses notification to inform others of a participant's status change (e.g., online/offline), and *NESSIE* [104] uses notification to inform others of a task that has been completed by a participant.

In this chapter, a flexible notification framework is presented, which can be used to describe and compare a range of notification strategies used in existing collaborative systems, and to guide the design of notification components for new collaborative systems. In the proposed framework, the notification policy that determines when and what to notify is separated from the notification mechanism that determines how to notify [125]. The notification policy part of the framework consists of a set of basic and generic parameters, which can be used to define a spectrum of notification policies suitable for meeting different collaboration needs. The notification mechanism part consists of a set of basic and generic technical components, which can be used to support various notification policies. The flexible notification framework has been applied to the design of the notification component for a flexible collaborative editing system that is able to support unconstrained, responsive, real-time collaborative editing; unconstrained, syncretic, non-real-time collaborative editing, and smooth, flexible switching between real-time and non-real-time collaborative editing.

The rest of the chapter is organized as follows: a flexible notification framework is discussed in the following section. Then next sections systematically present the notification component for a flexible group editor. Some related work is reviewed after that. Finally, the chapter is concluded with a summary of contributions and future work.

4.2 A flexible notification framework

The flexible notification framework consists of a notification *policy* part and a notification *mechanism* part. To achieve flexible notification, two directions of notifications are differentiated. One is the *ON* (Outgoing Notification) direction, which is about when, what, and how changes made by a user are propagated to others. The other is the *IN* (Incoming Notification) direction, which is about when, what, and how changes made by other users are accepted and reflected on a user's interface. Two parameters, *frequency* and *granularity*, are provided to define various notification policies.

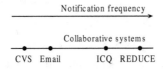

Figure 4.1: Relation between notification frequency and collaborative systems

4.2.1 Notification frequency

The frequency parameter determines the "when" aspect of notification, that is, when a notification is to be propagated/ accepted. According to the frequency of notification, we can sort collaborative systems in a linear order, with less frequently notifying systems ordered before more frequently notifying systems. As shown in Figure 4.1, non-real-time collaborative systems, such as *CVS* and the *Email* system, occupy the left spectrum of notification frequencies, and real-time collaborative systems, such as *ICQ* and *REDUCE*, are using the right spectrum of notification frequencies.

System-triggered	I: Instant
	S: Scheduled
User-triggered	U: User-controlled

Figure 4.2: Notification frequency parameter values

The frequency parameter may take different values, which have been adopted in various collaborative systems. As shown in Figure 4.2, values for *ON/IN*, denoted as *ONF/INF*, can be classified into two categories: system-triggered and user-triggered. In system-triggered notification, the system automatically propagates/accepts notification. If *ONF = I*, changes made by a user would be instantly propagated to remote sites, and if *INF = I*, changes made by remote users would be instantly accepted and reflected on the local user interface. *ICQ* [73] is an example of using *INF = I*, where arriving messages are instantly reflected on the local user interface. If *ONF/INF = S*, the system propagates/accepts notifications as scheduled. Scheduling strategies are application-dependent and may be based on some rules that are related to external events. Scheduling rules could be either implicitly built in the application or explicitly configured by users. For example, in *REDUCE*, the *INF* has the following system built-in scheduling rule: a remote operation is accepted only when it is causally ready. In many email programs, new messages will be checked out in user-specified time intervals. If *ONF/INF = U*, the propagation or acceptance of notifications is triggered by the user's explicit commands. For example, in *CVS*, changes made by a user are not made available to others unless the user issues the *commit* command.

Different collaborative systems usually take different notification frequency parameter values. For example, as shown in Figure 4.3, in *CVS*, all participants have the same parameter values: $ONF/INF = U$. So, changes made by a user are not propagated unless s/he issues the *commit* command, and these changes are not applied to another user's copy unless that user issues the *update* command. In *ICQ*, all participants have the same parameter values: $ONF = U$ and $INF = I$. So, a message is not sent out unless the user hits the *Send* button, and when the message arrives at a remote site, it will be displayed on the remote user's interface instantly. In *REDUCE*, all participants have the same parameter values: $ONF = I$ and $INF = S$. So, each editing operation generated at a site is instantly propagated and when it arrives at another site, it is executed when causally ready.

	CVS	Email	ICQ	REDUCE
ONF	*U*	*U/S*	*U*	*I*
INF	*U*	*U/S*	*I*	*S*

Figure 4.3: Frequency parameter values used in example systems

A collaborative system may allow different participants to have different notification parameter values. For example, in the *email* system, consider a scenario with two users *User A* and *User B* working as follows: suppose *User B* sent *User A* an email but *User A* was away from her/his office. Before her/his departure, s/he has configured her/his email system with the capability of periodically checking new email at specified time intervals and automatically replying to every received email with a pre-described message telling s/he is on vacation. So, when the message from *User B* was received by *User A*'s email system, it was automatically replied to with the pre-described message. *User B* can check this message manually or be automatically notified by this message if s/he has configured her/his email system with the capability of periodically checking new email at specified time intervals. So, as shown in

Figure 4.3, frequency parameter values for *User A* are: $ONF = S$ and $INF = S$, and frequency parameter values for *User B* are: $ONF = U$ and $INF = U/S$.

4.2.2 Notification granularity

The granularity parameter determines the "what" aspect of notification, that is, what changes are going to be included in a notification for propagation/acceptance. The granularity parameter may also take different values, which have been adopted in various collaborative systems. Values for *ON/IN*, denoted as *ONG/ING*, can be either *A* (All) or *S* (Selective). If *ONG/ING* = *A*, all changes accumulated since last propagation/acceptance are propagated/accepted. Most existing collaborative systems adopt this granularity policy. For example, in *CVS*, when a user issues the *commit* command, all changes accumulated since the last *commit* operation are propagated.

If *ONG/ING* = *S*, users are allowed to select changes among those that have been accumulated since the last propagation/acceptance to propagate/accept. Notification with selective granularity is flexible and usually triggered by users with explicit selection criteria. If selection criteria can be pre-defined, notification could also be automatically triggered by the system. Selection criteria are application dependent and some typical examples are as follows:

- Time criterion: a user can selectively propagate/accept changes made within a certain period of time.

- Object criterion: a user can selectively propagate/accept changes made to certain objects.

- Type criterion: a user can selectively propagate/accept certain types of changes.

- Version criterion: a user can selectively propagate/accept changes made in certain versions of a shared artifact.

- User criterion: a user can selectively notify certain users of her/his changes or selectively accept changes made by certain users.

These criteria can be used as filters for the notifying site to select certain notifications to propagate, or for the notified site to select certain notifications to accept. Carzaniga et al. presented a systematic approach to select appropriate collection of events using filters and patterns [22, 21]. Although its primary goal is not to support notification with selective granularity, most of the ideas can be directly applied or extended to define selection criteria for selective granularity.

	ICQ	CVS	Netmeeting	Email
ONF	A	A	A/S	A/S
INF	A	A/S	A	A/S

Figure 4.4: Granularity parameter values used in example systems

Different collaborative systems usually take different notification granularity parameter values. For example, as shown in Figure 4.4, in ICQ, $ONG = A$ and $ING = A$, in the sense that all composed messages that have not been propagated will be sent out as a whole with a single click of the $Send$ button, and all messages sent to a user, which have been buffered in the relay server will pop up on the screen altogether once the user turns up online. In CVS, $ONG = A$ because when a user issues the $commit$ command, all changes accumulated since the last $commit$ operation will be propagated altogether. But $ING = S$ may be taken if a user issues the $update$ command to update her/his working copy with a specified version from the repository. The selection is based on the $version$ criterion.

In $Netmeeting$ videoconference system [87], $ONG = S$ is supported in the sense that a user is able to selectively share some applications in her/his windows desktop environment. The selection is based on the $object$ criterion. But $ING = A$ is the only option in the sense that users are unable to control the update of shared applications.

In other words, a user has to accept updates to all applications that have been shared by others. In *Email* system, both $ONG = S$ and $ING = S$ are supported in the sense that a user is able to configure her/his email system with the capability of automatically delivering messages composed within a specified time period or checking out messages sent from certain users. The selection could be based on *time*, *type*, and/or *user* criteria.

Generally speaking, if the frequency of notification is high, notification tends to have a small granularity, and $ONG/ING = A$ is usually used. If the frequency of notification is low, notification may have a large granularity if $ONG/ING = A$, or could also have a small granularity if $ONG/ING = S$. The notification frequency and granularity parameters, with a combination of various values, can be used to describe a range of notification strategies used in existing collaborative systems, and to guide the design of new notification strategies.

4.2.3 Notification mechanism

The "when" and "what" aspects of notification have been explored in the policy part; however, any notification policy has to be carried out by the underlining notification mechanism, which is the technique to deal with the "how" aspect of notification, that is, how changes are propagated and accepted.

To support a range of notification policies, notification buffers are needed to buffer changes in order to allow users to select any changes to propagate/accept at any time. In particular, an OB (Outgoing Buffer) is needed at each site to accept and buffer changes generated from the local interface so that the user at this site is able to select any local changes to propagate at any time. Furthermore, an ONE (Outgoing Notification Executor) component is needed at each site to carry out various outgoing notification policies, which manages OB at this site, selects a collection of changes from OB, and properly reformulates the selected changes to propagate.

Changes are propagated to remote sites across the Internet by the *NPP* (Notification Propagation Protocol) component that is distributed across the system. There are two alternatives to design the protocol. One is the *pull* approach in which the notified site pulls changes from *OB* at the notifying site. An example of using this approach is *CVS* in which a user uses the *update* command to pull changes made by other users into her/his working copy. The other is the *Push* approach in which the notifying site pushes changes into *IB* at the notified site. The *Publish/Subscribe* paradigm [3, 14] is a typical example of using this approach, where the publisher pushes certain messages to certain subscribers who are interested.

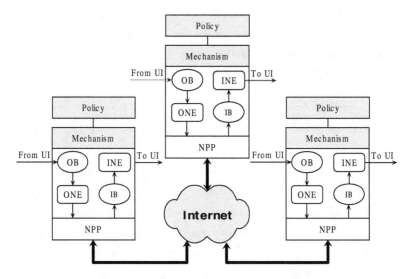

Figure 4.5: A flexible notification framework

At a notified site, notifications propagated from notifying sites are buffered into an *IB* (Incoming Buffer) by the *NPP* component. With the *IB*, the user at this site is able to select any changes made by other users to accept and reflect on the interface at any time. Similarly, an *INE* (Incoming Notification Executor) component is needed at each site to carry out various incoming notification policies, which manages *IB* at this site, selects a collection of changes from *IB*, and properly reformulates the selected changes to accept.

A flexible notification framework consisting of the above discussed components is shown in Figure 4.5. The policy part makes various application dependent notification policies by specifying frequency and granularity parameters with a combination of various values. The notification mechanism part consists of notification buffers for buffering changes made by local and remote users, notification executors for carrying out various outgoing and incoming notification policies, and the notification propagation protocol for propagating local notifications to remote sites and receiving notifications from remote sites. In the following sections, the framework is applied to the design of the notification component for a flexible group editor, which is able to support unconstrained, responsive, real-time collaborative editing; unconstrained, syncretic, non-real-time collaborative editing; and smooth, flexible switching between real-time and non-real-time collaborative editing.

4.3 Notification for flexible collaborative editing

As we know, collaborative editing allows a group of users to view and edit the same document over the network, where notification policies for meeting real-time collaboration needs have been used in various real-time systems like *REDUCE* [137], *DistEdit* [76], and *Groove* [95], while notification policies for meeting non-real-time collaboration needs have been used in various non-real-time systems like *WebDAV* [43, 44], *CVS* [10, 56], and *ClearCase* [1]. Our objective is to design the notification component for a flexible collaborative editing system, by applying the proposed flexible notification framework.

4.3.1 Related techniques

As consistency maintenance is a key issue in collaborative editing with replicated architecture, the major technical challenge of designing the notification component for the flexible collaborative editing system is how to design a notification mechanism, which is effective and efficient, to maintain consistency for both real-time and non-real-time collaborative editing. With such consistency maintenance mechanism supported by notification, switching between real-time and non-real-time collaborative editing can be supported in a smooth and flexible way simply by changing notification policies at any time.

Non-real-time systems usually do not capture individual changes made to the shared document. Instead, a notifying site infrequently propagates versions of the shared document at that site to remote sites for the purpose of consistency maintenance. At a notified site, one solution is to merge the remote version into the local version of the shared document by executing some merging algorithms. This solution has been widely used in various SCM systems such *CVS* [10, 56] and *ClearCase* [1]. Another solution is to keep either the local or the remote version of the shared document as the final version by means of mutual exclusion, which has been widely used in various Web-based coauthoring systems such as *WebDAV* [43, 44] and *BSCW* [68]. This approach does not suit real-time collaborative editing. First, it could take a long while for replicas to become consistent because frequent propagation of documents over the network and frequent execution of merging algorithms are both time-consuming. Moreover, it would not support unconstrained collaborative editing if mutual exclusion is used for concurrency control.

In contrast, real-time systems usually intercept and save individual changes made to the shared document as operations that are timestamped with state vectors [53, 78, 107] in order to capture causal/concurrent relations among operations. A notifying site frequently propagates these timestamped operations to remote sites, where they are executed under control of operational transformation algorithms for consistency maintenance. These algorithms, such as $dOPT$ [46], $adOPTed$ [109], GOT [137], or $GOTO$ [136], are complicated and have non-linear time complexity, which is acceptable for real-time collaborative editing systems owing to the limited number of operations to be transformed with, but unsuitable for non-real-time collaborative editing due to the large number of operations to be transformed with. Moreover, it is unrealistic to timestamp individual operations with state vectors for the following reasons: first, it is difficult to timestamp operations with fixed-dimension state vectors because non-real-time collaborative editing tends to have a large and unknown number of participants. Second, it is wasteful to timestamp individual operations because non-real-time collaborative editing does not propagate individual operations. Finally, it is complicated to manage state vectors for individual operations because operations saved in a log may need to be compressed from time to time in order to keep the log as small as possible [122].

Therefore the notification mechanism should avoid using state vectors to timestamp individual operations, and maintain consistency by operational transformation control algorithms that are efficient for both real-time and non-real-time collaborative editing. Moreover, the notification mechanism should include notification buffers OB and IB, notification algorithms ONE and INE, and a notification propagation protocol NPP, as suggested in Figure 4.5.

4.3.2 Notification buffers

At a site, notification buffer OB stores locally generated editing operations that have not been propagated to remote sites and notification buffer IB stores editing operations propagated from remote sites, which have not been executed at this site. On the one hand, operations in IB have not been executed at the time before operations in OB were generated. Therefore, according to Definition 1.1, given any operation

O_o in OB and O_i in IB, it could not be $O_i \rightarrow O_o$. On the other hand, operations in OB have not been propagated to any remote site at the time before operations in IB were generated, executed, and propagated from remote sites. Therefore, according to Definition 1.1, given any operation O_o in OB and O_i in IB, it could not be $O_o \rightarrow O_i$. According to Definition 1.2, operations in OB and IB at the same site must be mutually concurrent in the sense that given any operation O_o in OB and O_i in IB, it must be $O_o \parallel O_i$. As a result, timestamping editing operations with state vectors is not necessary any more because the identification of concurrent relation between operations has been achieved by notification buffers OB and IB.

Furthermore, notification buffers OB and IB at the same site have the following relation: $OB[1] \sqcup IB[1]$. Consider that a document whose initial state is S_0 is replicated at n sites. Then the first operation generated at each site should be contextually equivalent with each other. More precisely, it must be $OB_1[1] \sqcup OB_2[1] \sqcup \cdots \sqcup OB_n[1]$ because $CT_{OB_1}[1] = CT_{OB_2}[1] = \cdots = CT_{OB_n}[1] = S_0$. At any site k, the proposed notification propagation protocol ensures $IB_k[1] = OB_i[1]$ ($i = 1, 2, \cdots$, or n and $i \neq k$). Because $OB_k[1] \sqcup OB_i[1]$, then it must be $OB_k[1] \sqcup IB_k[1]$. Moreover, when some operations are propagated from OB_k or some operations are executed from IB_k, the proposed notification propagation protocol and notification algorithms always ensure $OB_k[1] \sqcup IB_k[1]$. The notification propagation protocol and notification algorithms will be described in later sections.

Finally, operations in OB and IB are *contextually serialized*. Contextual serialization of operations in a list is defined as follows:

Definition 4.1. Contextual serialization

Given a list L, operations in L are contextually serialized, *iff* L[i] $\mapsto$ L[i+1] ($1 \leq i \leq$ |L|-1), which may have the following possibilities:

1. L[i] $\rightarrow$ L[i+1], or

2. L[i+1] $\rightarrow$ L[i] and (L'[i], L'[i+1]) = **Transpose**(L[i+1], L[i]), or

3. L[i] ∥ L[i+1] and L'[i+1] = **IT**(L[i+1], L[i]).

Operations in OB were sorted in their natural causal order from left to right. Therefore according to Definition 4.1(1), they have been contextually serialized. OB could be compressed with the $COMET$ compression algorithm, presented in Section 3.14 of Chapter 3, for the sake of reducing its size and number of operations. Operations in compressed OB are still contextually serialized because the compression algorithm ensures them to meet Definition 4.1(1) or (2). Operations in IB are also contextually serialized because the proposed notification propagation protocol ensures they meet Definition 4.1(1), (2), or (3).

In sum, at any site, OB[i-1] ↦ OB[i] ($1 < i \leq$ |OB|) and IB[j-1] ↦ IB[j] ($1 < j \leq$ |IB|), and OB[1] ⊔ IB[1] and OB[i] ∥ IB[j] ($1 \leq i \leq$ |OB|, $1 \leq j \leq$ |IB|). As a result, operations are not necessary to be timestamped with state vectors and the efficient operational transformation control algorithm $SLOT$ can be used to control transformation between operations in OB and IB. As stressed in Section 3.4 of Chapter 3, the $SLOT$ transformation control algorithm is in linear time complexity. It is also simple in the sense that it does not need any exclusion transformation and avoids $TP2$ transformation property (Property 1.2 described in Section 3.4 of Chapter 3), which will be reasoned in a later section.

4.3.3   Notification algorithms

To propagate any operation O_x in OB_l at site l, the following two steps should be done: first, O_x must be transposed to the place between the last *propagated* operation and the first *unpropagated* operation in OB_l in order to support selective outgoing notification granularity. O_x should be transformed into such a form that it is contextually preceding all unpropagated operations. Consequently, when it arrives at remote site r, operations that are contextually preceding O_x in OB_l must have all arrived.

This step is done by the **LTranspose**(L) procedure defined in Section 2.3 of Chapter 2 and paves the way for maintaining contextual serialization in IB_r. Furthermore, according to Definition 4.1, operations in OB_l are still contextually serialized.

In the second step, O_x must be transformed against all operations in IB_l before propagation to ensure operations in IB_r must be either operations from OB_l that are contextually preceding O_x, or operations from other sites that are concurrent with O_x but have been transformed to be contextually preceding O_x. Consequently, when O_x arrives at remote site r, it can be simply appended in IB_r to maintain contextual serialization. On the other hand, operations in IB_l must also be transformed against O_x into such a form that they are contextually following O_x in order to correctly preserve their intentions [137]. Consequently, when O_x has been propagated, the first unpropagated operation in OB_l (i.e., the operation right after O_x) is still contextually equivalent with the first operation in IB_l.

The *AnyONE* outgoing notification algorithm selects a list of operations $[O_{P_1}, \cdots, O_{P_k}]$ from an outgoing buffer $OB = [O_1, \cdots, O_n]$ $(1 \leq P_1 \cdots P_k \leq n)$, transforms these operations, and propagates them as an outgoing notification. The algorithm can support various outgoing notification policies and is described as follows:

Algorithm 4.1. *AnyONE([$O_{P_1}, \cdots, O_{P_k}$]): [$O''_{P_1}, \cdots, O''_{P_k}$]*

Suppose $OB = [O_1, \cdots, O_m, \cdots, O_n]$. A pointer called $ILPO = \text{ID}(O_m)$ (Identifier of Last Propagated Operation) is maintained to remember the last propagated operation in OB. Any O_i $(1 \leq i \leq m)$ is a *propagated* operation and any O_j $(m < i \leq n)$ is an *unpropagated* operation. The following steps are executed to propagate the list of operations $[O_{P_1}, \cdots, O_{P_k}]$ where $m < P_1 < \cdots < P_k \leq n$.

1. Transpose $O_{P_1}, \cdots, O_{P_k}$ to the place after O_m by repeatedly using the *LTranspose* procedure: **for** $(i = 1; i \leq k; i++)$ **{** *LTranspose*(L[m+1, P_i]); **}**
   After that, OB becomes $[O_1, \cdots, O_m, O'_{P_1}, \cdots, O'_{P_k}, O'_{U_1}, \cdots, O'_{U_l}]$ where $m < U_1 < \cdots < U_l \leq n$ and $U_x \neq P_y$ $(1 \leq x \leq l$ and $1 \leq y \leq k)$.

2. If IB is empty, skip this step. Otherwise suppose $IB = [O_1, \cdots, O_r]$. Transform the selected list of operations $[O'_{P_1}, \cdots, O'_{P_k}]$ with all operations in IB by $SLOT([O'_{P_1}, \cdots, O'_{P_k}], IB)$. After that, OB becomes $[O_1, \cdots, O_m, O''_{P_1}, \cdots, O''_{P_k}, O'_{U_1}, \cdots, O'_{U_l}]$ and IB becomes $[O'_1, \cdots, O'_r]$.

3. Propagate the list of operations $[O''_{P_1}, \cdots, O''_{P_k}]$ in a notification message and set $ILPO$ to $ID(O''_{P_k})$.

To execute any operation O_y in IB_l at site l, the following two steps need to be done. First, O_y must be transposed to the left-most side of IB_l in order to support selective incoming notification granularity. O_y should be transformed into such a form that it is contextually preceding the rest of operations in IB_l. Secondly, O_y should be transformed with all *unpropagated* operations in OB_l to correctly preserve their intentions [137]. Operations in OB_l should be concurrent with operations in IB_l. But O_y must have already been transformed with those *propagated* operations in OB_l before propagation. So O_y only needs to be transformed with those *unpropagated* operations in OB_l. Consequently, when O_y is executed and removed from IB_1, the first operation in IB_l must still be contextually equivalent with the first *unpropagated* operation in OB_l.

The *AnyINE* incoming notification algorithm selects a list of operations $[O_{A_1}, \cdots, O_{A_k}]$ from an incoming buffer $IB = [O_1, \cdots, O_n]$ $(1 \leq A_1 \cdots A_k \leq n)$, transforms these operations, and executes them sequentially. The algorithm can support various incoming notification policies and is described as follows:

Algorithm 4.2. *AnyINE($[O_{A_1}, \cdots, O_{A_k}]$): $[O''_{A_1}, \cdots, O''_{A_k}]$*

Suppose $IB = [O_1, \cdots, \cdots, O_n]$. The following steps are executed to execute the list of operations $[O_{A_1}, \cdots, O_{A_k}]$ where $1 \leq A_1 < \cdots < A_k \leq n$.

1. Transpose $O_{A_1}, \cdots, O_{A_k}$ to the left-most position in IB by repeatedly using the *LTranspose* procedure: **for** $(i = 1; i \leq k; i++)$ **{** *LTranspose(L[1, A_i]);***}**

After that, IB becomes $[O'_{A_1}, \cdots, O'_{A_k}, O'_{U_1}, \cdots, O'_{U_l}]$ where $1 < U_1 < \cdots < U_l \leq n$ and $U_x \neq A_y$ ($1 \leq x \leq l$ and $1 \leq y \leq k$).

2. If OB contains no *unpropagated* operation, skip this step. Otherwise suppose $OB = [O_1, \cdots, O_m, \cdots, O_n]$ with $ILPO = ID(O_m)$. Transform the selected list of operations $[O'_{A_1}, \cdots, O'_{A_k}]$ with the list of *unpropagated* operations $[O_{m+1}, \cdots, O_n]$ by $SLOT([O_{m+1}, \cdots, O_n], [O'_{A_1}, \cdots, O'_{A_k}])$. After that, IB becomes $[O''_{A_1}, \cdots, O''_{A_k}, O'_{U_1}, \cdots, O'_{U_l}]$ and OB becomes $[O_1, \cdots, O_m, O'_{m+1}, \cdots, O'_n]$.

3. Execute operations $O''_{A_1}, \cdots, O''_{A_k}$ and remove them from IB. After that, $IB = [O'_{U_1}, \cdots, O'_{U_l}]$. Then set the pointer $ILAO$ (Identifier of Last Accepted Operation) to $ID(O''_{A_k})$ to remember the last accepted operation from IB.

4.3.4 Notification propagation protocol

As mentioned in a previous section, the notification propagation protocol is crucial for achieving contextual serialization. To support real-time notification policies, the notification propagation protocol should be push-based because the *pull* approach is unsuitable for supporting real-time notification policies [45]. Therefore, in the proposed notification propagation protocol, a notifying site will voluntarily push notifications to notified sites, where they will be waiting for acceptance. More importantly, notifications are contextually serialized, which can be implemented in many ways. Notification server are widely used in distributed collaborative systems for notification specification and filtering [22, 21, 116], notification message relaying [58, 105], and notification serialization [99, 125]. For instance, many publish-subscribe systems [3, 14, 152] use a notification server to receive subscription information from users and to send certain publications to those users who are interested. Therefore, we use the notification server as an example to illustrate the proposed notification propagation protocol for achieving contextual serialization [125].

Sequential propagation

To achieve contextual serialization, one approach is sequential propagation, where only one notification is outstanding at any time. In this case, the *Notification server* manages a token to control propagation of notifications and only the site that has been granted the token is able to propagate a notification. As shown in Figure 4.6, before propagating a notification, the notifying site sends a *Token-Request* message to the *Notification server*, waiting for the *Token-Grant* message from the *Notification server*. After being granted the token, the site propagates the notification piggybacked with the *Token-Release* message to the *Notification server*. When the *Notification server* receives the notification message, it forwards the notification to notified sites and makes the token available to other waiting sites (if any). When receiving a notification message, a notified site appends operations in the notification message into its IB.

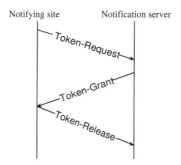

Figure 4.6: Sequential notification propagation protocol

Sequential propagation simplifies concurrency control because for any operation O_x in OB_k at site k, operations that have been propagated and are concurrent with O_x must all be in IB_k. As a result, O_x only needs to be transformed with all operations in IB_k before propagation at the notifying site. VIDOT *et al.* [143] proposed a total order based propagation protocol in order to simplify operational transformation control algorithm, which is also a sequential propagation protocol. However, sequential propagation in general is inefficient for supporting real-time notification policies because three extra messages *Token-Request*, *Token-Grant*, and *Token-Release* have to be exchanged between the *Notification server* and the notifying site to propagate each notification. Although the *Token-Release* message could be avoided by piggybacking it in the notification message and the *Token-Grant* message could possibly be avoided by piggybacking it in the notification message, there is no way to avoid the *Token-Request* message.

Concurrent propagation

An alternative approach to achieve contextual serialization is concurrent propagation, which allows a site to propagate its notification without first requesting the token, effectively eliminating the *Token-Request* message and efficiently supporting real-time notification policies. However, without the token, any site can propagate a notification at any time and multiple notifications could be outstanding at the same time, which makes concurrency control more difficult.

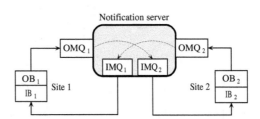

Figure 4.7: Concurrent notification propagation protocol

To tackle the issue of concurrency control, the *Notification server* maintains an *OMQ* (Outgoing Message Queue) and an *IMQ* (Incoming Message Queue) for each site to buffer notification messages into and out of the *Notification server*. As shown in Figure 4.7, outgoing notifications are propagated from *OB* at a notifying site to its corresponding OMQ at the *Notification server*. Propagated notifications are not removed from OB at the time of propagation, which instead are backed up there for a certain period in order to cope with concurrent outstanding notifications. The *Notification server* performs concurrency control and then delivers transformed notifications to other sites. In addition, all delivered notifications are also backed up in IMQ in order to cope with concurrent outstanding notifications.

In Figure 4.7, operations that are concurrent with a propagated operation from OB_1 could be in IB_1, on the way from IMQ_1 to IB_1, in IMQ_1, in OMQ_2, on the way from OB_2 to OMQ_2, or in OB_2. Therefore, concurrency control is first done at *Site 1* by performing operational transformation between operations to be propagated in OB_1 and all operations in IB_1. Concurrency control is then done at *Notification server* by enforcing mutually exclusive access to incoming messages queues and by performing operational transformation between operations in OMQ_1 and operations in IMQ_1. Concurrency control is finally done at *Site 2* by performing operational transformation between operations in IB_2 and *unpropagated* operations in OB_2. The challenge here is how to ensure each operation at any segment of the propagation path be transformed with all concurrent operations.

Because outstanding outgoing notifications are duplicated in OB at a notifying site and its corresponding OMQ at the *Notification server*, and outstanding incoming notifications are duplicated in IMQ for a notified site at the *Notification server* and IB at that site, a mechanism is needed to keep track of concurrent operations that need to be transformed with in order to achieve contextual serialization and to remove operations that have already been transformed with. To that end, in a notification message, in addition to a list of propagating operations L, there should be a reference called *ILTO* (Identifier of the Last Transformed Operation), which remembers the identifer of the last operation that the list of operations have been transformed with. The identifier of an operation consists of two fields: *Site-Id* (the identity number of the site which generates the operation) and *Seq-No* (the sequence number of the operation generated at that site). Furthermore, to ensure contextual serialization, access to the data structures of *IMQ*s inside the *Notification server* is serialized by mutual exclusion.

For a notification message at a notifying site, the list of propagating operations L is produced by the *AnyONE* outgoing notification algorithm: $L = \textbf{AnyONE}([O_{P_1}, \cdots, O_{P_k}])$ according to the specified outgoing notification policy and the *ILTO* reference is determined by the following *getILTO* function: $ILTO = \textbf{getILTO}(ILAO, IB)$.

Function 4.1. *getILTO(ILAO, IB): ILTO*

{   **if** $(|IB| == 0)$

    $ILTO = ILAO$;

  else

    $ILTO = \textbf{ID}(\text{IB}[|IB|])$;

  return *ILTO*;

}

Referring to Figure 4.7, when a notification message generated at the notifying site *Site 1* is propagated to the *Notification server*, it will be buffered in OMQ_1, waiting for access to *IMQ*s inside the *Notification server*. When access is granted for *Site 1*, the following steps will be repeatedly executed until there is no notification messages in OMQ_1 any more.

1. Obtain the first notification message in OMQ_1: $Msg = OMQ_1[1]$.

2. Remove notification messages that have been transformed with operations in *Msg.L* from IMQ_1 by the **removeMessage** (IMQ_1, *Msg.ILTO*) procedure.

3. Transform operations in *Msg.L* with operations in the remaining notification messages in IMQ_1 by the **transformMessage**(IMQ_1, *Msg.L*) procedure.

4. Update *Msg.ILTO* by the **updateILTO**(IMQ_1, *Msg.ILTO*) procedure.

5. Append the notification message *Msg* to *IMQ*s for all notified sites and push it to notified sites by the **pushMessage**(*Site-Id*, *Msg*) procedure.

6. Remove the notification message *Msg* from OMQ_1: **remove**($OMQ_1[1]$).

Finally, when the notification message *Msg* arrives at a notified site *Site 2*, the following steps will be executed:

1. Remove operations that have been transformed with operations in *Msg.L* from OB_2 by the **removeOperation** (OB_2, $ILPO_2$, *Msg.ILTO*) procedure.

2. Transform operations in *Msg.L* with the remaining *propagated* operations in OB_2 by **transformOperation**(OB_2, $ILPO_2$, *Msg.L*) procedure.

3. Append operations in *Msg.L* to IB_2, which will be executed by **AnyINE**($[O_{A_1}$, $\cdots, O_{A_k}]$) according to the specified incoming notification policy.

The **removeMessage**(*IMQ*, *Msg.ILTO*) procedure is defined to remove notification messages that have been transformed with operations in *Msg.L* from *IMQ*. *Msg.ILTO* records the identifier of the last operation in *IB*. If there exists an operation O in *IMQ* such that **ID**(O) = *Msg.ILTO*, then operations in *Msg.L* must have been transformed with all operations till O in *IMQ*. Consequently, all operations before and including O in *IMQ* should be removed.

Procedure 4.1. *removeMessage(IMQ, Msg.ILTO)*

```
{    for (i = 1; i ≤ |IMQ|; i++)
          if (ID(IMQ[i].L[|L|]) == Msg.ILTO)
              break;
     if (i ≤ |IMQ|)
          for (j = 1; j ≤ i; j++)
              remove(IMQ[1]);
}
```

The **transformMessage**(*IMQ, Msg.L*) procedure is defined to transform operations in *Msg.L* with operations in *IMQ*. Operations that have been transformed with operations in *Msg.L* have been removed from *IMQ*, therefore, the remaining operations in *IMQ* must have not been transformed with operations in *Msg.L*.

Procedure 4.2. *transformMessage(IMQ, Msg.L)*

{   **for** $(i = 1; i \leq |IMQ|; i{+}{+})$

       SLOT(*IMQ*[i].*L, Msg.L*);

}

The **updateILTO**(*IMQ, Msg.ILTO*) procedure is defined to update *Msg.ILTO* after operations in *Msg.L* have been transformed with operations in *IMQ*.

Procedure 4.3. *updateILTO(IMQ, Msg.ILTO)*

{   **if** $(|\text{IMQ}| > 0)$

       Msg.ILTO = **ID**(IMQ[|IMQ|].L[|L|]);

}

The **pushMessage**(*Site-Id, Msg*) procedure is defined to append notification message *Msg* to the message queue $IMQ_{Site-Id}$ and push it to the site *Site-Id*.

Procedure 4.4. *pushMessage(Site-Id, Msg)*

{ $IMQ_{Site-Id}$ += *Msg*;

       sendMsg2Site (*Msg, Site-Id*);

}

The **removeOperation**(*OB, ILPO, Msg.ILTO*) procedure is defined to remove propagated operations that have been transformed with operations in *Msg.L* from *OB*. *Msg.ILTO* records the identifier of the last transformed operation. If there exists an operation *O* in *OB* such that **ID**(*O*) = *Msg.ILTO*, then operations in *Msg.L* must have been transformed with all operations till *O* in *OB*. Consequently, all operations before and including *O* in *OB* should be removed.

Procedure 4.5. *removeOperation(OB, ILPO, Msg.ILTO)*

{ **if** (*ILPO* == *nil* **or** *ILPO.Site-Id* ≠ *Msg.ILTO.Site-Id*)

    return;

   else

   { **for** ($i = 1; i \leq |OB|; i$++)

        if (**ID**(OB[i]) == *Msg.ILTO* **or** OB[i]) == *ILPO*)

           break;

     if ($i \leq |OB|$ **and** **ID**(OB[i]) == *Msg.ILTO*)

       for ($j = 1; j \leq i; j$++)

       { **if** (**ID**(OB[1]) == *ILPO*)

          ILPO = *nil*;

         remove(OB[1]);

       }

   }

}

The **transformOperation**(*OB*, *ILPO*, *Msg.L*) procedure is defined to transform operations in *Msg.L* with propagated operations in *OB*. Operations that have been transformed with operations in *Msg.L* have been removed from *OB*, therefore, the remaining propagated operations in *OB* must have not been transformed with operations in *Msg.L*.

Procedure 4.6. *transformOperation(OB, ILPO, Msg.L)*

{ **if** (*ILPO* == *nil*)

    return;

   else

   { **for** ($i = 1; i \leq |OB|; i$++)

    { L += OB[i];

      if (**ID**(OB[i]) == *ILPO*)

        break;

```
        }
        SLOT(L, Msg.L);
    }
}
```

The *SCOP* (Symmetric Contextually-serialized Operation Propagation) concurrent notification propagation protocol is described as follows:

Protocol 4.1. *SCOP notification propagation protocol*

1. At any notifying site s, an outgoing notification message *Msg* is made up of $Msg.L = \mathbf{AnyONE}([O_{P_1}, \cdots, O_{P_k}])$ and $Msg.ILTO = \mathbf{getILTO}(ILAO_s, IB_s)$, which is propagated to the *Notification server*.

2. At the *Notification server*, *Msg* is appended to OMQ_s: $OMQ_s\ +\!= Msg$, waiting for exclusive access to *IMQ*s. When the access is granted, the following code will be executed:

```
while (|OMQ_s| > 0)
{   Msg = OMQ_s[1];
    removeMessage(IMQ_s, Msg.ILTO);
    transformMessage(IMQ_s, Msg.L);
    updateILTO(IMQ_s, Msg.ILTO);
    for (i = 1; i ≤ Number of notified sites; i++)
        pushMessage(i, Msg);
    remove(OMQ_s[1]);
}
```

3. At any notified site r, when a notification message *Msg* arrives, the following code will be executed:

```
removeOperation(OB_r, ILPO_r, Msg.ILTO);
transformOperation(OB_r, ILPO_r, Msg.L);
```

for $(i = 1; i \leq |Msg.L|; i{+}{+})$

$\quad IB_r \mathrel{+}= Msg.L[i];$

4.3.5 A comprehensive example

A comprehensive example is used to illustrate various technical contributions in supporting flexible collaborative editing, including notification buffers, notification algorithms, and the concurrent notification propagation protocol. As shown in Figure 4.8, consider that a document initially contained string *abcd* replicated at two sites *Site 1* and *Site 2*. The user at *Site 1* performed an operation $O_1 = \mathbf{Del}[1, 2, \text{bc}]$ to delete two characters from position 1 (i.e., characters *b* and *c*). Concurrently, the user at *Site 2* performed operation $O_2 = \mathbf{Del}[0, 1, \text{a}]$ to delete one character from position 0 (i.e., character *a*) and a subsequent operation $O_3 = \mathbf{Ins}[2, 1, \text{x}]$ to insert a character *x* at position 2 (i.e., between the character *c* and *d*).

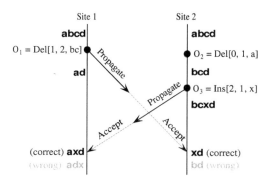

Figure 4.8: An example of flexible collaborative editing

When *Site 1* propagates operation O_1 to *Site 2*, *Site 2* selectively propagates operation O_3 to *Site 1* at the same time. When the notification on O_1 is accepted at *Site 2*, to correctly preserve O_1's intention, characters *b* and *c* should be deleted, resulting in the final document state xd at *Site 2*. However, executing O_1 as is would lead to the wrong document state bd. Similarly, when the notification on O_3 is accepted at *Site 1*, to correctly preserve O_3's intention, characters x should be inserted before character d, resulting in the final document state axd at *Site 1*. However, executing O_3 as is would lead to the wrong document state adx.

We use this example to illustrate how consistency is maintained under control of the *SCOP* notification propagation protocol in flexible collaborative editing. Before propagation of O_1 and O_3 from *Site 1* and *Site 2*, all message queues at the *Notification server* are empty. At *Site 1*, $OB_1 = [O_1]$ with $ILPO_1 = nil$, indicating there is no propagated operation in OB_1 and IB_1 is empty with $ILAO_1 = nil$, indicating there is no accepted operation at *Site 1*. At *Site 2*, $OB_2 = [O_2, O_3]$ with $ILPO_2 = nil$, indicating there is no propagated operation in OB_2 and IB_1 is empty with $ILAO_2 = nil$, indicating there is no accepted operation at *Site 2*.

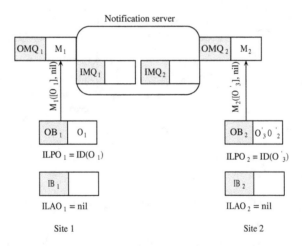

Figure 4.9: Generation of notification messages M_1 and M_2

Generation of notification messages M_1 and M_2

As shown in Figure 4.9, at *Site 1*, because O_1 is the only operation in OB_1 and IB_1 is empty, notification message M_1 is generated with $M_1.L = \textbf{AnyONE}([O_1])$ $= [O_1]$ and $M_1.ILTO = \textbf{getILTO}(IB_1, ILAO_1) = nil$. After M_1 is propagated, $ILPO_1 = \textbf{ID}(O_1)$. At *Site 2*, notification message M_2 is generated with $M_2.L = \textbf{AnyONE}([O_3]) = [O_3']$ and $M_2.ILTO = \textbf{getILTO}(IB_2, ILAO_2) = nil$. $OB_2 = [O_3', O_2'] = \textbf{LTranspose}(OB_1[1, 2])$ where $O_3' = \textbf{ET\_ID}(O_3, O_2) = \textbf{Ins}[3, 1, x]$ and $O_2' = \textbf{IT\_DI}(O_2, O_3') = \textbf{Ins}[0, 1, a]$. After M_2 is propagated, $ILPO_2 = \textbf{ID}(O_3')$.

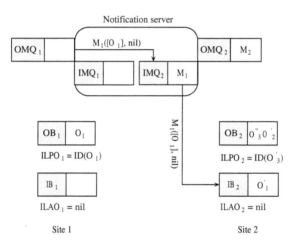

Figure 4.10: Propagation of notification message M_1

Propagation of notification message M_1

When notification message M_1 is propagated from *Site 1* to the *Notification server*, it is buffered in OMQ_1. When access is granted, the following steps will be executed as shown in Figure 4.10. Firstly, remove notification messages from IMQ_1 by **removeMessage**(IMQ_1, $M_1.ILTO$). Because IMQ_1 is empty and/or $M_1.ILTO$

$= nil$, nothing will be removed. Secondly, transform the operation in $M_1.L = [O_1]$ with operations in IMQ_1 by **transformMessage** (IMQ_1, $M_1.L$). Because IMQ_1 is empty, no transformation happens. Thirdly, update $M_1.ILTO$ by **updateILTO**(IMQ_1, $M_1.ILTO$). Because IMQ_1 is empty, $M_1.ILTO$ remains $Inil$. Fourthly, append M_1 to IMQ_2 and push it to *Site 2*. Finally remove M_1 from OMQ_1.

When M_1 arrives at *Site 2*, the following steps will be executed. Firstly, remove propagated operations from OB_2 by **removeOperation**(OB_2, $ILPO_2$, $M_1.ILTO$). Because $M_1.ILTO = nil$, no operation will be removed from OB_2. Secondly, transform the operation in $M_1.L = [O_1]$ with propagated operations in OB_2 (i.e., O_3') by **transformOperation**(OB_2, $ILPO_2$, $M_1.L$). After **SLOT**($[O_3']$, $[O_1]$), $M_1.L = [O_1']$ where $O_1' = \textbf{IT\_DI}(O_1, O_3') = \textbf{Del}[1, 2, bc]$ and $OB_2 = [O_3'', O_2']$ where $O_3'' = \textbf{IT\_ID}(O_3', O_1) = \textbf{Ins}[1, 1, x]$. Finally, append the operation in $M_1.L = [O_1']$ to IB_2.

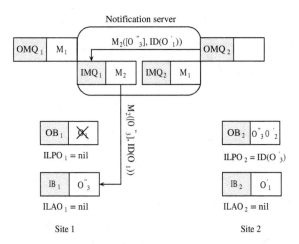

Figure 4.11: Propagation of notification message M_2

Propagation of notification message M_2

When notification message M_2 is propagated from *Site 2* to the *Notification server*, it is buffered in OMQ_2. When access is granted, the following steps will be executed as shown in Figure 4.11. Firstly, remove notification messages from IMQ_2 by **removeMessage**$(IMQ_2, M_2.ILTO)$. Because $M_2.ILTO = nil$, nothing will be removed. Secondly, transform the operation in $M_2.L = [O_3']$ with the operation in $M_1.L = [O_1]$ in IMQ_2 by **transformMessage** $(IMQ_2, M_2.L)$. After **SLOT**$([O_3'], [O_1])$, $M_2.L = [O_3'']$ where $O_3'' = \textbf{IT\_ID}(O_3', O_1) = \textbf{Ins}[1, 1, x]$ and $M_1.L = [O_1']$ where $O_1' = \textbf{IT\_DI}(O_1, O_3') = \textbf{Del}[1, 2, bc]$. Thirdly, update $M_2.ILTO$ by **updateILTO**$(IMQ_2, M_2.ILTO)$: $M_2.ILTO = \textbf{ID}(IMQ_2[1].L[1]) = \textbf{ID}(O_1')$. Fourthly, append M_2 to IMQ_1 and push it to *Site 1*. Finally remove M_2 from OMQ_2.

When M_2 arrives at *Site 1*, the following steps will be executed. Firstly, removing propagated operations from OB_1 by **removeOperation**$(OB_1, ILPO_1, M_2.ILTO)$. Because $\textbf{ID}(OB_1[1]) = \textbf{ID}(O_1) = M_2.ILTO = ILPO_1$, O_1 should be removed from OB_1. After then, OB_1 is empty and $ILPO_1 = nil$. Secondly, transform operations in $M_2.L$ with propagated operations in OB_1 by **transformOperation**$(OB_1, ILPO_1, M_2.L)$. Because OB_1 is empty and/or $ILPO_1 = nil$, no transformation happens. Finally, append the operation in $M_2.L = [O_3'']$ to IB_1.

Acceptance of notifications

To accept the remote notification on operation O_3 from *Site 2*, *Site 1* executes **AnyINE**$([O_3''])$ as shown in Figure 4.12. Because there is no unpropagated operation in OB_1, O_3'' is executed as is on the current document state ad to generate a new document state axd, which correctly preserves O_3's intention. Then O_3'' is removed from IB_1 and $ILAO_1$ is set to $ID(O_3'')$. To accept the remote notification on operation O_1 from *Site 1*, *Site 2* executes **AnyINE**$([O_1'])$ as shown in Figure 4.12. Firstly, because $ILPO_2 = \textbf{ID}(O_3')$, O_1' will be transformed with the unpropagated operation O_2' in OB_2 by **SLOT**$([O_1'], [O_2'])$. After then, $OB_2 = [O_3'', O_2'']$ where $O_2'' = $ **IT_DD**$(O_2', O_1') = $ **Del**$[0, 1, a]$ and $O_1'' = $ **IT_DD**$(O_1', O_2') = $ **Del**$[0, 2, bc]$. Secondly, O_1'' is executed on the current document state $bcxd$ to generate a new document state xd, which correctly preserves O_1's intention. Finally, O_1' is removed from IB_2 and $ILAO_2$ is set to $ID(O_1'')$.

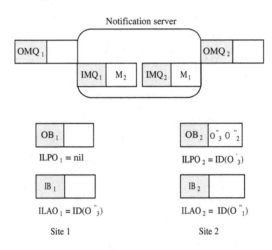

Figure 4.12: Acceptance of notifications on operations O_1 and O_3

Analogically, when the notification on operation O_2 is propagated from *Site 2* and accepted at *Site 1*, its intention will be correctly preserved, and the two sites will be convergent in the document state xd.

4.4   Discussions on propagation protocols

In this section, we discuss how the *SCOP* notification propagation protocol is able to maintain consistency for flexible collaborative editing. The consistency model proposed for real-time collaborative editing is also suitable for addressing consistency criteria in flexible collaborative editing, where consistency is maintained if the properties of convergence, intention, and causality are preserved [137].

Optimistic concurrency control based on operational transformation technology is used for consistency maintenance in the *SCOP* notification propagation protocol. Therefore intention is preserved by operational transformation functions. Moreover, collaborating sites and the *Notification server* form a star-like topology with the *Notification server* at the center of the topology, relaying notification messages from all collaborating sites. In this sense, the *Notification server* has the function of being the central *propagator*, which is able to preserve causality among notification messages [134]. We now discuss the preservation of convergence by the *SCOP* protocol, where three essential technical components have been identified.

4.4.1   SLOT transformation control algorithm

The first technical component is the *SLOT* transformation control algorithm. As already discussed in Section 3.4 of Chapter 3, the *SLOT* transformation control algorithm is able to preserve convergence in the sense that is illustrated as follows: given any two list of operations L_1 and L_2 generated at two sites, where $L_1[i] \mapsto L_1[i+1]$ ($1 \leq i < |L_1|$) and $L_2[j] \mapsto L_1[j+1]$ ($1 \leq j < |L_2|$), if $L_1[1] \sqcup L_2[1]$ and $L_1[i] \parallel L_2[j]$ ($1 \leq i \leq |L_1|$, $1 \leq j \leq |L_2|$), then $\mathbf{SLOT}(L_1, L_2) = (L_1', L_2')$ can be performed to derive two lists of operations L_1' and L_2' that can be executed at the two sites respectively to preserve convergence in the sense $L_1 \circ L_2' \equiv L_2 \circ L_1'$. Moreover, if $\mathbf{SLOT}(L_1, L_2) = (L_1', L_2')$, then operations in the compound list $L = L_1 \circ L_2'$ or $L_2 \circ L_1'$ must have been contextually serialized in the sense that $L[k] \mapsto L[k+1]$ where $1 \leq k < |L_1|+|L_2|$. We first prove that notification propagation protocol based on sequential propagation is able to preserve convergence.

Theorem 4.1. *Given n lists of operations $L_1, \cdots, L_n$ concurrently generated at n sites, under control of sequential notification propagation protocol, all sites are convergent when all operations have been transformed and executed at these sites.*

Proof: Sequential notification propagation protocol ensures at most one outstanding notification at any moment. Any notifying site that wants to propagate a notification must first request the token from the *Notification server*, (if granted) then transform operations in its *OB* with all operations in its *IB*, and finally propagate and append transformed operations to the *IB*s at all notified sites and remove them from its *OB*. For the sake of illustration, we denote L_i^{jk} ($1 \leq i \neq j \neq k \leq n$) as the transformed form of L_i after L_i has been transformed with L_j and L_k. Suppose these n sites will be granted the token in the order of from 1 to n.

For $n = 2$, OB_1 stores the list of operations L_1 generated at *Site 1* and OB_2 stores the list of operations L_2 generated at *Site 2*. When *Site 1* is granted the token to propagate the list of operations L_1, L_1 will be propagated and removed from OB_1, and then appended to IB_2 at *Site 2* as-is because IB_1 is empty. Subsequently, when *Site 2* is granted the token to propagate the list of operations L_2, it must $OB_1 = [\ ]$ and $IB_1 = [\ ]$, and $OB_2 = L_2$ and $IB_2 = L_1$. Because $OB_2[i] \mapsto OB_2[i+1]$ ($1 \leq i < |L_2|$) and $IB_2[j] \mapsto IB_2[j+1]$ ($1 \leq j < |L_1|$), and $OB_2[1] \sqcup IB_2[1]$ and $OB_2[i] \parallel IB_2[j]$ ($1 \leq i \leq |L_2|, 1 \leq j \leq |L_1|$), *Site 2* will first transform OB_2 with IB_2 by **SLOT**(L_2, L_1) = (L_2^1, L_1^2), then propagate and remove L_2^1 from OB_2, and finally append L_2^1 to IB_1 at *Site 1*. After that, $IB_1 = L_2^1$ and $IB_2 = L_1^2$. According to Theorem 3.2 in Chapter 3, it must be $L_1 \circ L_2^1 \equiv L_2 \circ L_1^2$. When operations in IB_1 have been executed at *Site 1* and operations in IB_2 have been executed at *Site 2*, the two sites would be convergent in the sense that $L_1 \circ L_2^1 \equiv L_2 \circ L_1^2$. Moreover, the compound list of $L_1 \circ L_2^1$ or $L_2 \circ L_1^2$ is contextually serialized.

Suppose the theorem holds for $n = m$ in the sense that $L_1 \circ L_2^1 \circ L_3^{12} \circ \cdots \circ L_m^{1 \cdots m-1} \equiv L_2 \circ L_1^2 \circ L_3^{12} \cdots \circ L_m^{1 \cdots m-1} \equiv \cdots \equiv L_m \circ L_1^m \circ L_2^{1m} \circ L_3^{12m} \circ \cdots \circ L_{m-1}^{1 \cdots m} \ \square$. Moreover, operations in the compound list of $L_1 \circ L_2^1 \circ L_3^{12} \circ \cdots \circ L_m^{1 \cdots m-1}$ is contextually serialized. We will prove the theorem holds for $n = m+1$.

For $n = m+1$, when *Site m+1* is granted the token to propagate the list of operations L_{m+1}, it must be $OB_1 = [\ ]$ and $IB_1 = L_2^1 \circ L_3^{12} \circ \cdots \circ L_m^{1\cdots m-1}$ at *Site 1*, $OB_2 = [\ ]$ and $IB_2 = L_1^2 \circ L_3^{12} \circ \cdots \circ L_m^{1\cdots m-1}$ at *Site 2*, $\cdots$, $OB_m = [\ ]$ and $IB_m = L_1^m \circ L_2^{1m} \circ L_3^{12m} \circ \cdots \circ L_{m-1}^{1\cdots m}$ at *Site m*, and $OB_{m+1} = L_{m+1}$ and $IB_{m+1} = L_1 \circ L_2^1 \circ L_3^{12} \circ \cdots \circ L_m^{1\cdots m-1}$ at *Site m+1*. Because $OB_{m+1}[i] \mapsto OB_{m+1}[i+1]$ $(1 \le i < |L_{m+1}|)$, $IB_{m+1}[j] \mapsto IB_{m+1}[j+1]$ $(1 \le j < |L_1|+|L_2|+\cdots+|L_m|)$, $OB_{m+1}[1] \sqcup IB_{m+1}[1]$ and $OB_{m+1}[i] \parallel IB_{m+1}[j]$ $(1 \le i \le |L_{m+1}|, 1 \le j \le |L_1|+|L_2|+\cdots+|L_m|)$, *Site m+1* will first transform OB_{m+1} with IB_{m+1} by $SLOT(L_{m+1}, L_1 \circ L_2^1 \circ L_3^{12} \circ \cdots \circ L_m^{1\cdots m-1}) = (L_{m+1}^{1\cdots m}, L_1^{m+1} \circ L_2^{1m+1} \circ L_3^{12m+1} \circ \cdots \circ L_m^{1\cdots m-1m+1})$, then propagate and remove $L_{m+1}^{1\cdots m}$ from OB_{m+1}, and finally append $L_{m+1}^{1\cdots m}$ to IB_1 at *Site 1*, IB_2 at *Site 2*, $\cdots$, and IB_m at *Site m* respectively. After that, $IB_1 = L_2^1 \circ L_3^{12} \circ \cdots \circ L_m^{1\cdots m-1} \circ L_{m+1}^{1\cdots m}$, $IB_2 = L_1^2 \circ L_3^{12} \circ \cdots \circ L_m^{1\cdots m-1} \circ L_{m+1}^{1\cdots m}$, $\cdots$, $IB_m = L_1^m \circ L_2^{1m} \circ L_3^{12m} \circ \cdots \circ L_{m-1}^{1\cdots m} \circ L_{m+1}^{1\cdots m}$, and $IB_{m+1} = L_1^{m+1} \circ L_2^{1m+1} \circ L_3^{12m+1} \circ \cdots \circ L_m^{1\cdots m-1m+1}$. According to Theorem 3.2 in Chapter 3, it must be $L_{m+1} \circ L_1^{m+1} \circ L_2^{1m+1} \circ L_3^{12m+1} \circ \cdots \circ L_m^{1\cdots m-1m+1} \equiv L_1 \circ L_2^1 \circ L_3^{12} \circ \cdots \circ L_m^{1\cdots m-1} \circ L_{m+1}^{1\cdots m} \ \Diamond$.

When operations in IB_1, IB_2, $\cdots$, IB_m, IB_{m+1} have been executed at *Site 1*, *Site 2*, $\cdots$, *Site m*, and *Site m+1* respectively, these $m+1$ sites would be convergent in the sense that $L_1 \circ L_2^1 \circ L_3^{12} \circ \cdots \circ L_m^{1\cdots m-1} \circ L_{m+1}^{1\cdots m} \equiv L_2 \circ L_1^2 \circ L_3^{12} \circ \cdots \circ L_m^{1\cdots m-1} \circ L_{m+1}^{1\cdots m} \equiv \cdots \equiv L_m \circ L_1^m \circ L_2^{1m} \circ L_3^{12m} \circ \cdots \circ L_{m-1}^{1\cdots m} \circ L_{m+1}^{1\cdots m} \equiv L_{m+1} \circ L_1^{m+1} \circ L_2^{1m+1} \circ L_3^{12m+1} \circ \cdots \circ L_m^{1\cdots m-1m+1}$, which can be reasoned as follows. On the one hand, it can be derived from $\Box$ that $L_1 \circ L_2^1 \circ L_3^{12} \circ \cdots \circ L_m^{1\cdots m-1} \circ L_{m+1}^{1\cdots m} \equiv L_2 \circ L_1^2 \circ L_3^{12} \circ \cdots \circ L_m^{1\cdots m-1} \circ L_{m+1}^{1\cdots m} \equiv \cdots \equiv L_m \circ L_1^m \circ L_2^{1m} \circ L_3^{12m} \circ \cdots \circ L_{m-1}^{1\cdots m} \circ L_{m+1}^{1\cdots m}$. On the other hand, it can be derived from $\Diamond$ that $L_1 \circ L_2^1 \circ L_3^{12} \circ \cdots \circ L_m^{1\cdots m-1} \circ L_{m+1}^{1\cdots m} \equiv L_{m+1} \circ L_1^{m+1} \circ L_2^{1m+1} \circ L_3^{12m+1} \circ \cdots \circ L_m^{1\cdots m-1m+1}$. Therefore the theorem holds if $n = m+1$.

For sequential notification propagation protocol, concurrency control is done only at the notifying site by transforming operations in OB with operations in IB because

198

the protocol ensures operations that have been propagated and are concurrent with operations in *OB* must have all been in *IB*. By contrast, for concurrent notification propagation protocol, it is inadequate to do concurrency control only at the notifying site because operations that have been propagated and are concurrent with operations in *OB* may not all be in *IB*.

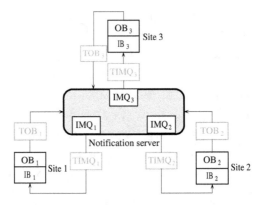

Figure 4.13: Compare concurrent propagation to sequential propagation

For example, as shown in Figure 4.13, operations that have been propagated and concurrent with operations in OB_1 could be in IB_1, in $TIMQ_1$ (i.e., on the way from the *Notification server* to IB_1), in IMQ_1 (i.e., inside the *Notification server*), or in TOB_2 (i.e., on the way from OB_2 to the *Notification server*). But we can compare concurrent notification propagation protocol to sequential notification propagation protocol by extending *IB* at a local site to *VIB* (virtual *IB*), which consists of the entire propagation path from a remote site to the local site via the *Notification server*, and by enforcing mutual exclusion at the *Notification server* to achieve serialization. In Figure 4.13, VIB_1 at *Site 1* could consist of IB_1, $TIMQ_1$, IMQ_1, and TOB_2. Therefore, concurrency control is done by transforming operations in OB_1 with operations in VIB_1 in the process of propagation. Since VIB_1 consists of several segments distributed on the way between a notifying site, the *Notification server*, and a notified site, transformation should be distributed accordingly at different places along a propagation path. More precisely, because $VIB_1 \equiv IB_1 \circ TIMQ_1 \circ IMQ_1 \circ TOB_2$, **SLOT**$(OB_1, VIB_1) = (OB'_1, VIB'_1)$ can be decoupled into: **SLOT**$(OB_1, IB_1) = (OB^1_1, IB^1_1)$; **SLOT**$(OB^1_1, TIMQ_1) = (OB^2_1, TIMQ^1_1)$; **SLOT**$(OB^2_1, IMQ_1) = (OB^3_1, IMQ^1_1)$; and **SLOT**$(OB^3_1, TOB_2) = (OB^4_1, TOB^1_2)$, where $OB'_1 \equiv OB^4_1$ and $VIB'_1 = IB^1_1 \circ TIMQ^1_1 \circ IMQ^1_1 \circ TOB^1_2 \lozenge$. For the *SCOP* notification propagation protocol to preserve convergence, there are two other essential technical components to ensure each *SLOT* transform meet its precondition.

4.4.2 Mutual exclusion at the notification server

As we know, in sequential notification propagation protocol, contextual serialization of *IB* is achieved by sequential propagation of notifications and transformation by *SLOT* control algorithm. By comparison, in concurrent notification propagation protocol, besides transformation by *SLOT* control algorithm, mutually exclusive access to buffers inside the *Notification server* is also essential to ensure contextual serialization of *VIB* for the sake of meeting preconditions of *SLOT* transformations (refer to $\lozenge$). We can easily give a counter example that contextual serialization is not achieved without mutual exclusion.

In Figure 4.13, suppose operations O_1 and O_2 that were concurrently generated at *Site 1* and *Site 2* gain access to IMQ_1, IMQ_2, and IMQ_3 at the *Notification server* at the same time. Because IMQ_1 is empty, O_1 will be appended to IMQ_2 and IMQ_3 as-is. At the same time, because IMQ_2 is also empty (O_1 has not been appended yet), O_2 will be appended to IMQ_1 and IMQ_3 as-is. As a result, IMQ_3 would become $[O_1, O_2]$ or $[O_2, O_1]$, which is not contextually serialized in either case. In contrast, if *Site 1* gains access to IMQ_1, IMQ_2, and IMQ_3 exclusively, *Site 2* would not be able to gain access before O_1 has been appended to IMQ_2 and IMQ_3.

So when *Site 2* gains access, it will transform O_2 with O_1 in IMQ_2 by **SLOT**$([O_2]$, $[O_1]) = ([O_2'], [O_1'])$, and then append O_2' to IMQ_1 and IMQ_3. As a result, IMQ_3 would become $[O_1, O_2']$, which has been contextually serialized.

4.4.3   Backup of outstanding notifications

Propagated operations are backed up in the left part of *OB* to cope with outstanding outgoing notifications from a notifying site to the *Notification server* (i.e., operations in *TOB* as shown in Figure 4.13). Incoming notifications are backed up in the left part of *IMQ* to cope with outstanding incoming notifications from the *Notification server* to a notified site (i.e., operations in *TIMQ* as shown in Figure 4.13). Backup of outstanding notifications is essential for the *SCOP* protocol to avoid missing notifications. Missing notifications could cause some concurrent operations to miss out the chance of being transformation with each other, or make some *SLOT* transformations (refer to $\Diamond$) unable to meet their preconditions. For example, in Figure 4.13, suppose O_1 and O_2 were concurrently generated at *Site 1* and *Site 2*. If O_1 is propagated at the time when O_2 is on the way from the *Notification server* to IB_1, then the two operations will never have a chance of being transformed with each other if they have not been properly backed up somewhere. First, if O_2 has not arrived at IB_1, O_1 will not be transformed with O_2 at *Site 1*. Second, if O_2 is not backed up in IMQ_1, O_1 will not be transformed with O_2 at the *Notification server*. Finally, if O_2 is not backed up in OB_2, O_1 will not be transformed with O_2 at *Site 2*.

But backup of outstanding notifications may cause some notifications to appear more than once in *VIB*, which makes *VIB* as a whole not contextually serialized and makes some *SLOT* transformations (refer to $\Diamond$) violate their preconditions. For example, in Figure 4.13, suppose O_1 and O_2 were concurrently generated at *Site 1* and *Site 2*. If O_2 was propagated first, O_2 would be backed up in OB_2 at *Site 2*, then be backed up in IMQ_1 at the *Notification server*, and finally arrive in IB_1 at *Site*

1. As a result, O_2 would appear in VIB_1 three times. At *Site 1*, O_1 is transformed with O_2 in IB_1 by **SLOT**$([O_1], [O_2]) = ([O_1'], [O_2'])$ at the time of propagation, whose precondition has been met because $O_1 \sqcup O_2$. Then at the *Notification server*, O_1' is transformed with O_2 in IMQ_1 by **SLOT**$([O_1'], [O_2]) = ([O_1''], [O_2'])$ whose precondition has been violated because it does not hold $O_1' \sqcup O_2$. Finally at *Site 2*, O_1'' is transformed with O_2 in OB_2 by **SLOT**$([O_1''], [O_2]) = ([O_1'''], [O_2'])$ whose precondition has been violated because it does not hold $O_1'' \sqcup O_2$.

Therefore, backup notifications in either *OB* or *IMQ* should be removed at appropriate time to ensure all *SLOT* transformations (refer to $\Diamond$) meet their preconditions and to collect garbage for the sake of saving space and reducing search time. To that end, each notification carries a reference called *ILTO*, which is the identifier of the last operation that operations in the notification have been transformed with. With *ILTO* updated accordingly after each *SLOT* transformation, it is able to identify and remove operations that have been transformed with in every segment of a *VIB*. For the above example, when O_1 is transformed with O_2 at the time of propagation at *Site 1*, the notification should consist of $L = [O_1']$ and $ILTO = \mathbf{ID}(O_2)$. When the notification arrives at the *Notification server*, *ILTO* identifies that O_2 in IMQ_1 has been transformed with operations in the notification. So, O_2 is removed from IMQ_1. When the notification arrives at *Site 2*, *ILTO* identifies that O_2 in OB_2 has been transformed with operations in the notification. So, O_2 is removed from OB_2.

Intuitively, when a notification goes through the *Notification server* to various notified sites, it should carry a different value of *ILTO* to a different notified site in order to correctly identify which operations from that site have been transformed with and should be removed accordingly [134]. But in the *SCOP* protocol, a notification carries the same value of *ILTO* to all notified sites, which is the identifier of the last operation (from whichever site) that operations in the notification have been transformed with. *ILTO* is first collected at the notifying site by the *getILTO* function, which should be the identifier of the last operation in its *IB* if *IB* is not empty. When the notification arrives at the *Notification server*, its *ILTO* provides adequate information to identify which operations have been transformed with and should be removed from *IMQ* because operations that appear in both *IB* and *IMQ* should be in the same order. Then operations in the notification will be transformed with operations in the remaining notifications in *IMQ*, and *ILTO* will be updated by the *updateILTO* function, which is the identifier of the last operation in *IMQ* (if any).

When the notification arrives at the notified site whose notifications gained access to the *Notification server* just before that notification did, *ILTO* in the notification will provide adequate information to identify which operations have been transformed with and should be removed from *OB* at this site. When the notification arrives at other notified sites, its operations must have not been transformed with any propagated operations in *OB*s at those sites. The reason why a single value of *ILTO* is adequate to identify all transformed operations in *OB* at all notified sites is that *IMQ*s at the *Notification server* and *IB*s at all sites are contextually serialized all the time. Here is an example to illustrate this point. In Figure 4.13, suppose O_1, O_2, and O_3 were concurrently generated at *Site 1*, *Site 2*, and *Site 3*. Three notifications $M_1.L = [O_1]$ and $M_1.ILTO = nil$, $M_2.L = [O_2]$ and $M_2.ILTO = nil$, and $M_3.L = [O_3]$ and $M_3.ILTO = nil$ were propagated to the *Notification server* at the same time. Suppose M_1, M_2, and M_3 gain access to the *Notification server* sequentially. When M_3 gains access, it must be $IMQ_3 = [M_1, M_2]$. Therefore $M_3.ILTO$ will be updated to $\mathbf{ID}(O_2)$, which will help remove O_2 from OB_2 when arriving at *Site 2*. When M_3 arrives at *Site 1*, nothing will be removed from OB_1 because M_2 arrived at *Site 1* before M_3 did and O_1 has already been removed at the time when M_2 arrived. At the *Notification server*, when M_2 gained access, it must be $IMQ_2 = [M_1]$. Therefore, $M_2.ILTO$ would be updated to $\mathbf{ID}(O_1)$, which helped remove O_1 from OB_1 when arriving at *Site 1*.

At this stage, we are able to explain why transformation with the *SLOT* control algorithm has voided *TP2* (Property 1.2) under control of either the sequential notification propagation protocol or the *SCOP* concurrent notification propagation protocol. The reason is that an operation will be transformed with any concurrent operation only once by **SLOT** (*OB*, *IB*) before propagation if under control of the sequential notification propagation protocol, or by **SLOT** (*OB*, *VIB*) that are distributed at various places if under control of the *SCOP* concurrent notification propagation protocol. As a result, under no circumstance could an operation be transformed with a pair of operations in different orders.

4.5 System design and implementation

The flexible notification technique has been implemented in a web-based flexible collaborative editing system *NICE* for the purpose of testing the correctness, demonstrating the feasibility, and providing a vehicle to explore system design and implementation issues, do usability study, and drive future research. *NICE* is a web-based flexible collaborative editing system that supports unconstrained, responsive, real-time collaborative editing; unconstrained, syncretic, non-real-time collaborative editing; and smooth, flexible switching between real-time and non-real-time collaborative editing.

4.5.1 System configuration

The web-based *NICE* flexible collaborative editing system assembles the architecture used for the web-based *REDUCE* real-time collaborative editing system [137, 138]. The *NICE* server is a *Linux* server that accommodates a web server and a web-based document manager implemented with *CGI* scripts, which is a Microsoft Windows *Explorer*-like file manager for Linux file system. The *NICE* session manager is a Java application running on the *NICE* server for managing the joining and leaving events. The difference is that the *propagator* in *REDUCE* for relaying editing operations has been replaced by the *Notification server* in *NICE*, which does concurrency control for flexible collaborative editing, as described in Section 4.3. The *NICE* editor is a Java applet running inside a Java-enabled web browser at a collaborating site. The *NICE* editor communicates with the session manager to join/leave a collaborative editing session and communicates with the *Notification server* to send and receive notifications.

The *Notification server* at the *NICE* server and multiple collaborating sites form a star-like communication topology with the *Notification server* at the center of the star. There are two main reasons for adopting the star-like topology. One is the security restrictions imposed by the web browsers, which restrict a Java applet to directly communicate only with the web server from which it is downloaded. As a result, it is impossible for a *NICE* editor applet to communicate directly with other *NICE* editor applets. The other reason is that the *SCOP* concurrent notification propagation protocol presented in Section 4.7 requires a *Notification server* to be connected with all collaborating sites in order to perform concurrency control for flexible collaborative editing.

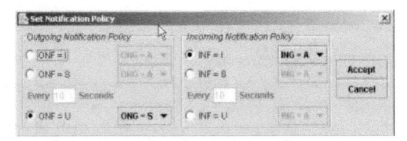

Figure 4.14: Configure notification policies

As shown in Figure 4.14, unconstrained, responsive, real-time collaborative editing is supported by configuring real-time notification policies like $ONF = I$ and $INF =$

I, while unconstrained, syncretic, non-real-time collaborative editing is supported by configuring non-real-time notification policies like $ONF = U$ and $INF = U$. Smooth, flexible switching between real-time and non-real-time collaborative editing is supported by allowing any participant to change to any notification policies at any time. In Figure 4.14, $ONF = U$ and $ONG = S$, so the user is more likely working in the mode of non-real-time collaborative editing.

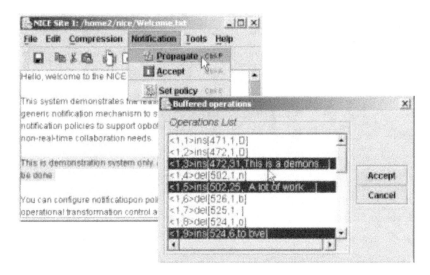

Figure 4.15: User-controlled notification with selective granularity

As shown in Figure 4.15, a notification will be propagated at any time when the user manually presses the *propagate* menu/button and the granularity of the notification is selected from the local outgoing notification buffer OB. Incoming notification policies can be configured in a similar way and any granularity of incoming notification can be accepted from the incoming notification buffer IB at any time. Furthermore, any participant is allowed to change to any notification policies at any time without any restriction and the change of notification policies would not cause distraction to any other participant.

4.5.2 A scenario of flexible collaborative editing

In this scenario, the *NICE* flexible collaborative editing system is for an online examination where a shared exam sheet consists of several questions. Each student is given two minutes to answer each question. Once the time for a question is up, the students' answers will be automatically sent to the examiner and students will not be allowed to answer that question again. Instead, the student will have to continue on the next question. For the examiner, on the one hand, although answers from students are continuously arriving, the examiner only wishes to accept answers in a way controlled by herself/himself to avoid being disturbed by arriving messages when s/he is focusing on reviewing. In other words, s/he will manually accept a group of answers after the previous group of answers have already been processed. On the other hand, after all students have completed their questions, the examiner will send marks and comments on questions to students question-by-question in the order that is easiest for commentation by the examiner. For students, they are anxious to know their exam results. So, marks and comments from the examiner will be instantly accepted to reflect in students' exam sheets. Therefore, the exam period is a non-real-time collaborative editing session with students' notification policies set to $ONF = S$ (Every 120 seconds), $ONG = A$, $INF = I$, and $ING = A$ and the examiner's notification policies set to $INF = U$, $ING = A$, $ONF = U$, and $ONG = S$.

After the examiner has commentated on all students' answers to those questions, s/he arranges a discussion session on this exam, where students are allowed to freely speak their opinions, suggestions, or even complaints about the exam, and the examiner is just one ordinary member in the discussion session who exchanges her/his opinions and suggestions with students and replies to students' complaints. Therefore, the discussion period is a real-time collaborative editing session with the examiner's and students' notification policies set to $INF = I$, $ING = A$, $ONF = I$, and $ONG = A$. In this online exam scenario, students and the examiner first do non-real-time collaborative editing of the shared exam sheet in the form of answering questions and reviewing answers in the exam period. Then they switch to real-time collaborative editing of the shared exam sheet, in the form of brainstorming about the questions, students' answers, and the examiner's comments, within the discussion period. This example demonstrates the usefulness of the *NICE* flexible collaborative editing system in supporting flexible collaborative editing where unconstrained responsive real-time collaborative editing and unconstrained syncretic non-real-time collaborative editing are needed in different phases or situations, and that switching between real-time and non-real-time collaborative editing should be smooth and flexible.

4.6 Related work

To support non-real-time notification policies, a challenging issue in flexible collaborative editing is to keep notification buffers small. This issue is similar in nature to the issue of controlling log scale in flexible operation-based merging. Because notification buffers are contextually serialized at any time, the *COMET* log compression algorithm presented in Chapter 3 can be directly applied to compress notification buffers in flexible collaborative editing.

Ramduny et al. discussed some key issues for notification servers [105]. Their work focused on a conceptual framework to guide the design of notification servers while our work covers both a generic framework and algorithms to tackle technical issues involved in notification. Some issues have been raised in [105]. For example, the concept of "pace impedance" has been proposed to allow the notification pace between the notifying site and the notification server to be different from that between the notification server and the notified side. This issue has been addressed in our work by separating outgoing and incoming notification policies. Some issues addressed in our work such as concurrency control were not mentioned them.

NESSIE [104] provided an application-independent generic notification infrastructure for asynchronous application sharing systems. Because its goal was to provide task-based group awareness, notifications were made on the granularity of tasks instead of individual events. As a result, it is unsuitable to be used for notification service in synchronous applications. Another major difference between their work [104] and our work is they focused on the issues of using notification to support group awareness while our work focuses on the issues of using notification to support consistency maintenance.

NSTP (Notification Service Transfer Protocol) [99] provided a simple and general application-independent notification service for sharing artifacts in synchronous multi-user applications. Its goal was to provide notification service for synchronous applications and it did not address issues related to the support of asynchronous applications. Moreover, because changes are allowed to be made on shared artifacts, a centralized locking-based serialization protocol was designed for concurrency control. This solution is simple and independent of applications, but the notification server has to maintain all shared artifacts and could become a bottleneck as the number of shared artifacts grows.

4.7 Conclusions and future work

In this chapter, we propose a flexible notification framework to unify real-time and non-real-time collaborative systems, which can be used to describe and compare a range of notification strategies used in existing collaborative systems, and to guide the design of notification components for new collaborative systems. In this framework, the policy part uses two parameters *frequency* and *granularity* with a combination of various values to define a spectrum of notification polices. The mechanism part uses a set of basic components including notification buffers, notification executors, and notification propagation protocol to carry out various notification policies.

The proposed framework has been applied to the design of the notification component for a flexible collaborative editing system that is able to support unconstrained, responsive, real-time collaborative editing; unconstrained, syncretic, non-real-time collaborative editing; and smooth, flexible switching between real-time and non-real-time collaborative editing. In the notification component, we use separate outgoing and incoming notification buffers to support various notification policies. The major contribution is the extension of the operational transformation technique, originally proposed for consistency maintenance in real-time collaborative editing, to support consistency maintenance in flexible collaborative editing. It includes a new transformation control algorithm that has a linear time complexity, two notification algorithms that support propagation and acceptance of any notifications at any time, and a notification propagation protocol that is efficient for both real-time and non-real-time collaborative editing.

All technical solutions have been implemented in an Internet-based flexible collaborative editing system *NICE* for the purpose of testing the correctness, demonstrating the feasibility, and providing a vehicle to explore system design and implementation issues, do a usability study, and drive future research. In this system, unconstrained, responsive, real-time collaborative editing is supported by configuring real-time notification policies and unconstrained, syncretic, non-real-time collaborative editing is supported by configuring non-real-time notification policies. Furthermore, smooth, flexible switching between real-time and non-real-time collaborative editing is supported by allowing any participant to change to any notification policies at any time. In the future, we plan to do more theoretical work in order to formally prove the correctness of notification algorithms and the concurrent notification propagation protocol for supporting flexible collaborative editing. Another future work is to realize notification policies that can be intuitively understood by end users in terms of the semantics of applications. Other future work includes investigation of other key issues in flexible collaborative editing, such as undo, locking, and group awareness.

Chapter 5

An Internet-based collaborative programming environment

An Internet-based collaborative programming environment *RECIPE* [127] has been designed and implemented to motivate and drive our research on collaborative programming and to provide a vehicle for exploring system design and implement issues, and gaining initial feedback on Internet-based collaborative programming. *RECIPE* provides a platform for integrating various cutting-edge techniques from the research on collaborative editing for supporting collaborative programming presented in Chapter 2, Chapter 3, and Chapter 4.

This chapter is organized as follows: the overview of the system is described in the following section. The next section presents the configuration of the system and a description of collaborative sessions supported by the system. A scenario of collaborative programming by using the system is illustrated after that. Finally, the chapter is concluded with a summary of contributions and future work.

5.1 Overview

RECIPE is a web-based collaborative programming environment that allows a group of geographically distributed programmers to work together on the same source code for design, implementation of individual components, and integration of individual components over the Internet. First, it supports non-real-time collaborative programming in the implementation phase by allowing individual programmers to do coding, debugging, testing, and documentation of individual components that belong to the same source code. Second, it supports real-time collaborative programming in the design phase by allowing a group of programmers to define new components, structure relations between components, and make specifications for components in a source code, by means of brainstorming and frequent interaction. Finally, it supports real-time collaborative programming in the integration phase by allowing a group of programmers to debug, test, and document the source code with integrated components by means of discussion and frequent interaction.

RECIPE is still in its initial stage and it supports collaborative programming only in *Unix* environments on the basis of a *shell* terminal. It supports both collaboration-transparent and collaboration-aware applications that were implemented in different ways for different reasons. On the one hand, not much research has been done on collaborative compiling, collaborative debugging, or collaborative testing and it is non-trivial to design and implement collaboration-aware collaborative compilers, collaborative debuggers, or collaborative testers. Therefore, applications running inside a *shell* terminal (e.g., compiling or debugging applications), including the *shell* application itself, are shared transparently to support real-time collaborative interactive compiling, debugging and testing. On the other hand, we have done a lot of research on collaborative editing and have designed and implemented several collaboration-aware collaborative editors ranging from a real-time collaborative editor *REDUCE* [137], a non-real-time collaborative editor with integrated version control support *FORCE* [124], and a flexible collaborative editor *NICE* [125]. These collaboration-aware collaborative editors have been integrated in the *RECIPE* environment for supporting collaborative editing of the same source code in different phases or situations in a collaborative programming process.

In particular, the *REDUCE* real-time collaborative editor is used in the design phase for a group of programmers to design the source code by means of brainstorming and frequent interaction. *REDUCE* real-time collaborative editor is also used in the integration phase for a group of programmers to debug, test, and document the source code with integrated individual components implemented by individual programmers by means of discussion and frequent interaction. The collaborative *highlighting* tool, presented in Chapter 2, has proven very useful in supporting real-time gesture communication on the same source code file. The *FORCE* non-real-time collaborative editor with integrated version control support is used in the implementation phase for programmers to work on different components belonging to the same source code because these programmers do not need frequent interaction. The *NICE* flexible collaborative editor is used in the implementation phase for programmers to work on the same component because these programmers may sometimes need to collaboratively edit the same component by means of frequent interaction, or sometimes need to independently edit different parts of the same component for isolated functions with little interaction.

5.2   System configuration

The system configuration of the web-based *RECIPE* collaborative programming environment is shown in Figure 5.1. The *RECIPE* server is a Linux server that accommodates a web server, a *RECIPE Server* daemon process, and sources code files of software projects to be carried out by means of collaborative programming. The *RECIPE Server* is a Java application, which resides at a well-known Internet address, waiting for connection requests from *RECIPE* clients. Once a connection is established, a thread *SCH* (Server Connection Handler) inside the *RECIPE Server* process is spawned to communicate with that client and the main thread of *RECIPE Server* keeps waiting for new connection requests. The *SCH* thread controls the source code files, manages participants' joining/leaving events, and transparently converts single-user *Unix* applications running inside a shell terminal into corresponding multi-user collaborative applications.

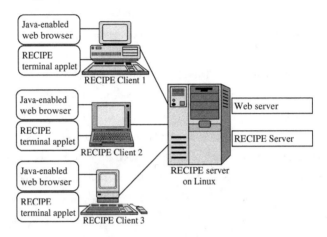

Figure 5.1: System configuration of the web-based RECIPE environment

Converting single-user applications to multiple collaborative applications is done transparently as follows: first, the *SCH* thread receives inputs from the *RECIPE* client that is connected with, analyzes these inputs, and distributes them to handlers corresponding to different single-user applications. Furthermore, the *SCH* thread collects outputs from those handlers and broadcasts them to the *RECIPE* client that is connected with.

A *RECIPE* client emulates the *Unix* shell terminal program and it is a Java applet running inside a Java-enabled web browser at a collaborating site. The *RECIPE* client applet at a collaborating site makes connection requests to the *RECIPE Server* daemon process at the *RECIPE* sever. Once a connection is established, it buffers key strokes generated at the local site, processes key strokes into string-based commands, and sends the commands to the *SCH* thread that is connected with. It also receives outputs from the *SCH* thread that is connected with, processes the outputs, executes instructions encapsulated in the outputs, and displays non-instruction outputs in the terminal window. As shown in Figure 5.2, the *RECIPE* terminal applet looks like a typical *Unix* terminal and the way of logging into the *RECIPE* environment is also like that of logging into a *Unix* system by providing a valid *Linux* account and password.

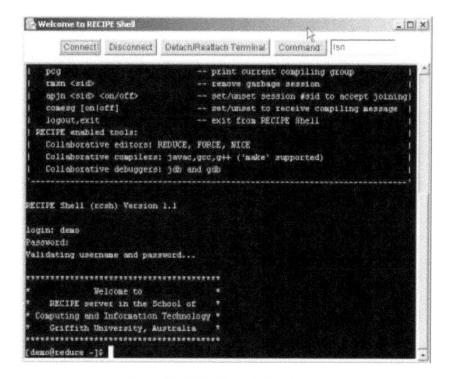

Figure 5.2: RECIPE terminal applet

5.3 Four kinds of collaborative sessions

There are four kinds of collaborative sessions supported by *RECIPE* to meet different needs in a collaborative programming process, these are:

- *RCSH* - Collaborative shell session to share every application running inside the shell terminal including the shell application itself with others.

- *COMP* - Collaborative compiling session to share compiling applications such as *javac*, *gcc*, *g++*, or *make* with others.

- *DEBG* - Collaborative debugging session to share debugging applications such as *jdb* or *gdb* with others.

- *EDIT* - Collaborative editing session to support collaborative editing of the same source code file.

As mentioned in Section 5.1, *RCSH*, *COMP*, and *DEBG* collaborative sessions are achieved in the collaboration-transparent way by converting the single-user shell application, single-user compiling applications, and single-user debugging applications to corresponding multi-user collaborative applications without touching their source code. The *EDIT* collaborative session supports real-time, non-real-time, or flexible collaborative editing of the same source code file for design, coding, debugging, testing, and documentation by specially designed collaboration-aware collaborative editors *REDUCE*, *FORCE*, or *NICE*.

Any collaborative session that has not been made sharable remains a private session. When a user logs into the *RECIPE* environment, it is by default that none of the collaborative sessions s/he owns is sharable. In this case, the user works in single-user mode, where the *RECIPE Server* daemon process is simply a remote access server like the *telnet* server and the *RECIPE* client applet is simply a remote access client like the *telnet* terminal. A user may choose to share different collaborative sessions in different phases or situations during a collaborative programming process. For example, in the design phase, a user may choose to share *EDIT* sessions that are related to a software project. In the implementation phase, if a user is independently working on an individual component, s/he may choose not to share anything. By comparison, if a user is collaboratively working on the same individual component with some other users, s/he could choose to share *EDIT*, *COMP*, and *DEBG* sessions that are related to the coding, debugging, testing, and documentation of the component, or simply choose to share the *RCSH* session with those collaborators.

In the integration phase, because all users could be involved in debugging, testing, and documentation of various individual components in the integration process, every user could simply choose to share her/his *RCSH* session with others to avoid sharing many individual sessions tediously. Making a *RCSH* session sharable is able to achieve the function similar to that provided by Sun's *SharedShell* system [139], which is a terminal program that enables multiple users to interact together by replicating a terminal window of one computer onto other computers. However, the primary goal of *SharedShell* is to facilitate customer support engineers or system administrators to diagnose and resolve software problems on remote customers' computers. Therefore, its support for collaborative programming is limited. It should be mentioned that sharing a *RCSH* session makes the user who owns the session lose privacy. Therefore, during a collaborative programming process, if a user has the possibility of doing private activities such as processing email, s/he would choose to share individual *EDIT*, *COMP*, and *DEBG* sessions rather than her/his *RCSH*, for the sake of keeping privacy.

A user makes a session sharable by issuing the *apjn* command. As shown in Figure 5.3, user *hfshen* makes the *EDIT* session of real-time collaboratively editing the Java source code file */home/hfshen/reduce/RE.java* sharable by explicitly issuing the *apjn* command to share collaborative session ♯4. A user joins a collaborative session by issuing the *join* command. As shown in Figure 5.3, user *hfshen* joins the *DEBG* collaborative session of collaboratively debugging the program */gdb/array* with *gdb* collaborative debugger by issuing the *join* command to join collaborative session ♯3 owned by user *demo*.

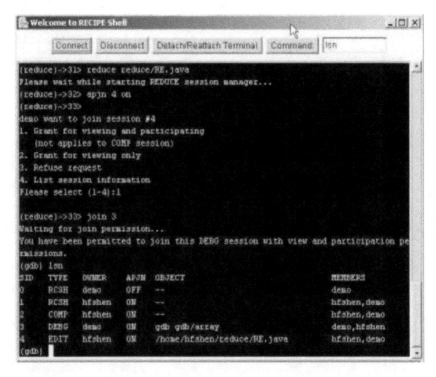

Figure 5.3: Four kinds of collaborative session supported by RECIPE

Joining a collaborative session is controlled by the *request-authorize* access control protocol, where the user who wants to join a collaborative session will make a joining request to the session owner and the session owner may grant the user with full permission(i.e., option 1: view and participate) or restricted permission (i.e., option 2: view only), or even reject the joining request. Moreover, a session owner can change the granted permission to any user at any time. As shown in Figure 5.3, user *demo* makes a request to the session owner *hfshen* for joining session ♯4 of collaboratively editing the Java source code file */home/hfshen/reduce/RE.java* with the real-time collaborative editor *REDUCE* and the session owner *hfshen* grants user *demo* with full permission (i.e., view and participate).

5.4   A collaborative programming experiment

In this section, we will describe a collaborative programming experiment that has been done with the *RECIPE* environment. This experiment demonstrates how the Internet-based collaborative programming environment is useful in supporting collaborative testing, debugging, and documentation of the same source code by collaborators geographically distributed over the Internet.

Haifeng is a PhD student at Griffith University, Australia. He was implementing a new undo component for the *REDUCE* system, which was designed by his supervisor Professor Sun. Haifeng found a problem when testing the undo component but could not figure out where the bug was because he did not have enough knowledge about the algorithms. Prof. Sun was on leave in Singapore at that time. So they scheduled a time to collaboratively debug the program. The code was stored on the *RECIPE* server machine at Griffith University. Then at the scheduled time, Haifeng and Prof. Sun both logged into the *RECIPE* server from their own machines located within Griffith University and in Singapore respectively.

Firstly, Haifeng made his *RCSH* session sharable. By joining Haifeng's *RCSH* session, Prof. Sun got a replicated terminal window of Haifeng's terminal window on his machine. Haifeng then executed the undo component and showed Prof. Sun the error message produced by executed program. With his expertise on the algorithms,

Prof. Sun had an idea how to debug the program. He let Haifeng start debugging the *undo* class with the *jdb* utility. Prof. Sun could also start the debugging utility from his replicated terminal window and the reason why he let Haifeng do that was simply because he did not know Haifeng's programming environment well.

Prof. Sun set a breakpoint at the method *anyUndo* and executed the *undo* program. When the program suspended at the breakpoint, he printed the value of the global variable *HB* and found it was incorrect. Then Prof. Sun set another breakpoint at the *undoCA* method before the previous breakpoint and re-executed the program. When the program suspended at the *undoCA* method, he printed *HB*'s value and found it was correct. So Prof. Sun concluded the bug was hidden between the two methods. He then let Haifeng start a session to edit the source code file *undo.java* with the *REDUCE* real-time group editor and then joined the session. By reading the source code, Prof. Sun found the *undoCA* method did not properly timstamp undo operations, leading to an incorrect *HB*. So, he let Haifeng modify the source code (Haifeng knew *Java* language better than Prof. Sun did.), and at the same time wrote some online comments for the *undoCA* method to explain why and how a change was made there.

Finally changes made to the source code *undo.java* by both of them were saved. Haifeng then compiled the source code and executed the program again. As expected, the bug had been fixed. From this experiment, it can be seen how collaborative programming is effective. Apparently, without Prof. Sun's expertise on the algorithms, it would have taken a very long time for Haifeng to find the bug. On the other hand, without Haifeng's rich experience with the programming environment and language, it would also have taken too long for Prof. Sun to fix the bug, not to mention that a busy professor may not have the time to do it!

5.5 Conclusions and future work

In this chapter, we describe an Internet-based collaborative programming environment that provides an ideal platform for integrating various cutting-edge techniques from the research on collaborative editing for supporting collaborative programming. In particular, the collaborative highlighting technique has proven very useful for a group of programmers to improve their real-time gesture communication on source code files. The flexible operation-based merging technique has proven useful and efficient for individual programmers to implement different components in a source code with little interaction, by means of supporting unconstrained, syncretic, non-real-time collaborative editing and version control of the same source code. The flexible notification technique has proven useful and flexible for programmers to implement the same component in a source code, by means of supporting flexible collaborative editing of the same component.

The Internet-based collaborative programming environment has served a good purpose for motivating and driving our research on collaborative programming, providing a testbed to test the correctness of proposed techniques, and providing a vehicle to explore system design and implement issues and gain initial feedback on Internet-based collaborative programming. The environment has been demonstrated at a major international conference [120], and has been available for public demonstration for quite some time. A variety of evaluations from researchers, industrial engineers, and end users have helped test the correctness of proposed techniques and provided initial feedback of the usability of those techniques.

Common feedback from evaluators is that users do not intend to accept those specially designed collaboration aware editors used by *REDUCE*, *FORCE*, and *NICE*. Users are used to various word processing editors like Microsoft Word [17], source code editors like *Emacs* [20], or integrated development environments like Java Net-Beans [16]. They are reluctant to get collaboration support at the cost of sacrificing their favourite editors. Another major feedback is that it is inconvenient to use different collaborative editors from *REDUCE*, *FORCE*, to *NICE* in different phases or situations. It is desirable to use a single collaborative editor for all phases or situations. This feedback is valuable to our future research.

Another project, *CoWord* (Collaborative Word) project [133], is a platform of transparently integrating cutting-edge techniques from the research on collaborative editing into the commonly used single-user editor Microsoft *Word* [17], without touching its source code. It intercepts edit-related events such as keyboard strokes and mouse down, up, and movements from the Microsoft *Word* application. These events are assembled as edit operations, which will be propagated and replayed on another *Word* application to support real-time collaborative editing, as that achieved by the *REDUCE* real-time collaborative editor. User inputs are not restricted by floor control, and optimistic concurrency control by operational transformation is used for consistency maintenance.

Version control is another very desirable feature in addition to collaborative editing in supporting collaborative programming, which keeps track of the evolvement of documents [77]. On the one hand, a document collaboratively edited by multiple users would evolve more quickly but be more error-prone, therefore, version control of the document would be of great benefit to keep track of its evolvement and restore its older versions. On the other hand, any version of a document should be able to be collaboratively edited by multiple users, if necessary. For example, if the present document being collaboratively edited by a group of users has a major flaw that is difficult to recover from, a previous version of the document in which that flaw did not exist can be checked out and collaboratively edited. We plan to integrate the flexible operation-based merging technique to *CoWord* for the purpose of supporting flexible version control, as that achieved by the *FORCE* non-real-time collaborative editor since the state-based merging technique is not applicable to binary *Word* documents. Furthermore, we also plan to integrate the flexible notification technique to the *CoWord* to make it support flexible collaborative editing, as that achieved by the *NICE* collaborative editor.

The *RECIPE* environment is still in its initial stage and will continue to motivate and drive our future research. As collaborative debugging and collaborative testing are equally as important as collaborative editing in supporting collaborative programming and our research on collaborative debugging and collaborative testing is still preliminary, we plan to do more systematic research on collaborative debugging and collaborative testing for supporting collaborative programming.

Chapter 6

Conclusions and future work

Software systems are getting larger and more complex, while the requirements are becoming vaguer and more rapidly changing. These trends make current software development more and more likely a team work. To integrate multiple developers into a coherent structured management process and make team software development a positive-sum game for both higher productivity and better quality, many team software development methodologies have been proposed and practised. An emerging methodology is collaborative programming, which allows a group of programmers to work together on the same source code for design, implementation of individual components, and integration of individual components. Compared with other team software methodologies such as pair programming or software configuration management that only address the needs in some phases or situations, collaborative programming is more adaptive to the variety of different phases or situations in a team software development process. Collaborative programming is the response to many surveys on team software development and collaborative writing, calling for technology to be flexible and permissive, and allowing groups to change strategies and processes at any time during a team project.

Because collaborative programming is to support collaboration on the basis of shared source code, while source code has to be manipulated by means of editing, a core technical component in collaborative programming is collaborative editing that allows a group of programmers to view and edit the same source code. To support different phases or situations in an Internet-based collaborative programming process, collaborative editing must meet the requirements of supporting unconstrained, responsive, real-time collaborative editing; unconstrained, syncretic, non-real-time collaborative editing; and smooth, flexible switching between real-time and non-real-time collaborative editing. This thesis research contributes several novel techniques to address these requirements, and an Internet-based collaborative programming environment that integrates these novel techniques.

Unconstrained, responsive, real-time collaborative editing is needed in the design and integration phases of a collaborative programming process, where programmers collaboratively edit the same source code with high interaction by means of brainstorming, exchanging ideas, or close discussion. In a highly interactive environment, group awareness is essential to improve the quality of real-time interaction. We contribute a collaborative highlighting technique for supporting gestural communication, which is more effective than others in improving the quality of real-time interaction on text-based source code documents. The major contribution to the operational transformation technique is the extension of the technique, originally proposed for consistency maintenance in real-time collaborative editing, to support group awareness, by means of collaborative highlighting. It includes a package of operational transformation functions and transformation control algorithms for consistency maintenance in collaborative highlighting, and a flexible undo solution that has the capability of undoing any highlighting operation at any time.

Unconstrained, syncretic, non-real-time collaborative editing is needed in the implementation phase of a collaborative programming process for programmers to work on different components of a source code. We contribute a flexible operation-based merging technique that is efficient and has the capability of textually integrating all changes concurrently made by multiple users and automatically detecting and resolving syntactic conflicts according to application-dependent user-specified policies. The major contribution to the operational transformation technique is the extension of the technique, originally proposed for supporting unconstrained, responsive, real-time collaborative editing, to support unconstrained, syncretic, non-real-time collaborative editing. It includes a log compression algorithm, a textual merging algorithm, and a syntactic merging algorithm.

Smooth, flexible switching between real-time and non-real-time collaborative editing is needed in the implementation phase of a collaborative programming process for programmers who are working on the same component to sometimes collaboratively edit the same component with frequent interaction or sometimes independently edit different parts of the same component for isolated functions with little interaction. We contribute a flexible notification technique to support flexible collaborative editing by integrating unconstrained, responsive, real-time collaborative editing and unconstrained, syncretic, non-real-time collaborative editing, and allowing smooth, flexible switch between them. The major contribution to the operational transformation technique is the extension of the technique, originally proposed for consistency maintenance in real-time collaborative editing, to support consistency maintenance in flexible collaborative editing. It includes a new transformation control algorithm that has a linear time complexity, two notification algorithms that support propagation and acceptance of any notifications at any time, and a notification propagation protocol that is efficient for both real-time and non-real-time collaborative editing.

An Internet-based collaborative programming environment has been designed and implemented to integrate those novel techniques for the purpose of testing the correctness and demonstrating the feasibility and usefulness of those techniques, and providing a vehicle for exploring system design and implement issues, gaining initial feedback on Internet-based collaborative programming, and driving our future research on Internet-based collaborative programming.

In the future, we will continue validating and developing these techniques, apply and extend these techniques to other areas, and explore other research issues in the area of collaborative programming. In particular, we are in the process of applying the collaborative highlighting technique to support other group awareness features to improve the quality of real-time interaction, such as collaborative font-changing, collaborative size-changing, collaborative italicizing, collaborative underlining, and so on. We are also investigating how to develop the collaborative highlighting technique into a generic approach for handling consistency maintenance and flexible undo of general updating operations. We have carried out an experiment to measure the performance of the *COMET* log compression algorithm and the efficiency difference between operation-based merging and state-based merging with the *FORCE* system. We plan to systematically perform a statistics study on the compression algorithm and the flexible operation-based merging technique. Furthermore, we will investigate how to develop the compression algorithm into a generic data compression algorithm that can be used to compress general event queues. We will also investigate how to apply the flexible operation-based merging technique to semantic merging and how to extend the flexible operation-based merging technique to support distributed repositories in SCM systems.

We have done some theoretical work on formally proving that the *SLOT* transformation control algorithm is able to maintain consistency in non-real-time collaborative editing and the sequential notification propagation protocol is able to maintain consistency in flexible collaborative editing. We plan to do more theoretical work on formally proving that the *SCOP* concurrent notification propagation protocol is able to maintain consistency in flexible collaborative editing, and the *TP2* condition has been avoided in the *SLOT* transformation control algorithm under control of the *SCOP* concurrent notification propagation protocol. Moreover, we are investigating other key issues such as undo, locking, group awareness, and so on in flexible collaborative editing.

Furthermore, we are working on a generic collaboration-transparent approach to integrate cutting-edge techniques on real-time collaborative editing, non-real-time collaborative editing, flexible version control, and flexible collaborative editing into widely used single-used editors or word processing systems without modifying their source code. An important contribution will be a set of programming user interface specifications that must be provided by those single-user systems to support transparent marriage between cutting-edge techniques and popular systems. While our contributions on collaborative programming have been mainly made on collaborative editing, we plan to explore more research issues in the area of collaborative programming, such as collaborative compiling, collaborative debugging and so on. In addition, we also intend to apply or extend the proposed techniques on real-time collaborative editing, non-real-time collaborative editing, flexible version control, and flexible collaborative editing to other relevant research areas such as web coauthoring and versioning [43, 70], distributed simulation [59], and grid computing [57], in order to tackle some research issues in those areas.

Appendix A

More selective undo examples

This appendix includes four more selective undo examples, illustrating how the *SUIT* undo algorithm presented in Chapter 2 is able to handle situations where the undo of a highlighting operation is mixed with a concurrent highlighting/insertion/deletion operation, or concurrent undo of a highlighting/insertion/deletion operation.

The first example is that undoing a highlighting operation is mixed with a concurrent highlighting operation. Consider a document with characters a, b, c, d, and e, replicated at two sites as shown in Figure A.1. *Site 1* performed a highlighting operation $H_1 = \mathbf{Hlt}[0, 4, [\langle 0, 4, \text{null}\rangle]]$ to highlight characters a, b, c, and d in dark. Subsequently, *Site 2* performed a highlighting operation $H_2 = \mathbf{Hlt}[1, 4, [\langle 1, 3, \text{dark}\rangle, \langle 4, 1, \text{null}\rangle]]$ to highlight characters b, c, d, and e in grey. Concurrently with H_2, *Site 1* issues the command of undoing H_1.

At *Site 1*, after the execution of H_1, characters a, b, c, and d are highlighted in dark and $HB = [H_1]$. To undo H_1, $\mathbf{SUIT}(\mathbf{Id}(H_1), HB)$ simply executes H_1's inverse operation $\overline{H_1} = \mathbf{makeInverse}(H_1) = \mathbf{Uhlt}[0, 4, [\langle 0, 4, \text{null}\rangle]]$ because H_1 is the only operation in *HB*. After that, characters a, b, c, and d are dehighlighted and $HB = [^*H_1]$. Then the undo command carrying $\mathbf{Id}(H_1)$ is propagated to *Site 2*. When the remote highlighting operation H_2 arrives, $\mathbf{PICOT}(H_2, HB)$ simply executes H_2 as-is because H_2 is totally after H_1. After that, characters b, c, d and e are highlighted in grey, $\mathbf{OHL}(H_2)$ is replaced with new *OHRs* in $[\langle 1, 4, \text{null}\rangle]$, and $HB = [^*H_1, H_2]$.

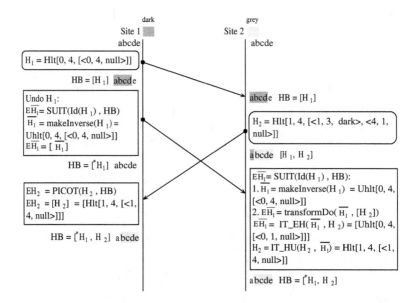

Figure A.1: Undoing a highlighting operation is mixed with a concurrent highlighting operation

At *Site 2*, after the execution of H_1 and H_2, character a is highlighted in dark, characters b, c, d, and e are highlighted in grey, and $HB = [H_1, H_2]$ where $H_1 = \mathbf{Hlt}[0, 4, [\langle 0, 4, \text{null}\rangle]]$ and $H_2 = \mathbf{Hlt}[1, 4, [\langle 1, 3, \text{dark}\rangle, \langle 4, 1, \text{null}\rangle]]$. When the remote undo command arrives, if the undo command were carrying $\overline{H_1}$'s execution form $E\overline{H_1} = \mathbf{Uhlt}[0, 4, [\langle 0, 4, \text{null}\rangle]]$ rather than $\mathbf{Id}(H_1)$, the execution of $E\overline{H_1}$ would dehighlight characters a, b, c, and d, which is obviously wrong because part of H_2's effect has been removed. The reason is the derivation of $E\overline{H_1}$ at *Site 1* had no knowledge about the concurrent highlighting operation H_2 performed at *Site 2*. Therefore the undo command should carry $\mathbf{Id}(H_1)$ with which *Site 2* executes $\mathbf{SUIT}(\mathbf{Id}(H_1),\ HB)$ to derive $E\overline{H_1}$ locally.

SUIT(**Id**(H_1), *HB*) is executed to derive $E\overline{H_1}$ at *Site 2* as follows: first, find H_1 = HB[1] with a matching of **Id**(H_1). Second, make H_1's inverse operation $\overline{H_1}$ = **makeInverse**(H_1) = **Uhlt**[0, 4, [$\langle 0,\ 4,\ null \rangle$]]. Third, derive $\overline{H_1}$'s execution form $E\overline{H_1}$ by transforming $\overline{H_1}$ with the operation in HB[2] by $E\overline{H_1}$ = **transformDo**($\overline{H_1}$, HB[2]). After that, $E\overline{H_1}$ = **IT_EH**($\overline{H_1}$, H_2) = **Uhlt**[0, 4, [$\langle 0,\ 1,\ null \rangle$]] and H_2 = **IT_HU**(H_2, $\overline{H_1}$) = **Hlt**[1, 4, [$\langle 1,\ 4,\ null \rangle$]]. Finally, execute $E\overline{H_1}$ and mark H_1 and $\overline{H_1}$ as a do-undo pair. After that, character a is dehighlighted while characters b, c, d, and e remain highlighted in grey, and *HB* = [$^*H_1$, H_2].

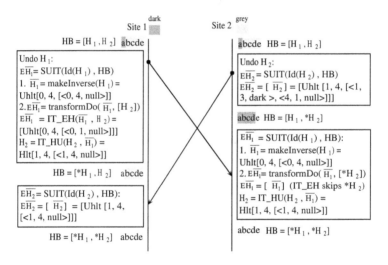

Figure A.2: Undoing a highlighting operation is mixed with concurrent undo of another highlighting operation

The second example is that undoing a highlighting operation is mixed with undoing another highlighting operation. Consider the example in Figure 2.5. After H_1 and H_2 have both been executed at *Site 1* and *Site 2*, the two sites are convergent with character a highlighted in dark and characters b, c, d, and e highlighted in grey, and $HB = [H_1, H_2]$ where $H_1 = \mathbf{Hlt}[0, 4, [\langle 0, 4, \text{null}\rangle]]$ and $H_2 = \mathbf{Hlt}[1, 4, [\langle 1, 3,$ dark$\rangle, \langle 4, 1, \text{null}\rangle]]$. As shown in Figure A.2, *Site 1* issues a command to undo H_1 while *Site 2* issues another command to undo H_2 at the same time.

At *Site 1*, $\mathbf{SUIT}(\mathbf{Id}(H_1), HB)$ is executed to undo H_1 as follows: firstly, find $H_1 = HB[1]$ with a matching of $\mathbf{Id}(H_1)$. Second, make H_1's inverse operation $\overline{H_1}$ = $\mathbf{makeInverse}(H_1) = \mathbf{Uhlt}[0, 4, [\langle 0, 4, \text{null}\rangle]]$. Third derive $\overline{H_1}$'s execution form $E\overline{H_1}$ by transforming $\overline{H_1}$ with the operation in HB[2] by $E\overline{H_1} = \mathbf{transformDo}(\overline{H_1},$ HB[2]). After that, $E\overline{H_1} = \mathbf{IT\_EH}(\overline{H_1}, H_2) = [\mathbf{Uhlt}[0, 4, [\langle 0, 1, \text{null}\rangle]]]$ and $H_2 = IT\_HU(H_2, \overline{H_1}) = \mathbf{Hlt}[1, 4, [\langle 1, 4, \text{null}\rangle]]$. Finally, execute $E\overline{H_1}$ and mark H_1 and $\overline{H_1}$ as a do-undo pair. After that, character a is dehighlighted while characters b, c, d, and e remain highlighted in grey, and $HB = [^*H_1, H_2]$. When the remote undo command carrying $\mathbf{Id}(H_2)$ arrives, because H_2 is the last operation in HB, $\mathbf{SUIT}(\mathbf{Id}(H_2), HB)$ simply executes H_2's inverse operation $\overline{H_2} = \mathbf{makeInverse}(H_2) = \mathbf{Uhlt}[1, 4, [\langle 1, 4,$ null$\rangle]]$ to undo H_2. After that, characters b, c, d, and e are dehighlighted, and $HB = [^*H_1, ^*H_2]$.

At *Site 2*, because H_2 is the last operation in HB, $\mathbf{SUIT}(\mathbf{Id}(H_2, HB)$ simply executes H_2's inverse operation $\overline{H_2} = \mathbf{makeInverse}(H_2) = \mathbf{Uhlt}[1, 4, [\langle 1, 3, \text{dark}\rangle, \langle 4, 1, \text{null}\rangle]]$ to undo H_2. After that, characters b, c, and d are recovered to be highlighted in dark and character e is dehighlighted while character a remains highlighted in dark, and $HB = [H_1, ^*H_2]$. When the remote undo command carrying $\mathbf{Id}(H_1)$ arrives, $\mathbf{SUIT}(\mathbf{Id}(H_1), HB)$ is executed to undo H_1 as follows: first, find $H_1 = HB[1]$ with a matching of $\mathbf{Id}(H_1)$. Second, make H_1's inverse operation $\overline{H_1} = \mathbf{makeInverse}(H_1)$ = $\mathbf{Uhlt}[0, 4, [\langle 0, 4, \text{null}\rangle]]$. Third, $E\overline{H_1} = \overline{H_1}$ because $^*H_2$ is a do-undo pair and $H_2 = \mathbf{IT\_HU}(H_2, \overline{H_1}) = \mathbf{Hlt}[1, 4, [\langle 1, 4, \text{null}\rangle]]$. Finally, execute $E\overline{H_1}$ and mark H_1 and $\overline{H_1}$ as a do-undo pair. After that, characters a, b, c, and d are dehighlighted, and $HB = [^*H_1, ^*H_2]$.

The third example is that undoing a highlighting operation is mixed with a concurrent insertion/deletion operation. Still consider the example in Figure 2.5. After H_1 and H_2 have both been executed at *Site 1* and *Site 2*, the two sites are convergent with character a highlighted in dark, characters b, c, d, and e highlighted in grey, and $HB = [H_1, H_2]$ where $H_1 = \mathbf{Hlt}[0, 4, [\langle 0, 4, null\rangle]]$ and $H_2 = \mathbf{Hlt}[1, 4, [\langle 1, 3, dark\rangle,$ $\langle 4, 1, null\rangle]]$. As shown in Figure A.3, while *Site 1* performs a deletion operation E $= \mathbf{Del}[3, 1, d]$ to delete the character at position 3 (i.e., character d), *Site 2* issues a command to undo H_2 at the same time.

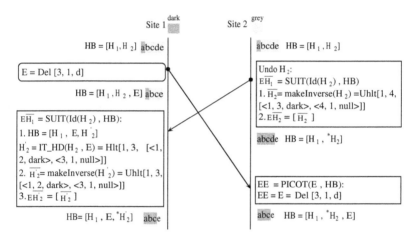

Figure A.3: Undoing a highlighting operation is mixed with a concurrent insertion/deletion operation

At *Site 1*, after the execution of E, character d is deleted, and $HB = [H_1, H_2,$ $E]$. When the remote undo command carrying $\mathbf{Id}(H_2)$ arrives, $\mathbf{SUIT}(\mathbf{Id}(H_2),$ $HB)$ is executed to undo H_2 as follows: first, find $H_2 = HB[2]$ with a matching of $\mathbf{Id}(H_2)$. Second, transform and shift the deletion operation E to the left side of H_2. After that $HB = [H_1, E, H_2']$ where $H_2' = \mathbf{IT\_HD}(H_2, E) = \mathbf{Hlt}[1, 3, [\langle 1, 2, dark\rangle, \langle 3, 1,$

null$\rangle$]] and $H_2' = \mathrm{HB}[3]$. Third, make H_2''s inverse operation $\overline{H_2'} = \textbf{makeInverse}(H_2')$ $= \textbf{Uhlt}[1, 3, [\langle 1, 2, \text{dark}\rangle, \langle 3, 1, \text{null}\rangle]]$. Fourth, $E\overline{H_2'} = \overline{H_2'}$ because H_2' is the last operation in HB. Finally, execute $E\overline{H_2'}$ and mark H_2' and $\overline{H_2'}$ as a do-undo pair. After that, characters b and c are recovered to be highlighted in dark and character e is dehighlighted, and $HB = [H_1, E, {}^*H_2']$.

At *Site 2*, $\textbf{SUIT}(\textbf{Id}(H_2), HB)$ is executed to undo H_2. Because H_2 is the last operation in HB, H_2's inverse operation $\overline{H_2} = \textbf{makeInverse}(H_2) = \textbf{Uhlt}[1, 4, [\langle 1, 3, \text{dark}\rangle, \langle 4, 1, \text{null}\rangle]]$ will be executed as-is. After that, characters b, c, and d are recovered to be highlighted in dark and character e is dehighlighted , and $HB = [H_1, {}^*H_2]$. When the remote deletion operation E arrives, because there is no other insertion/deletion operation in HB, $\textbf{PICOT}(E, HB)$ simply executes E as-is. After that, character d is deleted and $HB = [H_1, {}^*H_2, E]$.

The last example is that undoing a highlighting operation is mixed with concurrent undoing an insertion/deletion operation. As a follow-up of the above example in Figure A.3, as shown in Figure A.4, *Site 1* issues a command to undo the deletion operation E in $HB = [H_1, E, {}^*H_2']$ where $H_1 = \textbf{Hlt}[0, 4, [\langle 0, 4, \text{null}\rangle]]$, $E = \textbf{Del}[3, 1, \text{d}]$, and $H_2' = \textbf{Hlt}[1, 3, [\langle 1, 2, \text{dark}\rangle, \langle 3, 1, \text{null}\rangle]]$. At the same time, *Site 2* issues another command to undo the undone highlighting operation H_2 (i.e., to redo H_2) in $HB = [H_1, {}^*H_2, E]$ where $H_1 = \textbf{Hlt}[0, 4, [\langle 0, 4, \text{null}\rangle]]$, $H_2 = \textbf{Hlt}[1, 4, [\langle 1, 3, \text{dark}\rangle, \langle 4, 1, \text{dark}\rangle]]$, and $E = \textbf{Del}[3, 1, \text{d}]$.

At *Site 1*, $\textbf{SUIT}(\textbf{Id}(E), HB)$ is executed to undo E as follows: first, find operation $E = \mathrm{HB}[2]$ with a matching of $\textbf{Id}(E)$. Second, make E's inverse operation $\overline{E} = \textbf{makeInverse}(E) = \textbf{Ins}[3, 1, \text{d}]$. Third, $E\overline{E} = \overline{E}$ because ${}^*H_2$ is a do-undo pair but $H_2' = \textbf{IT\_HI}(H_2', \overline{E}) = \textbf{Hlt}[1, 4, [\langle 1, 3, \text{dark}\rangle, \langle 4, 1, \text{null}\rangle]]$. Finally, execute $E\overline{E}$ and mark E and $\overline{E}$ as a do-undo pair. After that, character d is inserted at position 3 (i.e., after character c), and $HB = [H_1, {}^*E, {}^*H_2']$. It should be mentioned that deletion operations should save deleted characters as well as their attributes in order to recover those characters with correct attributes when they are undone. In this example, when E was executed, character d and its highlighting attribute in dark were saved in E. Therefore, when $E\overline{E}$ is executed to undo E, character d would be highlighted in dark and inserted at position 3.

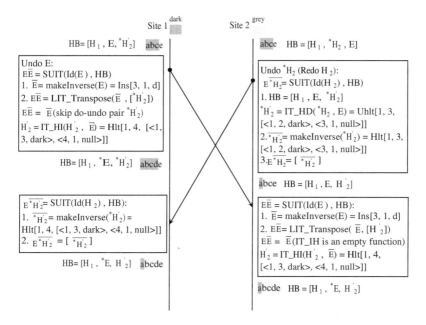

Figure A.4: Undoing a highlighting operation is mixed with concurrent undo of an insertion/deletion operation

When the remote undo command carrying $\mathbf{Id}(H_2)$ arrives, $\mathbf{SUIT}(\mathbf{Id}(H_2)$, $HB)$ simply executes $^*H_2'$'s inverse operation $\overline{^*H_2'} = \mathbf{makeInverse}(^*H_2') = \mathbf{Hlt}[1, 4, [\langle 1, 3, dark\rangle, \langle 4, 1, null\rangle]]$. After that, characters b, c, d, and e are highlighted in grey while character a remains highlighted in dark, and $HB = [H_1, {}^*E, H_2']$.

At $Site\ 2$, $\mathbf{SUIT}(\mathbf{Id}(H_2)$, $HB)$ is executed to undo the undone operation H_2

(i.e., to undo H_2) as follows: first, find operation $H_2 = $ HB[2] with a matching of **Id**(H_2). Second, transform and shift the deletion operation E to the left side of $^*H_2$. After that, $HB = [H_1, E, {^*H'_2}]$ where $^*H'_2 = $ **IT_HD**($^*H_2$, E) = **Uhlt**[1, 3, [$\langle 1, 2,$ dark$\rangle$, $\langle 3, 1,$ null$\rangle$]] and $^*H'_2 = $ HB[3]. Third, make $^*H'_2$'s inverse operation $\overline{^*H'_2} = $ **makeInverse**($^*H'_2$) = **Hlt**[1, 3, [$\langle 1, 2,$ dark$\rangle$, $\langle 3, 1,$ null$\rangle$]]. Fourth, $E^{\overline{^*H'_2}} = \overline{^*H'_2}$ because $^*H'_2$ is the last operation in HB. Finally, execute $E^{\overline{^*H'_2}}$ and remove the mark of do-undo pair for $^*H'_2$. After that, characters b, c, and e are highlighted in grey while character a remains highlighted in dark, and $HB = [H_1, E, H'_2]$.

When the remote undo command carrying **Id**(E) arrives, **SUIT**(**Id**(E), HB) is executed to undo E as follows: first, find operation $E = $ HB[2] with a matching of **Id**(E). Second, make E's inverse operation $\overline{E} = $ **makeInverse**(E) = **Ins**[3, 1, d]. Third, $E^{\overline{E}} = \overline{E}$ because there is no insertion/deletion operation in HB[3] and $H'_2 = $ **IT_HI**(H'_2, $\overline{E}$) = **Hlt**[1, 4, [$\langle 1, 3,$ dark$\rangle$, $\langle 4, 1,$ null$\rangle$]]. Finally, execute $E^{\overline{E}}$ and mark E and $\overline{E}$ as a do-undo pair. After that, character d is highlighted in dark (as explained in the above paragraph) and inserted at position 3 (i.e., after character c), and $HB = [H_1, {^*E}, H'_2]$. But because character d falls into the highlighting region covered by H'_2, it is then highlighted in grey.

Appendix B

Formal proofs of theorems and properties

This appendix includes formal proofs of Theorem 3.1 and Property 3.2 described in Chapter 3.

Theorem 3.1 Given a log L, if $L_c = \mathbf{COMET}(L)$, then it must be $L_c = L_\Gamma$.

Proof:

1. When $|\mathrm{L}| = 1$, $L_\Gamma = L$ and $L_c = \mathbf{COMET}(L) = L$. Therefore $L_c = L_\Gamma$. The theorem holds.

2. Assume the theorem holds when $|\mathrm{L}| = n$. That is, given a $L = [O_1, \cdots, O_n]$, if $L_c = \mathbf{COMET}(L) = [D_1, \cdots D_r, I_1, \cdots, I_s]$, D_i $(1 \leq i \leq r)$ are disjointed deletion operations, I_j $(1 \leq j \leq s)$ are disjointed insertion operations, and $D_i \odot I_j$.

3. When $|\mathrm{L}| = n{+}1$, $L = [O_1, \cdots, O_n, O_{n+1}]$, $L_c = \mathbf{COMET}(L) = \mathbf{COMET}([O_1, \cdots, O_n, O_{n+1}]) = \mathbf{COMET}([[O_1, \cdots, O_n], [O_{n+1}]]) = \mathbf{COMET}([\mathbf{COMET}([O_1, \cdots, O_n]), \mathbf{COMET}([O_{n+1}])]) = \mathbf{COMET}([[D_1, \cdots, D_r, I_1, \cdots, I_s], [O_{n+1}]]) = \mathbf{COMET}([D_1, \cdots, D_r, I_1, \cdots, I_s, O_{n+1}])$.

    (a) If O_{n+1} is an insertion operation, then for $\forall\, D_i$ $(1 \leq i \leq r)$, $D_i \odot O_{n+1}$, according to Definition 3.3. Therefore $L_c = \mathbf{COMET}([D_1, \cdots, D_r, I_1, \cdots, I_s, O_{n+1}]) = [D_1, \cdots, D_r, \mathbf{COMET}([I_1, \cdots, I_s, O_{n+1}])]$.

237

i. Given $\forall\, I_j$ $(1 \le j \le s)$, if $I_j \odot O_{n+1}$, then $L_c = \textbf{COMET}([D_1, \cdots,$ $D_r, I_1, \cdots, I_s, O_{n+1}]) = [D_1, \cdots, D_r, I_1, \cdots, I_s, O_{n+1}]$ where all operations are disjointed. Therefore the theorem holds.

ii. If $\exists\, I_k$ $(1 \le k \le s)$, where $I_k \oplus O_{n+1}$ or $I_k \ominus O_{n+1}$, O_{n+1} will be merged into I_k by operational merging. Then, $\textbf{COMET}([I_1, \cdots, I_k, \cdots, I_s,$ $O_{n+1}]) = [I_1, \cdots, I'_k, \cdots, I_s]$ where all operations are disjointed. As a result, $L_c = \textbf{COMET}([D_1, \cdots, D_r, I_1, \cdots, I_s, O_{n+1}]) = [D_1, \cdots,$ $D_r, I_1, \cdots, I'_k, \cdots, I_s]$ where all operations are disjointed. Therefore the theorem holds.

(b) If O_{n+1} is a deletion operation,

i. Given $\forall\, D_i$ $(1 \le i \le r)$ or $\forall\, I_j$ $(1 \le j \le s)$, if $D_i \odot O_{n+1}$ and $I_j \odot O_{n+1}$, then $L_c = \textbf{COMET}([D_1, \cdots, D_r, I_1, \cdots, I_s, O_{n+1}])$ $= \textbf{COMET}([D_1, \cdots, D_r, O'_{n+1}, I'_1, \cdots, I'_s]) = [\textbf{COMET}([D_1, \cdots,$ $D_r, O'_{n+1}]), \textbf{COMET}([I'_1, \cdots, I'_s])]$. The deletion operation O_{n+1} would never create new adjacent relations among $[D_1, \cdots, D_r]$, so $\textbf{COMET}([D_1, \cdots, D_r, O'_{n+1}]) = [D_1, \cdots, D_r, O'_{n+1}]$ where all deletion operations are disjointed. However, the deletion operation O_{n+1} may create a new adjacent relation between I_l and I_q $(1 \le l, q \le s)$. As a result, $\textbf{COMET}([I'_1, \cdots, I'_s]) = [I'_1, \cdots, I''_l, \cdots, I'_{q-1}, I'_{q+1}, \cdots, I'_s]$ where all insertion operations are disjointed. So $L_c = \textbf{COMET}([D_1,$ $\cdots, D_r, I_1, \cdots, I_s, O_{n+1}]) = [D_1, \cdots, D_r, O'_{n+1}, I'_1, \cdots, I'_s]$ or $[D_1,$ $\cdots, D_r, O'_{n+1}, I'_1, \cdots, I''_l, \cdots, I'_{q-1}, I'_{q+1}, \cdots, I'_s]$ where all operations are disjointed. Therefore the theorem holds.

ii. Given $\forall\, I_j$ $(1 \le j \le s)$, where $I_j \odot O_{n+1}$, but $\exists\, D_k$ $(1 \le k \le r)$, where $D_k \oplus O_{n+1}$ or $D_k \ominus O_{n+1}$, then O_{n+1} will be merged into D_k. So L_c $= \textbf{COMET}([D_1, \cdots, D_r, I_1, \cdots, I_s, O_{n+1}]) = [\textbf{COMET}([D_1, \cdots,$

$D_r, O'_{n+1}])$, **COMET**$([I'_1, \cdots, I'_s])]$. **COMET**$([D_1, \cdots, D_r, O'_{n+1}])$ $= [D_1, \cdots, D'_k, \cdots, D'_r]$ where all deletion operations are disjointed. O_{n+1} may create a new adjacent relation between I_l and I_q $(1 \leq l, q \leq s)$. As a result, **COMET**$([I'_1, \cdots, I'_s]) = [I'_1, \cdots, I''_l, \cdots, I'_{q-1}, I'_{q+1}, \cdots, I'_s]$ where all insertion operations are disjointed. So $L_c =$ **COMET**$([D_1, \cdots, D_r, I_1, \cdots, I_s, O_{n+1}]) = [D_1, \cdots, D'_k, \cdots, D'_r, I'_1, \cdots, I'_s]$ or $[D_1, \cdots, D'_k, \cdots, D'_r, I'_1, \cdots, I''_l, \cdots, I'_{q-1}, I'_{q+1}, \cdots, I'_s]$ where all operations are disjointed. Therefore the theorem holds.

iii. Given $\forall D_i$ $(1 \leq i \leq r)$, where $D_i \odot O_{n+1}$ but $\exists I_k$ $(1 \leq k \leq s)$, where $I_k \oplus O_{n+1}$.

   A. If O_{n+1} can be totally merged into I_k, $L_c =$ **COMET**$([D_1, \cdots, D_r, I_1, \cdots, I_s, O_{n+1}]) = [D_1, \cdots, D_r, \textbf{COMET}([I_1, \cdots, I_s, O_{n+1}])] = [D_1, \cdots, D_r, I_1, \cdots, I'_k, \cdots, I'_s]$ where all operations are disjointed. Therefore the theorem holds.

   B. If I_k can be totally merged into O_{n+1}, $L_c =$ **COMET**$([D_1, \cdots, D_r, I_1, \cdots, I_s, O_{n+1}]) =$ **COMET**$([D_1, \cdots, D_r, O'_{n+1}, I'_1, \cdots, I'_{k-1}, I'_{k+1}, \cdots, I'_s]) = [D_1, \cdots, D_r, O'_{n+1}, \textbf{COMET}([I'_1, \cdots, I'_{k-1}, I'_{k+1}, \cdots, I'_s])$ where D_i $(1 \leq i \leq r)$ and O'_{n+1} are disjointed deletion operations. If O_{n+1} creates a new adjacent relation between I_l and I_q $(1 \leq l, q \leq s)$, **COMET**$([I'_1, \cdots, I'_{k-1}, I'_{k+1}, \cdots, I'_s]) = [I'_1, \cdots, I'_{k-1}, I'_{k+1}, \cdots, I''_l, \cdots, I'_{q-1}, I'_{q-1}, \cdots, I'_s]$ where all insertion operations are disjointed. So $L_c = [D_1, \cdots, D_r, O'_{n+1}, I'_1, \cdots, I'_{k-1}, I'_{k+1}, \cdots, I'_s]$ or $[D_1, \cdots, D_r, O'_{n+1}, I'_1, \cdots, I'_{k-1}, I'_{k+1}, \cdots, I''_l, \cdots, I'_{q-1}, I'_{q-1}, \cdots, I'_s]$ where all operations are disjointed. Therefore the theorem holds.

   C. If I_k and O_{n+1} can be partially merged, $L_c =$ **COMET**$([D_1, \cdots, D_r, I_1, \cdots, I_s, O_{n+1}]) =$ **COMET**$([D_1, \cdots, D_r, I_1, \cdots, I'_k, O'_{n+1},$

$$I'_{k+1}, \cdots, I'_s]) = \textbf{COMET}([D_1, \cdots, D_r, O''_{n+1}, I'_1, \cdots, I''_k, \cdots, I'_s])$$
$$= [D_1, \cdots, D_r, O''_{n+1}, \textbf{COMET}([I'_1, \cdots, I''_k, \cdots, I'_s])] \text{ where } D_i$$

$(1 \leq i \leq r)$ and O''_{n+1} are disjointed deletion operations. If O_{n+1} creates a new adjacent relation between I_l and I_q $(1 \leq l, q \leq s)$,

$$\textbf{COMET}([I'_1, \cdots, I''_k, \cdots, I'_s]) = [I'_1, \cdots, I''_k, \cdots, I''_l, \cdots, I'_{q-1},$$

$I'_{q+1}, \cdots, I'_s]$ where all insertion operations are disjointed. So L_c

$$= [D_1, \cdots, D_r, O''_{n+1}, I'_1, \cdots, I''_k, \cdots, I'_s] \text{ or } [D_1, \cdots, D_r, O''_{n+1},$$

$I'_1, \cdots, I''_k, \cdots, I''_l, \cdots, I'_{q-1}, I'_{q+1}, \cdots, I'_s]$ where all operations are disjointed. Therefore the theorem holds.

iv. If $\exists\, D_k$ $(1 \leq k \leq r)$ and I_p $(1 \leq p \leq s)$ where D_k $(\oplus/\ominus)$ O_{n+1} and $I_p \oplus O_{n+1}$, it can be deduced from (ii) and (iii) that operations in $L_c = \textbf{COMET}([D_1, \cdots, D_r, I_1, \cdots, I_s, O_{n+1}])$ are also disjointed. Therefore the theorem holds.

Property 3.2 *Operational Merging Property (OMP)*

Given any two operations O_a and O_b, where $O_a \mapsto O_b$, if $\textbf{OM}(O_a, O_b) = (O'_a, O'_b)$, then $[O_a, O_b] \equiv [O'_a, O'_b]$.

Proof: First reason the $\textbf{OM\_II}(O_a, O_b)$ function. Suppose $CT_{O_a} = S$, containing a sequence of n characters $C_1 \cdots C_n$. $O_a = \textbf{Ins}[i, r, X_1 \cdots X_r]$ $(0 \leq i \leq n)$ is to insert a sequence of r characters $X_1 \cdots X_r$ at position i.

1. If $O_a \odot O_b$, then $\textbf{OM\_II}(O_a, O_b) = (O'_a, O'_b) = (O_a, O_b)$. As a result, $S \circ [O_a, O_b] = S \circ \textbf{OM\_II}(O_a, O_b) = S \circ [O'_a, O'_b]$. So it holds that $[O_a, O_b] \equiv [O'_a, O'_b]$.

2. If $O_a \ominus O_b$, then it must be $O_b = \textbf{Ins}[i, s, Y_1 \cdots Y_s]$ to insert a sequence of s characters $Y_1 \cdots Y_s$ just left to the string inserted by O_a, or $O_b = \textbf{Ins}[i+r, s, Y_1 \cdots Y_s]$ to insert a sequence of s characters $Y_1 \cdots Y_s$ just right to the string inserted by O_a. As a result, $\textbf{OM\_II}(O_a, O_b) = (O'_a, I)$ where $O'_a = \textbf{Ins}[i, s+r, Y_1 \cdots Y_s X_1 \cdots X_r]$ or $\textbf{Ins}[i, r+s, X_1 \cdots X_r Y_1 \cdots Y_s]$.

- $S_a = S \circ [O_a] = C_1 \cdots C_i X_1 \cdots X_r C_{i+1} \cdots C_n$ and $S \circ [O_a, O_b] = S_a \circ [O_b] = C_1 \cdots C_i Y_1 \cdots Y_s X_1 \cdots X_r C_{i+1} \cdots C_n$ or $C_1 \cdots C_i X_1 \cdots X_r Y_1 \cdots Y_s C_{i+1} \cdots C_n$.

- $S \circ [O'_a] = C_1 \cdots C_i Y_1 \cdots Y_s X_1 \cdots X_r C_{i+1} \cdots C_n$ or $C_1 \cdots C_i X_1 \cdots X_r Y_1 \cdots Y_s C_{i+1} \cdots C_n$.

- As a result, $S \circ [O_a, O_b] = S \circ [O'_a] = S \circ \textbf{OM\_II}(O_a, O_b)$. So it holds that $[O_a, O_b] \equiv [O'_a]$.

3. If $O_a \oplus O_b$, then it must be $O_b = \textbf{Ins}[j, s, Y_1 \cdots Y_s]$ where $i < j < i+r$ to insert a sequence of s characters within the string inserted by O_a. As a result, $\textbf{OM\_II}(O_a, O_b) = (O'_a, I)$ where $O'_a = \textbf{Ins}[i, r+s, X_1 \cdots X_{j-i} Y_1 \cdots Y_s X_{j-i+1} \cdots X_r]$.

  - $S_a = S \circ [O_a] = C_1 \cdots C_i X_1 \cdots X_r C_{i+1} \cdots C_n$ and $S \circ [O_a, O_b] = S_a \circ [O_b] = C_1 \cdots C_i X_1 \cdots X_{j-i} Y_1 \cdots Y_s X_{j-i+1} \cdots X_r C_{i+1} \cdots C_n$.

  - $S \circ [O'_a] = C_1 \cdots C_i X_1 \cdots X_{j-i} Y_1 \cdots Y_s X_{j-i+1} \cdots X_r C_{i+1} \cdots C_n$.

  - As a result, $S \circ [O_a, O_b] = S \circ [O'_a] = S \circ \textbf{OM\_II}(O_a, O_b)$. So it holds that $[O_a, O_b] \equiv [O'_a]$.

Then reason the $\textbf{OM\_DD}(O_a, O_b)$ function. Suppose $CT_{O_a} = S$, containing a sequence of n characters $C_1 \cdots C_n$. $O_a = \textbf{Del}[i, r, C_{i+1} \cdots C_{i+r}]$ $(0 \le i \le n)$ is to delete a sequence of r characters $C_{i+1} \cdots C_{i+r}$ at position i.

1. If $O_a \odot O_b$, then $\textbf{OM\_DD}(O_a, O_b) = (O'_a, O'_b) = (O_a, O_b)$. As a result, $S \circ [O_a, O_b] = S \circ \textbf{OM\_DD}(O_a, O_b) = S \circ [O'_a, O'_b]$. So it holds that $[O_a, O_b] \equiv [O'_a, O'_b]$.

2. If $O_a \ominus O_b$, then it must be $O_b = \textbf{Del}[j, i-j, C_{j+1} \cdots C_i]$ where $j < i$ to delete a sequence of $i-j$ characters just left to the string deleted by O_a at position j, or $O_b = \textbf{Del}[i, s, C_{i+r+1} \cdots C_{i+r+s}]$ to delete a sequence of s characters just right to the string deleted by O_a at position i. As a result, $\textbf{OM\_DD}(O_a, O_b) = (O'_a, I)$ where $O'_a = \textbf{Del}[j, i-j+r, C_{j+1} \cdots C_{i+r}]$ or $\textbf{Del}[i, r+s, C_{i+1} \cdots C_{i+r+s}]$.

- $S_a = S \circ [O_a] = C_1 \cdots C_i C_{i+r+1} \cdots C_n$ and $S \circ [O_a, O_b] = S_a \circ [O_b] = C_1 \cdots C_j C_{i+r+1} \cdots C_n$ or $C_1 \cdots C_i C_{i+r+s+1} \cdots C_n$.

- $S \circ [O'_a] = C_1 \cdots C_j C_{i+r+1} \cdots C_n$ or $C_1 \cdots C_i C_{i+r+s+1} \cdots C_n$.

- As a result, $S \circ [O_a, O_b] = S \circ [O'_a] = S \circ \mathbf{OM\_DD}(O_a, O_b)$. So it holds that $[O_a, O_b] \equiv [O'_a]$.

3. If $O_a \oplus O_b$, then it must be $O_b = \mathbf{Del}[j, s, C_{j+1} \cdots C_i C_{i+r+1} \cdots C_{r+s+j}]$ where $j < i$ and $s > i\text{-}j$. As a result, $\mathbf{OM\_DD}(O_a, O_b) = (O'_a, I)$ where $O'_a = \mathbf{Del}[j, r+s, C_1 \cdots C_j C_{r+s+j+1} \cdots C_n]$.

- $S_a = S \circ [O_a] = C_1 \cdots C_i C_{i+r+1} \cdots C_n$ and $S \circ [O_a, O_b] = S_a \circ [O_b] = C_1 \cdots C_j C_{r+s+j+1} \cdots C_n$.

- $S \circ [O'_a] = C_1 \cdots C_j C_{r+s+j+1} \cdots C_n$.

- As a result, $S \circ [O_a, O_b] = S \circ [O'_a] = S \circ \mathbf{OM\_DD}(O_a, O_b)$. So it holds that $[O_a, O_b] \equiv [O'_a]$.

Finally reason the $\mathbf{OM\_ID}(O_a, O_b)$ function. Suppose $CT_{O_a} = S$, containing a sequence of n characters $C_1 \cdots C_n$. $O_a = \mathbf{Ins}[i, r, X_1 \cdots X_r]$ $(0 \leq i \leq n)$ is to insert a sequence of r characters $X_1 \cdots X_r$ at position i.

1. If $O_a \odot O_b$, then $\mathbf{OM\_ID}(O_a, O_b) = (O'_a, O'_b) = (O_a, O_b)$. As a result, $S \circ [O_a, O_b] = S \circ \mathbf{OM\_ID}(O_a, O_b) = S \circ [O'_a, O'_b]$. So it holds that $[O_a, O_b] \equiv [O'_a, O'_b]$.

2. $O_a \oplus O_b$, then it must be one of the following possibilities:

   (a) $O_b = \mathbf{Del}[i, r, X_1 \cdots X_r]$ to delete the r characters $X_1 \cdots X_r$ inserted by O_a at position i. As a result, $\mathbf{OM\_ID}(O_a, O_b) = [I, I]$.

   - $S_a = S \circ [O_a] = C_1 \cdots C_i X_1 \cdots X_r C_{i+1} \cdots C_n$ and $S \circ [O_a, O_b] = S_a \circ [O_b] = C_1 \cdots C_i C_{i+1} \cdots C_n = C_1 \cdots C_n = S$

- $S \circ \mathbf{OM\_ID}(O_a, O_b) = S \circ [\,] = S$
- As a result, $S \circ [O_a, O_b] = S \circ [\,] = S \circ \mathbf{OM\_ID}(O_a, O_b)$. So it holds that $[O_a, O_b] \equiv [\,]$.

(b) $O_b = \mathbf{Del}[j,\ s,\ C_{j+1}\cdots C_i X_1 \cdots X_r C_{i+1} \cdots C_{s+j-r}]$ where $j < i$ and $s > i\text{-}j\text{+}r$ to delete a sequence of $i\text{-}j$ characters left to the string inserted by O_a, the entire string $X_1 \cdots X_r$ inserted by O_a, and a sequence of $s\text{+}j\text{-}i\text{-}r$ characters right to the string inserted by O_a. As a result, $\mathbf{OM\_ID}(O_a, O_b) = [I, O_b']$ where $O_b' = \mathbf{Del}[j,\ s\text{-}r,\ C_{j+1}\cdots C_{s+j-r}]$.

  - $S_a = S \circ [O_a] = C_1 \cdots C_i X_1 \cdots X_r C_{i+1} \cdots C_n$ and $S \circ [O_a, O_b] = S_a \circ [O_b] = C_1 \cdots C_j C_{s+j-r+1} \cdots C_n$
  - $S \circ \mathbf{OM\_ID}(O_a, O_b) = S \circ [O_b'] = C_1 \cdots C_j C_{s+j-r+1} \cdots C_n$
  - As a result, $S \circ [O_a, O_b] = S \circ O_b' = S \circ \mathbf{OM\_ID}(O_a, O_b)$. So it holds that $[O_a, O_b] \equiv [O_b']$.

(c) $O_b = \mathbf{Del}[j,\ s,\ X_{j-i+1}\cdots X_{s+j-i}]$ where $i < j < i\text{+}r$ and $s < r\text{+}i\text{-}j$ to delete part of the string inserted by O_a. As a result, $\mathbf{OM\_ID}(O_a, O_b) = [O_a', I]$ where $O_a' = \mathbf{Ins}[i,\ r\text{-}s,\ X_1 \cdots X_{j-i} X_{s+j-i+1} \cdots X_r]$.

  - $S_a = S \circ [O_a] = C_1 \cdots C_i X_1 \cdots X_r C_{i+1} \cdots C_n$ and $S \circ [O_a, O_b] = S_a \circ [O_b] = C_1 \cdots C_i X_1 \cdots X_{j-i} X_{s+j-i+1} \cdots X_r C_{i+1} \cdots C_n$
  - $S \circ \mathbf{OM\_ID}(O_a, O_b) = S \circ [O_a'] = C_1 \cdots C_i X_1 \cdots X_{j-i} X_{s+j-i+1} \cdots X_r C_{i+1} \cdots C_n$
  - As a result, $S \circ [O_a, O_b] = S \circ S [O_a'] = \circ \mathbf{OM\_ID}(O_a, O_b)$. So it holds that $[O_a, O_b] \equiv [O_a']$.

(d) $O_b = \mathbf{Del}[j,\ s,\ C_{j+1}\cdots C_i X_1 \cdots X_{s+j-i}]$ where $j < i$ and $i\text{-}j < s < r\text{+}i\text{-}j$ to delete a sequence of $i\text{-}j$ characters left to the string inserted by O_a and a left part of the string inserted by O_a. As a result, $\mathbf{OM\_ID}(O_a, O_b) =$

$[O'_a, O'_b]$ where $O'_a = \textbf{Ins}[i,\ r\text{-}s+i\text{-}j,\ X_{s+j-i+1}\cdots X_r]$ and $O'_b = \textbf{Del}[j,\ i\text{-}j,$
$C_{j+1}\cdots C_i]$.

- $S_a = S \circ [O_a] = C_1\cdots C_i X_1 \cdots X_r C_{i+1}\cdots C_n$ and $S \circ [O_a, O_b] = S_a \circ$
  $[O_b] = C_1\cdots C_j X_{s+j-i+1}\cdots X_r C_{i+1}\cdots C_n$.

- $S'_a = S \circ [O'_a] = C_1\cdots C_i X_{s+j-i+1}\cdots X_r C_{i+1}\cdots C_n$ and $S \circ [O'_a, O'_b] =$
  $S'_a \circ [O'_b] = C_1\cdots C_j X_{s+j-i+1}\cdots X_r C_{i+1}\cdots C_n$.

- As a result, $S \circ [O_a, O_b] = S \circ [O'_a, O'_b] = S \circ \textbf{OM\_ID}(O_a, O_b)$. So
  it holds that $[O_a, O_b] \equiv [O'_a, O'_b]$.

(e) $O_b = \textbf{Del}[j,\ s,\ X_{j-i+1}\cdots X_r C_{i+1}\cdots C_{s+j-r}]$ where $i < j \le r+i$ and $s > r+i\text{-}$
j to delete a right part of the string inserted by O_a and a sequence of $s\text{-}r+j\text{-}$
i characters right to the string inserted by O_a. As a result, $\textbf{OM\_ID}(O_a,$
$O_b) = [O'_a, O'_b]$ where $O'_a = \textbf{Ins}[i,\ j\text{-}i,\ X_1\cdots X_{j-i}]$ and $O'_b = \textbf{Del}[j,\ s\text{-}r+j\text{-}i,$
$C_{i+1}\cdots C_{s+j-r}]$.

- $S_a = S \circ [O_a] = C_1\cdots C_i X_1 \cdots X_r C_{i+1}\cdots C_n$ and $S \circ [O_a, O_b] = S_a \circ$
  $[O_b] = C_1\cdots C_i X_1 \cdots X_{j-i} C_{s+j-r+1}\cdots C_n$.

- $S'_a = S \circ [O'_a] = C_1\cdots C_i X_{+1}\cdots X_{j-i} C_{i+1}\cdots C_n$ and $S \circ [O'_a, O'_b] = S'_a$
  $\circ [O'_b] = C_1\cdots C_i X_1 \cdots X_{j-i} C_{s+j-r+1}\cdots C_n$.

- As a result, $S \circ [O_a, O_b] = S \circ [O'_a, O'_b] = S \circ \textbf{OM\_ID}(O_a, O_b)$. So
  it holds that $[O_a, O_b] \equiv [O'_a, O'_b]$.

Appendix C

Sample code

This appendix gives an example of the **Syntactic-Conflict** (SMR, O_r, O_l, CT) function that emulates the state-based merging behavior.

Function C.1. *Syntactic-Conflict(Oa, O_b, CT): true/false*
{ if $\mathbf{T}(O_a) == Ins$ and $\mathbf{T}(O_b) == Ins$ and $\mathbf{getLineOfOffset}(\mathbf{P}(O_b))$-1
$\leq \mathbf{getLineOfOffset}(\mathbf{P}(O_a)) \leq \mathbf{getLineOfOffset}(\mathbf{P}(O_b))$+1
   return *true*;
else if $\mathbf{T}(O_a) == Ins$ and $\mathbf{T}(O_b) == Del$ and $\mathbf{getLineOfOffset}(\mathbf{P}(O_b))$-1
$\leq \mathbf{getLineOfOffset}(\mathbf{P}(O_a)) \leq \mathbf{getLineOfOffset}(\mathbf{P}(O_b)+\mathbf{N}(O_b))$+1
   return *true*;
else if $\mathbf{T}(O_a) == Del$ and $\mathbf{T}(O_b) == Ins$ and $\mathbf{getLineOfOffset}(\mathbf{P}(O_a))$-1
$\leq \mathbf{getLineOfOffset}(\mathbf{P}(O_b)) \leq \mathbf{getLineOfOffset}(\mathbf{P}(O_a)+\mathbf{N}(O_a))$+1
   return *true*;
else if $\mathbf{T}(O_a) == Del$ and $\mathbf{T}(O_b) == Del$ and ($\mathbf{getLineOfOffset}(\mathbf{P}(O_b))$-1
$\leq \mathbf{getLineOfOffset}(\mathbf{P}(O_a)) \leq \mathbf{getLineOfOffset}(\mathbf{P}(O_b)+\mathbf{N}(O_b))$+1 **or**
$\mathbf{getLineOfOffset}(\mathbf{P}(O_a))$-1 $\leq \mathbf{getLineOfOffset}(\mathbf{P}(O_b))$
$\leq \mathbf{getLineOfOffset}(\mathbf{P}(O_a)+\mathbf{N}(O_a))$+1)
   return *true*;
else
   return *false*;
}

Bibliography

[1] L. Allen, G. Fernandez, K. Kane, D. Leblang, D. Minard, and J. Posner. ClearCase MultiSite: Supporting geographically distributed software development. In *Software Configuration Management: Selected Papers of the ICSE SCM-4 and SCM-5 Workshops*, pages 194–214. Springer Verlag, 1995.

[2] R. M. Baecker, D. Nastos, I. R. Posner, and K. L. Mawby. The user-centred iterative design of collaborative writing software. In *Proceedings of ACM INTER-CHI'93 Conference on Human Factors in Computing Systems*, pages 399–405. ACM Press, 1993.

[3] G. Banavar, T. Chandra, B. Mukherjee, and J. Nagarajarao. An efficient multicast protocol for content-based publish-subscribe systems. In *Proc. of International Conference on Distributed Computing Systems*, pages 262–272. IEEE computer society, 1999.

[4] K. Beck. Embracing Change with Extreme Programming. *IEEE Transactions on computer*, 32(10):70–77, October 1999.

[5] K. Beck. *Extreme Programming explained : embrace change*. Addison-Wesley, 2000.

[6] J. Begole, M. B. Rosson, and C. A. Shaffer. Flexible collaboration transparency: supporting worker independence in replicated application-sharing systems. *ACM Transactions on Computer-Human Interaction*, 6(2):95–132, June 1999.

[7] H. Berghel. Who won the Mosaic War? *Communications of the ACM*, 41(10):13–16, October 1998.

[8] T. Berlage. A Selective Undo Mechanism for Graphical User Interfaces Based on Command Objects. *ACM Transactions on Computer-Human Interaction*, 1(3):269–294, September 1994.

246

[9] T. Berlage and A. Genau. A framework for shared applications with a replicated architecure. In *Proc. of ACM Symposium on User Interface Software and Technology*, pages 249–257. ACM Press, 1993.

[10] B. Berliner. Cvs ii:parallelizing software development. In *Proc. of 1990 Winter USENIX*, pages 341–352, 1990.

[11] V. Berzins. Software merge: semantics of combining changes to programs. *ACM Transactions on Programming Languages and Systems*, 16(6):1875–1903, November 1994.

[12] E. A. Bier and S. Freeman. Mmm: a user interface architecture for shared editors on a single screen. In *Proceedings of the 4th annual ACM symposium on User interface software and technology*, pages 79–86. ACM Press, October 1991.

[13] D. Binkley, S. Horwitz, and T. Peps. Program integration for languages with procedure calls. *ACM Transactions on Software Engineering Methodology*, 4(1):3–35, January 1995.

[14] K. P. Birman. The process group approach to reliable distributed computing. *Communications of the ACM*, 36(12):37–54, 1993.

[15] J. Blackburn, Ga. Scudder, and L. N. Van Wassenhove. Concurrent software development. *Communications of the ACM*, 43(11):200–214, November 2000.

[16] T. Boudreau, J. Glick, S. Greene, J. Woehr, and V. Spurlin. *NetBeans: The Definitive Guide*. O'Reilly and Associates, 2002.

[17] B. Bruck. *Essential Office 2000 Book*. Premier Press, Inc., 1999.

[18] J. Buffenbarger. Syntactic Software Merging. In *Software Configuration Management: Selected Papers SCM-4 and SCM-5*, pages 153–172. Springer Verlag, June 1995.

[19] M. Cagan. Untangling configuration management. In *Proc. of the 5th International Workshop on Software Configuration Management*, pages 35–52. Springer Verlag, 1995.

[20] D. Cameron, B. Rosenblatt, and E. S. Raymond. *Leanring GNU Emacs, 2nd Edition*. O'Reilly and Associates, 1996.

[21] A. Carzaniga, D. S. Rosenblum, and A. L. Wolf. Achieving scalability and expressiveness in an internet-scale event notification service. In *Proc. of ACM Conference on Distributed Computing*, pages 219–227. ACM Press, 2000.

[22] A. Carzaniga, D. S. Rosenblum, and A. L. Wolf. Evaluation of a Wide-Area Event Notification Service. *ACM Transactions on Computer Systems*, 19(3):332–383, 2001.

[23] D. Chen. *Consistency Maintenance in Collaborative Graphics Editing Systems*. PhD Thesis, Griffith University, Brisbane, Australia, 2001.

[24] D. Chen and C. Sun. Undoing Any Operation in Collaborative Graphics Editing Systems. In *Proc. of the ACM 2001 International Conference on Supporting Group Work*, pages 197–206. ACM Press, September 2001.

[25] R. Choudhary and P. Dewan. A general multi-user undo/redo model. In *Proc. of European Conference on Computer Supported Work*, pages 231–246, October 1995.

[26] A. Cockburn and L. Williams. The costs and benefits of pair programming. In *Proc. of eXtreme Programming and Flexible Processes in Software Engineering*, June 2000.

[27] B. Collins-Sussman. The subversion project: buiding a better CVS. *Linux Journal*, 2002(94):3–4, February 2002.

[28] R. Conradi and B. Westfechtel. Version models for software configuration management. *ACM Computing Surveys*, 30(2):232–282, June 1998.

[29] Bull Corporation. *FlowPath Functional Specification*. Bull S. A., Paris, France, 1992.

[30] IBM Corporation. *FlowMark-Managing Your Workflow, Version 2.3*. 1996.

[31] Microsoft Corporation. *Microsoft Internet Explorer 6 Resource Kit*. 2001.

[32] W. Courington. The network software environment. Technical Report Sun Technical Report FE197-001-98, Sun Microsystems Inc., February 1989.

[33] T. Crowley, P. Milazzo, E. Baker, H. Forsdick, and R. Tomlinson. Mmconf: an infrastructure for building shared multimedia applications. In *Proc. of the ACM Conference on Computer Supported Cooperative Work*, pages 329–342. ACM Press, September 1990.

[34] S. Dart. Concepts in configuration management systems. In *Proc. of the 3rd International Workshop on Software Configuration Management*, pages 1–18. Springer Verlag, June 1991.

[35] S. Dart. Content change management: Problems for web systems. In *Proc. of the 9th International Workshop on Software Configuration Management*, pages 1–17. Springer Verlag, September 1999.

[36] A. H. Davis, C. Sun, and J. Lu. Generalizing operational transformation to the standard general markup language. In *Proc. of the ACM Conference on Computer Supported Cooperative Work*, pages 58–67. ACM Press, November 2002.

[37] P. Dewan and J. Riedl. Toward computer-supported concurrent software engineering. *Computer*, 26(1):17–27, January 1993.

[38] P. Dourish. The parting of the ways: divergence, data management and collaborative work. In *Proc. of the Fourthe European Conference on Computer-Supported Cooperative Work*, pages 215–230, September 1995.

[39] P. Dourish. Consistency Guarantees: Exploiting Application Semantics for Consistency Management in a Collaboration Toolkit. In *Proc. of the Conference on Computer-Supported Cooperative Work*, pages 268–277. ACM Press, 1996.

[40] P. Dourish. Using metalevel techniques in a flexible toolkit for CSCW applications. *ACM Transactions on Computer Human Interaction*, 5(2):109–155, June 1998.

[41] P. Dourish and V. Bellotti. Awareness and Coordination in Shared Workspaces. In *Proc. of the Conference on Computer-Supported Cooperative Work*, pages 107–114. ACM Press, December 1992.

[42] P. Dourish and S. Bly. Portholes: Supporting awareness in a distributed work group. In *Proceedings of ACM CHI'92 Conference on Human Factors in Computing Systems*, Systems for Media-Supported Collaboration, pages 541–547. ACM Press, 1992.

[43] F. Dridi and G. Neumann. How to implement Web-based Groupware Systems based on WebDAV. In *Proc. of IEEE 8th International Workshops on Enabling Technologies: Infrastructure for Collaborative Enterprises*, June 1999.

[44] Jr. E. J. Whitehead and Y. Goland. Webdav: a network protocol for remote collaborative authoring on the web. In *Proceedings of the Sixth European conference on Computer supported cooperative work*, pages 291–310, August 1999.

[45] W. K. Edwards, E. D. Mynatt, K. Petersen, M. J. Spreitzer, D. B. Terry, and M. M. Theimer. Designing and implementing asynchronous collaborative

applications with bayou. In *Proc. of the 10th annual ACM symposium on User interface software and technology*, pages 119–128. ACM Press, October 1997.

[46] C.A. Ellis and S.J. Gibbs. Concurrency control in groupware systems. In *Proc. of ACM SIGMOD Conference on Management of Data*, pages 399–407. ACM Press, May 1989.

[47] C.A. Ellis, S.J. Gibbs, and G.L. Rein. Groupware: Some Issues and Experiences. *Communications of ACM*, 34(1):39–58, January 1991.

[48] R. Elmasri and S. B. Navathe. *Fundamentals of Database Systems*. The Benjamin/Cummings Publishing Company, Inc., 1989.

[49] Global Software Engineering. *Hydra, seven brains are smarter than one.* http://hydra.globalse.org.

[50] J. Estublier. Software configuration management: a roadmap. In *Proceedings of the conference on The future of Software engineering*, pages 279–289, May 2000.

[51] Jr. F. P. Brooks. *The Mythical Man-Month, Essays on Software Engineering*. Addision-Welsley, Reading, MA, USA.

[52] C. Fidge. Timestamps in message-passing systems that preserve the partial ordering. *Australian Computer Science Communications*, 10(1), February 1988.

[53] C. Fidge. Logical time in distributed computing systems. *Computer*, 24(8), August 1991.

[54] R. S. Fish, R. E. Kraut, and M. D. P. Leland. Quilt: a collaborative tool for cooperative writing. In *Proc. ACM SIGOIS and IEEECS TC-OA on Office information systems*, pages 30–37. ACM Press, April 1988.

[55] L. Fisher and T. White. *New Tools for New Times: The Workflow Paradigm*. Future Strategies Inc., Alameda, CA, USA, 1994.

[56] K. Fogel. *Open Source Development With CVS*. Coriolis Inc., 1999.

[57] I. Foster and C. Kesselman. *Computational Grids*. Morgan-Kaufman, 1999.

[58] L. Fuchs. Area: A cross-application notification service for groupware. In *Proceedings of the Sixth European Conference on Computer-Supported Cooperative Work*, pages 61–80, September 1999.

[59] R. M. Fujimoto. Parallel discrete event simulation. *Communications of the ACM*, 33(10):30–53, October 1990.

[60] D. Garfinkel, B. C. Welti, and T. W. Yip. HP SharedX: A Tool for Real-time Collaboration. *Hewlett-Packard Journal*, pages 23–36, April 1994.

[61] R. Gordon, G. Leeman, and G. Lewis. Concepts and implications of undo for interactive recovery. In *Proceedings of ACM Annual Conference*, pages 150–157. ACM Press, 1985.

[62] S. Greenberg, C. Gutwin, and A. Cockburn. Awareness through fisheye views in relaxed-wysiwis groupware. In *Proc. of Graphics Interface*, pages 28–38. Morgan-Kaufmann, May 1996.

[63] S. Greenberg and D. Marwood. Real time groupware as a distributed system: concurrency control and its effect on the interface. In *Proc. ACM Conference on Computer Supported Cooperative Work*, pages 207–217. ACM Press, November 1994.

[64] I. Greif and S. Sarin. Data sharing in group work. In *Proc. ACM Conference on Computer Supported Cooperative Work*, pages 175–183. ACM Press, December 1986.

[65] J. Grudin. Groupware and social dynamics: eight challenges for developers. *Communications of the ACM*, 37(1):92–105, January 1994.

[66] C. Gutwin and S. Greenberg. The effects of workspace awareness support on the usability of real-time distributed groupware. *ACM Transactions on Computer-Human Interaction*, 6(3):243–281, September 1999.

[67] J. M. Haake and B. Wilson. Supporting collaborative writing of hyperdocuments in SEPIA. In *Proc. ACM Conference on Computer Supported Cooperative Work*, pages 308–317. ACM Press, November 1992.

[68] T. Horstmann and R. Bentley. Distributed authoring on the web with the bscw shared workspace system. *ACM Standards View*, 5(1):9–16, March 1997.

[69] S. Horwitz and T. Peps. Integrating non-interfering versions of programs. *ACM Transactions on Programming Languages and Systems*, 11(3):345–387, July 1989.

[70] J. J. Hunt and J. Reuter. Using the web for document versioning: an implementation report for delta v. In *Proc. of the 23rd International Conference on Software Engineering*, pages 507–513. IEEE computer society, 2001.

[71] J. W. Hunt and M. D. McIlroy. An algorithm for differential file comparison. *Computing Science Technical Report*, (41), June 1976.

[72] J. W. Hunt and T. G. Szymanski. A fast algorithm for computing longest common subsequences. *Communications of ACM*, 20(5):350–353, 1977.

[73] ICQ. *ICQ is Online Happiness*. http://web.icq.com.

[74] A. Karsenty and M. Beaudouin-Lafon. An algorithm for distributed groupware applications. In *Proc. 13th Conference on Distributed Groupware Computing Systems*, pages 195–202, May 1993.

[75] A. M. Kermarrec and P. Druschel. The icecube approach to the reconciliation of divergent replicas. In *Proc. of ACM Symposium on Principles of Distributed Computing*, pages 210–218. ACM Press, August 2001.

[76] M. J. Knister and A. Prakash. Distedit: a distributed toolkit for supporting multiple group editors. In *Proceedings of the conference on Computer-supported cooperative work*, pages 343–355. ACM Press, September 1990.

[77] M. Koch. Design issues and model for a distributed multi-user editor. *Computer Supported Cooperative Work - An International Journal*, 3-4:359–378, March 1995.

[78] L. Lamport. Time, clocks and the ordering of events in a distributed system. *Communications of ACM*, 21(7):558–565, 1978.

[79] K. A. Lantz. An experiment in integrated multimedia conferencing. In *Proc. ACM Conference on Computer Supported Cooperative Work*, pages 267–275. ACM Press, December 1986.

[80] J. C. Lauwers. Collaboration transparency in desktop teleconferencing environments. In *Ph.D. dissertation, Technical Report CSL-TR-990-435*. Stanford University, Computer Systems Lab, CA, 1990.

[81] D. Li and R. Li. Transparent sharing and interoperation of heterogeneous single-user applications. In *Proc. of ACM Conference on Computer Supported Cooperative Work*, pages 246–255. ACM Press, November 2002.

[82] D. Li, L. Zhou, R. R. Muntz, and C. Sun. Operation Propagation in Real-Time Group Editors. *IEEE MultiMedia Special Issue on Multimedia Computer Supported Cooperative Work*, 7(4):55–61, 2000.

[83] A. Lie, R. Conradi, T. M. Didriksen, and E. A. Karlsson. Change oriented versioning in a software engineering database. *ACM SIGSOFT Software Engineering Notes*, 14(7):56–65, November 1989.

[84] E. Lippe and N. V. Oosterom. Operation-based merging. In *Proceedings of the Fifth ACM SIGSOFT Symposium on Software Development Environments*, pages 78–87. ACM Press, November 1992.

[85] B. Magnusson, U. Asklund, and S. Minr. Fine-grained revision control for collaborative software development. In *Proceedings of the 1st ACM SIGSOFT symposium on Foundations of software engineering*, pages 33–41. ACM Press, December 1993.

[86] L. McGuffin and G. Olson. ShrEdit: A Shared Electronic Workshpace. *CSMIL Technical Report*, 13, 1992.

[87] Microsoft Corporation. Microsoft NetMeeting 2.0: Overview and frequently asked questions. Technical report, Microsoft Corporation, July 1997.

[88] W. Miller and E. W. Myers. A file comparison program. *Software - Practice and Experience*, 15(1):1025–1040, 1985.

[89] M. Minasi, C. Anderson, B. M. Smith, and D. Toombs. *Mastering Windows 2000 Server (4th Edition)*. Sybex, 2002.

[90] M. M. Mller and W. F. Tichy. Case study: extreme programming in a university environment. In *Proceedings of the 23rd international conference on Software engineering*, pages 537–544. IEEE computer society, July 2001.

[91] J. H. Morris, M. Satyanarayanan, M. H. Coner, J. H. Howard, D. S. H. Rosenthal, and F. D. Smith. Andrew: A Distributed Personal Computing Environment. *Communications of ACM*, 29(3):184–201, March 1986.

[92] J. P. Munson and P. Dewan. A Flexible Object Merging Framework. In *Proceedings of ACM conference on Computer-supported cooperative work*, pages 231–242. ACM Press, October 1994.

[93] E. Myers. An O(ND) difference algorithm and its variations. *Algorithmica*, 1(2):251–266, 1986.

[94] D. Nachbar. Spiff – A Program for Making Controlled Approximate Comparisons of Files. In *Proceedings of the summer USENIX Conference*, pages 73–84, June 1988.

[95] Groove Networks. *Groove and Small Business, the low-cost, "no IT dept."
solution.* http://www.groove.net/.

[96] C.M. Neuwirth, R. Chandhok, D.S. Kaufer, P. Erion, J. Morris, and D. Miller.
Flexible Diff-ing In A Collaborative Writing System. In *Proc. ACM Confer-
ence on Computer Supported Cooperative Work*, pages 147–154. ACM Press,
November 1992.

[97] C.M. Neuwirth, D.S. Kaufer, R. Chandhok, and J. Morris. Issues in the Design
of Computer Support for Co-authoring and Commenting. In *Proc. ACM Conference on Computer Supported Cooperative Work*, pages 183–195. ACM Press,
October 1990.

[98] J. T. Nosek. Technical opinion: the case for collaborative programming. *Communications of the ACM*, 41(3):105–108, March 1998.

[99] J. F. Patterson, M. Day, and J. Kucan. Notification servers for synchronous
groupware. In *Proc. of ACM Conference on Computer Supported Cooperative
Work*, pages 122–129. ACM Press, 1996.

[100] K. Petersen, M. J. Spreitzer, D. B. Terry, M. M. Theimer, and A. J. De-
mers. Flexible update propagation for weakly consistent replication. In *Proc. of
the sixteenth ACM symposium on Operating systems principles*, pages 288–301.
ACM Press, October 1997.

[101] S. H. Phatak and B. R. Badrinath. Conflict resolution and reconciliation in
disconnected databases. In *Proc. of International Workshop on Mobility in
Database abd Distributed Systems*, pages 76–81, September 1999.

[102] I. R. Posner and R. M. Baecker. How people write together. In *Proceedings 25th
Hawaii International Conference on System Sciences*, volume 4, pages 127–138,
1992.

[103] A. Prakash and M. J. Knister. A framework for undoing actions in collaborative
systems. *ACM Transactions on Computer-Human Interaction*, 1(4):295–330,
September 1994.

[104] W. Prinz. Nessie: An awareness environment for cooperative settings. In *Proceedings of The Sixth European Conference on Computer Supported Cooperative
Work*, pages 391–410, September 1999.

[105] D. Ramduny, A. Dix, and T. Rodden. Exploring the design space for notification
servers. In *Proc. ACM Conference on Computer Supported Cooperative Work*,
pages 227–235. ACM Press, 1998.

[106] A. Rathbone. *Windows 3.11 for Dummies(3rd Edition)*. Hungry Minds, 1995.

[107] M. Raynal and M. Singhal. Logical time: capturing causality in distributed systems. *IEEE Computer Magazine*, 29(2):49–56, February 1996.

[108] M. Ressel and R. Gunzenhauser. Reducing the problems of group undo. In *Proc. of ACM Conference on Supporting Group Work*, pages 131–139. ACM Press, November 1999.

[109] M. Ressel, D. Nitsche-Ruhland, and R. Gunzenbauser. An integrating, transformation-oriented approach to concurrency control and undo in group editors. In *Proc. ACM Conference on Computer Supported Cooperative Work*, pages 288–297. ACM Press, November 1996.

[110] J. R. Rhyne and C. G. Wolf. Tools for supporting the collaborative process. In *Proceedings of the 5th annual ACM symposium on User interface software and technology*, pages 161–170. ACM Press, December 1992.

[111] T. Richardson, Q. Stafford-Fraser, K. R. Wood, and A. Hopper. Virtual network computing. *IEEE Internet Computing*, 2(1):33–38, January 1998.

[112] M. J. Rochkind. The source code control system. *IEEE Transactions on Software Engineering*, 1(4):364–370, December 1975.

[113] K. J. Rodham and S. R. Olsen Jr. Smart telepointers: Maintaining telepointer consistency in the presence of user interface customization. *ACM Transactions on Graphics*, 13(3):300–307, 1994.

[114] M. Roseman and S. Greenberg. GroupKit: a groupware toolkit for building real-time conferencing applications. In S. Greenberg, S. Hayne, and R. Rada, editors, *Groupware for Real-time Drawing: A Designer's guide*, pages 143–156. McGraw-Hill, 1995.

[115] M. Roseman and S. Greenberg. Building real-time groupware with group-kit, a groupware toolkit. *ACM Transactions on Computer-Human Interaction*, 3(1):66–106, March 1996.

[116] D. S. Rosenblum and A. L. Wolf. A design framework for internet-scale event observation and notification. In *Proc. of the 6th European Software Engineering Conference*, pages 344–360, September 1997.

[117] R. Sandberg, D. Goldberg, S. Kleiman, D. Walsh, and B. Lyon. The design and implementation of the sun network file system. In *Proceedings of the Summer USENIX Conference*, pages 119–130, June 1985.

[118] S. Sarin and I. Grief. Computer-based real-time conferences. *Computer*, 18(10):33–45, 1985.

[119] M.A. Sasse, M.J. Handley, and S.C. Chuang. Support for collaborative authoring via email: The messie environment. In *Proc. Third European Conference on Computer-Supported Cooperative Work*, pages 249–264, September 1993.

[120] Haifeng Shen and C. Sun. RECIPE: a prototype for Internet-based real-time collaborative programming. In *Proc. of ACM CSCW 2000 Workshop on Collaborative Editing Systems*, December 2000.

[121] Haifeng Shen and C. Sun. Operation-based revision control systems. In *Proc. of ACM GROUP 2001 Workshop on Collaborative Editing Systems*, September 2001.

[122] Haifeng Shen and C. Sun. A Log Compression Algorithm for Operation-based Version Control Systems. In *Proceedings of IEEE 26th Annual International Computer Software and Application Conference*, pages 867–872. IEEE computer society, August 2002.

[123] Haifeng Shen and C. Sun. Collaborative Highlighting for Real-time Group Editors. In *Proceedings of International Conference on Innovative Internet Computing Systems*, pages 39–50. Springer Verlag, June 2002.

[124] Haifeng Shen and C. Sun. Flexible Merging for Asynchronous Collaborative Systems. In *Proceedings of Tenth International Conference on Cooperative Information Systems*, pages 304–321. Springer Verlag, November 2002.

[125] Haifeng Shen and C. Sun. Flexible Notification for Collaborative Systems. In *Proceedings of ACM Conference on Computer-Supported Cooperative Work*, pages 77–86. ACM Press, November 2002.

[126] Haifeng Shen and C. Sun. Highlighting: A Gesturing Communication Tool for Real-time Collaborative Systems. In *Proceedings of the 5th IEEE International Conference on Algorithms and Architectures for Parallel Processing*, pages 180–187. IEEE computer society, October 2002.

[127] Haifeng Shen and C. Sun. RECIPE: A Web-based Environment for Supporting Real-time Collaborative Programming. In *Proceedings of International Conference on Networks, Parallel and Distributed Processing*, pages 283–288. ACTA Press, October 2002.

[128] Haifeng Shen and C. Sun. Improving real-time collaboration with highlighting. *International Journal of Future Generation Computer Systems*, August 2003.

[129] M. Stefik, D. G. Bobrow, G. Foster, S. Lanning, and D. Tatar. WYSIWIS Revised: Early Experiences with Multiuser Interface. In *Proceedings of ACM Conference on Computer Supported Cooperative Work*, pages 276–290. ACM Press, December 1986.

[130] M. Stefik, G. Foster, D. G. Bobrow, K. Kahn, S. Lanning, and L. Suchman. Beyond the chalkboard: computer support for collaboration and problem solving in meetings. *Communications of the ACM*, 3(1):32–47, January 1987.

[131] C. Sun. Undo any operation at any time in group editors. In *Proceedings of ACM Conference on Computer Supported Cooperative Work*, pages 191–200. ACM Press, December 2000.

[132] C. Sun. Undo as concurrent inverse in group editors. *ACM Transactions on Computer-Human Interaction*, 9(4):309–361, December 2002.

[133] C. Sun. Consistency maintenance in real-time collaborative editing systems. In *Mircosoft Research Lectures 2003*, February 2003.

[134] C. Sun and W. Cai. Capturing causality by compressed vector clock in real-time group editors. In *Proceedings of IEEE International Parallel and Distributed Processing Symposium*, pages 59–68. IEEE Computer Society, April 2002.

[135] C. Sun and D. Chen. Consistency maintenance in real-time collaborative graphics editing systems. *ACM Transactions on Computer-Human Interaction*, 9(1):1–41, March 2002.

[136] C. Sun and C.A. Ellis. Operational transformation in real-time group editors: Issues, algorithms, and achievements. In *Proceedings of ACM Conference on Computer Supported Cooperative Work*, pages 59–68. ACM Press, November 1998.

[137] C. Sun, X. Jia, Y. Zhang, Y. Yang, and D. Chen. Achieving convergence, causality-preservation, and intention-preservation in real-time cooperative editing systems. *ACM Transactions on Computer-Human Interaction*, 5(1):3 – 8, March 1998.

[138] C. Sun and Haifeng Shen. REDUCE Demo: a Web-based Real Time Group Editor. In *Demonstrations at ACM Conference on Computer Supported Cooperative Work*, December 2000.

[139] J. C. Tang, N. Yankelovich, and J. Begole. Sharedshell: A shared terminal for collaborative system administration. Technical Report Network Communities Report, Sun Microsystems Inc., June 1999.

[140] R. H. Thayer and M. Dorfman. *Software Engineering, Second Edition*. IEEE Computer Society Press, Los Alamitos, CA, 1997.

[141] H. Thimleby. *User Interface Design*. Addison-Wesley, Reading, MA, USA, 1990.

[142] W. F. Tichy. Rcs – a system for version control. *Software Practice and Experience*, 15(7):637–654, July 1985.

[143] N. Vidot, M. Cart, J. Ferri, and M. Suleiman. Copies convergence in a distributed real-time collaborative environment. In *Proceedings of ACM Conference on Computer Supported Cooperative Work*, pages 171–180. ACM Press, December 2000.

[144] X. Wang, J. Bu, and C. Chen. Achieving undo in bitmap-based collaborative graphics editing systems. In *Proceedings of ACM Conference on Computer supported cooperative work*, pages 68–76. ACM Press, November 2002.

[145] B. Westfechtel. Structure-oriented merging of revisions of software documents. In *Proc. of the 3rd International Workshop on Software Configuration Management*, pages 68–79. Springer Verlag, June 1991.

[146] Wiki. Pair programming facilities. In *Portland Pattern Repostory*, March 1999.

[147] Wiki. Programming in pairs. In *Portland Pattern Repostory*, June 1999.

[148] Wiki. Virutal pair programming. In *Portland Pattern Repostory*, June 2000.

[149] L. Williams, R. Kessler, W. Cunningham, and R. Jeffries. Strengthening the case for pair-programming. *Communications of the ACM*, 17(4):19–25, July 2000.

[150] L. A. Williams and R. R. Kessler. All i really need to know about pair programming i learned in kindergarten. *Communications of the ACM*, 43(5):108–114, May 2000.

[151] Y. Yang. A new conceptual model for interactive user recovery and command reuse facilities. In *Proceedings of the CHI'88 Conference on Human Factors in Computing Systems*, pages 165–170. ACM Press, 1988.

[152] Y. Zhao and R. Strom. Exploiting event stream interpretation in publish-subscribe systems. In *Proceedings of the twentieth annual ACM symposium on Principles of distributed computing*, pages 219–228. ACM Press, August 2001.

Index